# A PROUD ATHLETIC HISTORY

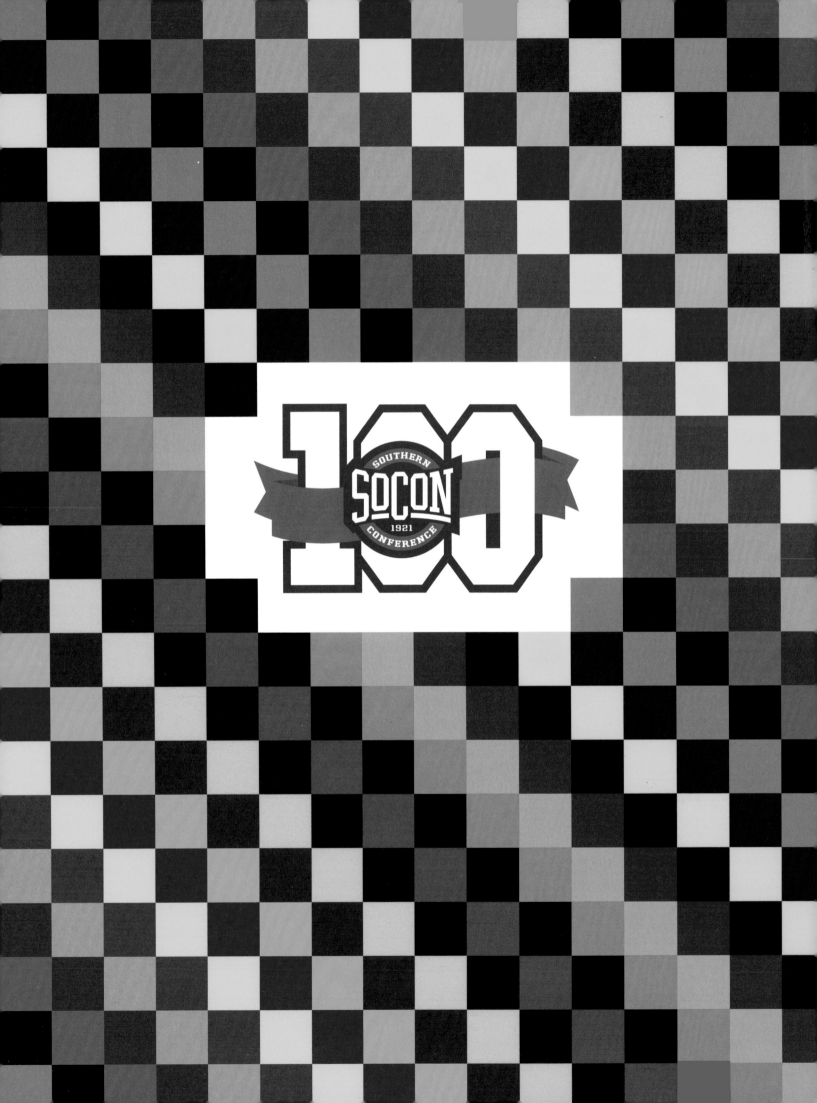

# A PROUD ATHLETIC HISTORY

## 100 YEARS OF THE SOUTHERN CONFERENCE

### JOHN IAMARINO

George,

It was a pleasure talking with you.
Hope you enjoy the book.

John Iamarino

MERCER UNIVERSITY PRESS
MACON, GEORGIA
2020

MUP/ H992

© 2020 by Mercer University Press
Published by Mercer University Press
1501 Mercer University Drive
Macon, Georgia 31207
All rights reserved

25 24 23 22 21 20        9 8 7 6 5 4 3 2 1

Books published by Mercer University Press
are printed on acid-free paper that meets the requirements of the American
National Standard for Information Sciences—Permanence of Paper
for Printed Library Materials.

Printed and bound in Canada.

This book is typeset in ITC Slimbach, Myriad Pro, and Undergrad
Interior and jacket design by Burt&Burt.

ISBN 978-0-88146-755-0

Iamarino, John, author.
A proud athletic history: 100 years of the Southern Conference
/John Iamarino.
Macon, Georgia: Mercer University Press, 2020.
Identifiers: LCCN 2020027589 | ISBN 9780881467550 (hardback)
LCSH: Southern Conference—History.
College sports—Southern States—History.
LCC GV351.3.S684 I36 2020 | DDC 796.04/30975--dc23

LC record available at https://lccn.loc.gov/2020027589

# ACKNOWLEDGMENTS

**IT WAS NOT MY ORIGINAL INTENTION** to be the sole participant in writing, assembling, and editing this book. With the Southern Conference about to celebrate its 100th anniversary, my initial plan was to serve as a traffic cop and direct all the pieces to the right place. But as I began researching in December of 2015 and began writing small bits of copy, I decided to just keep going. I had always thought I could write a book, having studied journalism in college and having spent two years with a newspaper chain. Now I had no excuse.

I made time as needed. I found a few slower periods in the office. I worked some evenings and weekends at home. I started coming into the office very early most mornings to get a couple hours of work done before the official start of the day. Soon enough, it became an irresistible challenge—complete a definitive history of the league without sacrificing my responsibilities as commissioner of the Southern Conference.

But none of this would have happened without a lot of help from a lot of good people.

I must start by saying thank you to the presidents and chancellors of the Southern Conference who supported this project right from the start. If they had delayed their support, this project might well have been a no-go.

Another early contributor was Mercer University women's basketball coach Susie Gardner, who highly recommended I contact Marc Jolley and Mercer University Press as a potential publisher. They had previously published Susie's first children's book, *1, 2, 3 Team!* in 2016. Marc was always positive and encouraging to me, and he and Marsha Luttrell never failed to provide answers to endless questions from this first-time author.

Among those who graciously gave me their time for either a telephone interview or an exchange of detailed emails were Bobby Cremins, Tom Davis, Rob Hjerling, Jim Jones, Bob McKillop, Danny Morrison, Les Robinson, Grace Roselli, Tony Skole, Alfred White, Steve White, Mike Wood, and Sam Wyche.

The office personnel at the Southern Conference headquarters in Spartanburg, South Carolina, were always supportive of this endeavor. Geoff Cabe and Sue Arakas have both lived a good deal of the conference's history from an insider's vantage point and were wonderful resources. Neither Phil Perry nor Haley Shotwell ever got annoyed with my request for a photo or help with cropping an image that my computer (or my lack of expertise) wouldn't allow. Paul Lollis was gracious in shooting photos of the building's exterior. Neili Akridge, my executive assistant, always made sure my obligations as commissioner were being met, even as I would sometimes immerse myself in book research for hours at a time.

Four SoCon interns made contributions to these efforts. Wofford College students Alex Hoots and Stephanie Lane were month-long volunteer interns who did needed research on conference historical events. Both Emily Fulton and Hannah Simmons had many other responsibilities during their 2018–19 internships with the SoCon but performed significant tasks for this project. Emily created two graphics used in the book and Hannah obtained photos and quotes from current Southern Conference student-athletes.

After much of the copy was written, I entered the phase of collecting photo images. This seemed a bit daunting at first when I realized permission to print would be required of all photos not taken or owned by the Southern Conference. But I experienced cooperation on virtually every front. I quickly realized how valuable a good archivist could be at a college or university library.

All the ones I contacted were cheerful, helpful, and generally went above and beyond the initial request. In particular, both Tessa Updike of the Citadel and Mary Kludy of VMI gave me valuable time during their busy days to look through materials, pick out images, and provide me with photo credits.

Additionally, special thanks go to archivists Brigette Kamsler (George Washington University), Jena Jones (Atlanta History Center), Mary Linnemann (University of Georgia), and Laurainne Ojo-Ohikuare (University of Maryland) for their timely cooperation.

Jon Scott of bigbluehistory.net, a site focused on Kentucky basketball, provided outstanding background into the early years of the Southern Conference basketball tournament and steered me toward some helpful research sites as well.

Media relations personnel were extremely helpful in providing scanned images and granting permission to publish. I'm grateful to all, particularly Hunter Reid (Furman), Wade Branner (VMI), Jay Blackman (Chattanooga), Daniel Hooker (Western Carolina), Brent Williamson (Wofford), Art Chase (Duke), Brian Laubscher (Washington & Lee), Brian Morrison (ACC), Steve Shutt (Wake Forest), and John Sudsbury (Sugar Bowl).

To my parents, Frank and Maryann—hey, all that money you spent for my journalism degree at St. Bonaventure finally paid off! Your son's a legitimate author.

And finally, to my wife, Mary Ann, and my son, P.J., I'm grateful for all your unwavering support and encouragement. I love you both.

*John Iamarino*
*Spartanburg, SC*
*July 2019*

# SOUTHERN CONFERENCE MEMBERSHIP

*in Chronological Order*

| INSTITUTION | JOINED | DEPARTED | INSTITUTION | JOINED | DEPARTED |
|---|---|---|---|---|---|
| Alabama* | 1921 | 1932 | The Citadel | 1936 | Present |
| Auburn* | 1921 | 1932 | Davidson | 1936 | 1988 |
| Clemson* | 1921 | 1953 | | 1992 | 2014 |
| Georgia* | 1921 | 1932 | Furman | 1936 | Present |
| Georgia Tech* | 1921 | 1932 | Richmond | 1936 | 1976 |
| Kentucky* | 1921 | 1932 | Wake Forest | 1936 | 1953 |
| Maryland* | 1921 | 1953 | William & Mary | 1936 | 1977 |
| Mississippi State* | 1921 | 1932 | George Washington | 1941 | 1970 |
| North Carolina* | 1921 | 1953 | West Virginia | 1950 | 1968 |
| North Carolina State* | 1921 | 1953 | East Carolina | 1964 | 1977 |
| Tennessee* | 1921 | 1932 | Appalachian State | 1971 | 2014 |
| Virginia* | 1921 | 1937 | Chattanooga | 1976 | Present |
| Virginia Tech* | 1921 | 1965 | Marshall | 1976 | 1997 |
| Washington & Lee* | 1921 | 1958 | Western Carolina | 1976 | Present |
| Florida | 1922 | 1932 | ETSU | 1978 | 2005 |
| Louisiana State | 1922 | 1932 | | 2014 | Present |
| Mississippi | 1922 | 1932 | Georgia Southern | 1991 | 2014 |
| South Carolina | 1922 | 1953 | UNCG | 1997 | Present |
| Tulane | 1922 | 1932 | Wofford | 1997 | Present |
| Vanderbilt | 1922 | 1932 | College of Charleston | 1998 | 2013 |
| VMI | 1923 | 2003 | Elon | 2003 | 2014 |
| | 2014 | Present | Samford | 2008 | Present |
| Sewanee (U. of the South) | 1924 | 1932 | Mercer | 2014 | Present |
| Duke | 1929 | 1953 | | | |

*Charter member

# NOTABLE EVENTS IN 1921

**FEBRUARY 5** New York Yankee owners Jacob Ruppert and Tillinghast Huston purchase twenty acres in the Bronx as the site for construction of the original Yankee Stadium, completed in 1923.

**FEBRUARY 24** The first transcontinental flight in less than twenty-four hours of flying time, from San Diego, California, to Jacksonville, Florida, is completed by First Lieutenant William Coney of the Army Air Service.

**MARCH 4** Warren G. Harding is inaugurated as the 29th president of the United States.

**JULY 2** Heavyweight champion Jack Dempsey knocks out Georges Carpentier of France in the fourth round. It is boxing's first $1 million gate. More than 91,000 spectators turn out in Jersey City, New Jersey.

**JULY 6** Anne Frances Robbins—later to be known as Nancy Reagan—is born in New York City.

*Warren G. Harding was inaugurated as the 29th president of the United States on March 4, 1921. (Public domain photo)*

**JULY 18** John Glenn is born in Cambridge, Ohio. He would become the first American to orbit the Earth in 1962 and would later serve as a US senator from Ohio.

**JULY 21** Nicola Sacco and Bartolomeo Vanzetti, two Italian-born anarchists, are found guilty of murdering a guard and paymaster at a Massachusetts shoe-manufacturing plant. They are electrocuted six years later.

**AUGUST 3** Judge Kenesaw Mountain Landis, newly appointed commissioner of baseball, permanently bars eight members of the Chicago White Sox from playing professionally in organized baseball. The eight, forever to be known as the Black Sox, had been charged with fixing the 1919 World Series.

**AUGUST 5** The first major league baseball game is broadcast live on radio when Pittsburgh station KDKA airs the Phillies vs. the Pirates from Forbes Field.

**SEPTEMBER 7**  The first Miss America beauty pageant is held in Atlantic City, New Jersey. The inaugural winner is Margaret Gorman, 16, a high school junior from Washington, DC.

**OCTOBER 13**  The New York Giants beat the New York Yankees, 1–0, to win the 1921 World Series five games to three. All eight games are played in New York's Polo Grounds.

**OCTOBER 25**  Bat Masterson, 67, a legendary figure from the American West, dies in New York City where he was a well-known sports writer and celebrity.

**NOVEMBER 9**  Dr. Albert Einstein is awarded the Nobel Prize in Physics, "especially for his discovery of the law of the photoelectric effect."

**NOVEMBER 11**  The Tomb of the Unknown Soldier is dedicated at Arlington National Cemetery.

*Sixteen-year-old Margaret Gorman of Washington, DC, was the first winner of the Miss America pageant. (Library of Congress, Prints & Photographs division)*

*A marble tomb is lowered into place as construction proceeds on the Tomb of the Unknown Soldier in Arlington, VA. (Public domain photo)*

## COST OF LIVING IN AMERICA IN 1921

| ITEM | COST |
|---|---|
| Quart of milk | 15 cents |
| Gallon of gas | 30 cents |
| Dozen eggs | 51 cents |
| Pound of butter | 52 cents |
| One-pound cut of sirloin steak | 39 cents |
| Six-cylinder, four-passenger Studebaker | $1,750 |
| Men's suit with two pair of trousers | $35 |
| Woman's summer hat | $5 |
| Woman's blouse | $7.95 |
| Man's silk shirt | $7.95 |

Source: US Department of Labor study, *Retail Prices, 1890 to 1927*;
1921 newspaper advertising.

## AMERICAN CULTURE IN 1921

### POPULAR SONGS

"April Showers"
"Ain't We Got Fun"
"There'll Be Some Changes Made"
"I'm Just Wild about Harry"

### POPULAR MOVIES

*The Four Horsemen of the Apocalypse* (Rudolph Valentino)
*The Kid* (Charlie Chaplin)
*The Sheik* (Rudolph Valentino)
*Through the Back Door* (Mary Pickford)

# THROUGH THE DECADES

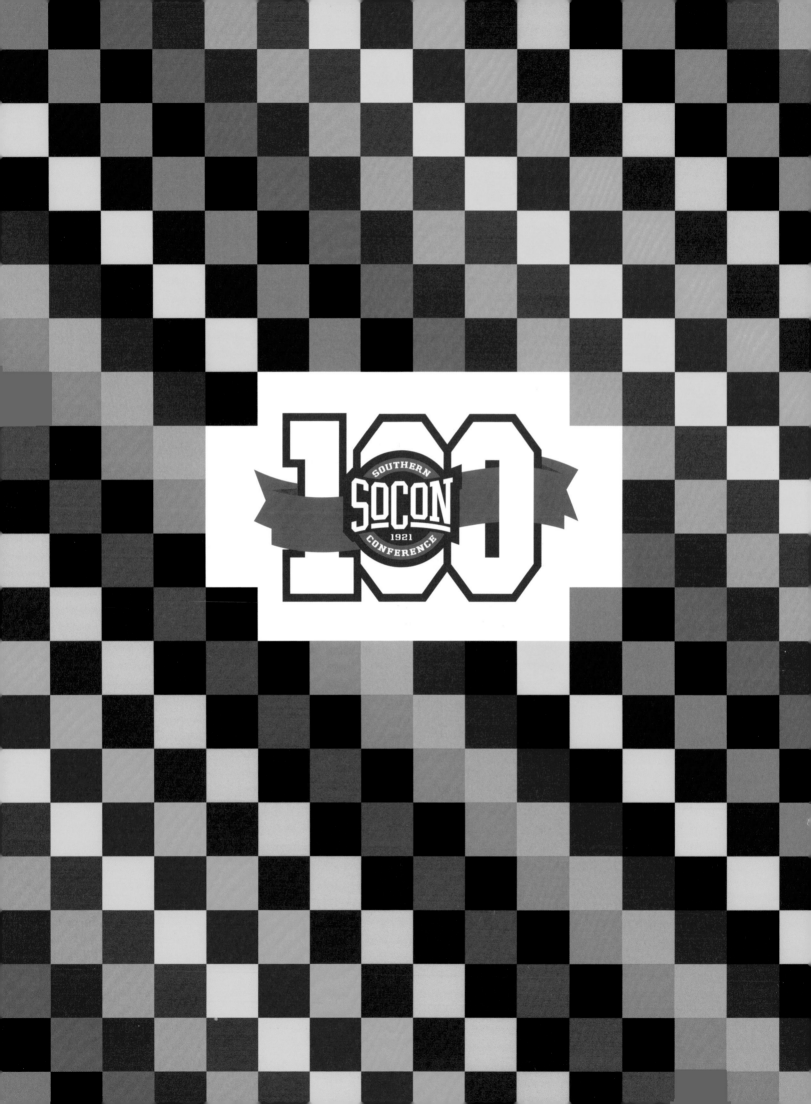

# THE
# 1920S

The new Southern Conference was founded with three primary sports in mind: football, basketball, and track and field. Football, which originated in the Northeast—the first collegiate game featured Princeton vs. Rutgers on November 6, 1869—gradually spread throughout the country and was becoming increasingly more popular in the South. So that was a must for the new league. Basketball featured smaller squad sizes, making train or automobile travel easier to make. And the third sport was track and field, one of the nation's most popular college sports at the time, given the attention paid to the Olympic Games. In fact, the first official NCAA championship was an outdoor track and field meet held in Chicago in 1921.

Two years later, in May of 1923, a dozen of the larger state schools gathered together at the ten-acre Cramton Bowl in Montgomery, Alabama, to participate in the first Southern Conference outdoor track and field championship. The event was not without controversy. At the invitation of the University of Virginia, seven of the conference's Northern schools got together to conduct their own meet, one not officially recognized by a majority of the twenty members.

"There has been a feeling that the far Southern [Conference] schools have kept too many of the events in their territory which made sending a full team of 16 men there almost too costly to consider," said one UVA observer.

A leather football helmet that belonged to Jack W. Simmons, Class of 1922 at the Citadel. (Tessa Updike, the Citadel archives)

At the Montgomery meet—the only one in which results were recorded for posterity—Mississippi State scored the most points, followed by LSU and Tennessee. The following year, SoCon track was divided into two championships. UVA hosted and won the northern version while Mississippi State repeated in the south. Indoor track would not become a conference sport until 1930 when the University of North Carolina offered its Indoor Athletic Center—popularly referred to as the "Tin Can"—as a competition venue.

The growing pains of a large, ambitious conference—an invitation to Duke in December of 1928 increased the membership to twenty-three—continued unabated. Wrote Norman Baxter in the *Washington Post*, "There are enough schools in the northern half of the Southern Conference for them to be self-sufficient in all matters athletic. The present body, with more than 20 members, is too unwieldy."

*VMI defeated the visiting Quantico Marines, 6–0, under soggy conditions in the 1923 season opener. (Virginia Military Institute archives)*

Early Southern Conference football standings seemed to support Baxter's opinion. In its inaugural season of 1922, the SoCon featured twenty teams playing anywhere from two to six league games. Five teams were unbeaten in conference play, led by North Carolina at 5-0. To find a more satisfying method of determining a champion rather than simple winning percentage, an Alabama alum named Champ Pickens donated a sterling silver cup to be awarded to the Southern Conference champion, as voted upon by a panel of sports writers. Vanderbilt was awarded the Pickens Trophy in 1923 with a 3-0-1 record in the conference. This did not sit well with the two Lexington, Virginia, schools, Washington & Lee (4-0-1) and VMI (5-1). But the Pickens Trophy method of selecting a champion remained in effect through the 1926 season.

Beginning in 1924, the Alabama Crimson Tide emerged as the dominant football program in the conference, winning twenty straight league games over three years on their way to consecutive national championships in 1925 and 1926. The architect of Alabama's rise was Wallace Wade, a former cavalry captain in the US Army from the small northwest Tennessee town of Trenton.

Wade's arrival in Tuscaloosa in 1923 triggered thirty-seven years of a legendary presence in the history of the Southern Conference—from Alabama to Duke to the commissioner's chair. His achievements during the conference's formative years led to his 2010 induction into the SoCon's Hall of Fame.

Alabama's Rose Bowl victory over the University of Washington on January 1, 1926, served notice that Southern football had truly arrived. At the time, most observers believed the Southern colleges played at a level below the powers in the East and West.

*In the conference's first decade, the LSU men's outdoor track and field team captured three consecutive championships (1927–29). The Tigers were coached by three different men during those three years, the first being FRANCIS (TAD) GORMLEY, who made a significant name for himself as a track coach in and around New Orleans and was an assistant coach for the US Olympic squad in the 1932 games in Los Angeles. Among the athletes he coached there were BABE DIDRIKSON, EDDIE TOLAN, RALPH METCALFE, and SoCon Hall of Famer PERCY BEARD of Auburn, who won a silver medal in the 110-meter hurdles.*

*Alabama's Pooley Hubert (No. 10) scored the first touchdown of the 1926 Rose Bowl, a landmark 20–19 win for the Crimson Tide over Washington. Hubert would later spend ten years as the head coach at VMI. (University of Alabama Athletics)*

When the Tide slumped in 1927, the void at the top of the SoCon was filled by Georgia Tech. Known in those days as the Golden Tornado, Tech did not lose a league game over the course of two years and topped off the run with an 8–7 Rose Bowl victory over California on New Year's Day, 1929. That game became famous for Cal's Roy Riegels recovering a Georgia Tech fumble and running sixty-five yards the wrong way, eventually being tackled on his own one-yard line. Tech blocked the ensuing punt for a safety and the two points stood up as the margin of victory.

An early version of what would later be known as "conference parity" revealed itself during the Roaring Twenties in Southern Conference basketball. In the eight seasons from 1921–22 through 1928–29, seven different programs claimed the SoCon's regular-season championship. They included a 1923–24 Tulane Green Wave squad that finished 22-1 overall and a perfect 10-0 in the conference, and the 1928–29 Generals of Washington & Lee, who lost only once in league play. A Southern Conference member until 1958, Washington & Lee would win two more regular-season league basketball titles in the 1930s.

As the good times rolled on and America kept "cool with Coolidge," colleges and universities invested more in their athletic programs. In Chapel Hill, North Carolina built Kenan Stadium in 1927. Two years later, rival Duke built a new stadium of its own. Originally called Duke Stadium, it later was renamed Wallace Wade Stadium. Both facilities remain in use today.

But while interest in the Southern Conference and collegiate sports continued to boom, national and global events would

*Vanderbilt's DONALD CRAM entered the record books as the first tennis champion in SoCon history when he won the 1928 tournament at New Orleans. A year later, freshman CLIFF SUTTER of Tulane captured the first of his three titles in four years. One of the first national champions coming from the Southern Conference, the New Orleans native firmly established himself as one of the best collegians in the South. In 1930, Sutter captured the NCAA championship, then repeated that honor again two years later as a senior. By that time he was ranked as high as No. 5 in the world. He eventually competed in the Davis Cup and played both Wimbledon and the US Open. He was inducted into the Sugar Bowl's Hall of Fame in 1980. Tulane posthumously dedicated a campus tennis court in his honor in 2002.*

CAROLINA 14    VIRGINIA
1927 THANKSGIVING

*Tucked away among the pine trees of Chapel Hill, Kenan Stadium opened in 1927 and remains the home of Tar Heel football. (University of North Carolina Athletics)*

soon curtail many capital projects on American campuses. On Tuesday, October 29, 1929, the stock market lost roughly 12 percent of its value, a $14 billion decline in one day. The nation soon learned a multitude of ominous new terms, things like "bank run" and "bread line" and "Hooverville." The Great Depression would serve as the backdrop for the first seismic changes in the Southern Conference as the new decade approached.

## A NEW CONFERENCE IS BORN

**AS AMERICA EMERGED** from the hardships and gloom of World War I, it entered a period known as the Roaring Twenties. A new dawn of optimism, technology, growth, and entertainment spread across the country. College athletics began to emerge as a staple of sporting fans' interest. It was in this environment that the Southern Conference was created.

Spearheaded by Dr. William Dudley of Vanderbilt University, a group of public and private institutions in the South had formed an umbrella administrative organization in 1894 called the Southern Intercollegiate Athletic Association (SIAA). To regulate competition, the SIAA set rules in a variety of areas, but primarily in amateurism and student-athlete eligibility. One of the major topics of dispute in the decade beginning in 1910 was the so-called one-year residence rule, more commonly known as "freshman eligibility."

The larger schools did not want freshmen to be able to compete until they'd spent a year in residence. Part of this concern was the use of "tramp athletes" who competed for, but seldom attended classes at multiple colleges in multiple years. "They go from college to college," said the University of Virginia's Albert Lefever at an address to the 1920 SIAA convention. "They are cajoled, flattered, tempted, and paid by false athletic leaders and false friends of athletics."

The smaller schools, with fewer students and less resources for freshmen-only teams, advocated for freshman eligibility.

In 1920, SIAA members formally voted to permit freshmen to be eligible. The decision did not sit well with the larger institutions. Dr. Steadman V. Sanford of the University of Georgia called for meetings on the campus of the University of Florida among the larger state institutions in December of that year. Talk centered around creating a separate, distinct alliance to establish "regulations that were long in force in the North, East and West," according to an historical note that preceded the first Southern Conference constitution.

At 4:15 P.M. on Friday, February 25, 1921, delegates from fifteen colleges and universities met at the Piedmont Hotel located on Peachtree Street NE in Atlanta to finalize plans for a new conference. Those in attendance included:

> University of Alabama
> Alabama Polytechnic Institute (*now Auburn*)
> Clemson College
> Georgia School of Technology
> University of Georgia
> University of Kentucky
> University of Maryland
> Mississippi Agricultural and Mechanical College (*now Mississippi State*)
> North Carolina State College
> University of North Carolina
> University of Tennessee
> Tulane University

## MEMORABLE MOMENTS

### MARCH 1, 1927

### VANDERBILT WINS ITS LONE SOUTHERN CONFERENCE TOURNAMENT

Down eight points at the half in an era when basketball scores were low, Vanderbilt "took all the Georgia Bulldogs had to offer, shook it off and plunged from the blackness of impending defeat to the championship," reported the *Nashville Banner* on Vandy's 46–44 victory at the 1927 Southern Conference Tournament. An overwhelming pro-Georgia crowd at Atlanta's Municipal Auditorium watched the Commodores earn their only Southern Conference basketball championship. With his team nursing a one-point lead late in the game, Vandy's Malcolm Moss scored three consecutive points, the final one coming on a technical foul when Georgia called a timeout it didn't have. Stated the *Banner*, "It was Josh Cody's last appearance as a Commodore coach and his boys had brought him a Southern championship."

University of Virginia
Virginia Polytechnic Institute
Washington and Lee University

The new organization would officially be called the Southern Intercollegiate Conference. It was agreed that all would be admitted as charter members "subject to ratification by their respective university authorities."

(Note: Tulane did not grant its athletic department permission to become a charter member, perhaps hesitating because Louisiana State University, while "expressing sympathy with the movement," had declined an invitation to attend the December meetings. Tulane and LSU would both join the following year when the conference added six more institutions to grow to a robust twenty members.)

Freshmen students would not be eligible to compete on varsity programs. Students had five years to play three years of varsity competition. The new constitution and bylaws would go into effect on January 1, 1922. Existing scheduling contracts and commitments would be honored. Dr. Sanford was named the first president of the organization. Annual dues were set at $25.

The group concluded its work when it resumed its meeting the following morning. It was noted in the minutes that the new conference's purpose was to "promote intercollegiate athletics in every form, to keep them in proper bounds by making them an incidental and not principal feature of intercollegiate and university life . . . and to strengthen the moral fibre of students."

At the request of Dr. Harry C. Byrd of Maryland, it was agreed that the announcement of the Southern Intercollegiate Conference would be held until representatives could provide it to "writers from the Sunday papers."

The established SIAA knew this was not a good development for its own existence. "Because the SIAA has persistently refused to take adequate steps for its own protection, purification and perpetuation," stated one institution's president, "there has arisen the Southern Intercollegiate Conference, whose shadow threatens the prestige, if not the very life of the SIAA."

*The North Carolina Tar Heels proved the most successful Southern Conference team in the early years of the league's basketball tournament, winning titles in 1922, '24, '25, and '26. Among UNC's key contributors were CARTWRIGHT CARMICHAEL (left) and JACK COBB (right). Carmichael became the program's first consensus All-American. Carmichael Arena on the Chapel Hill campus is named not in his honor, however, but for his brother, William. Cobb was the 1926 national Player of the Year as chosen by the Helms Foundation. In both the 1924 and '26 SoCon tournament championship games, he scored more than half of North Carolina's total points. (University of North Carolina Athletics)*

Since members of the new league still held some membership privileges in the SIAA, the similar names—both beginning with the words Southern Intercollegiate—were soon enough recognized as unwieldy and confusing. At its annual meeting in December of 1923, the minutes of the two-year-old league reflect the following action: "Amend Article I to read as follows: The name of this association shall be the Southern Conference."

The amendment was quickly adopted.

One hundred years later, the Southern Conference remains the fifth-oldest Division I athletic league in the NCAA. It was preceded only by the Big Ten Conference (1896), Missouri Valley Conference (1907), Pacific-12 Conference (1915), and the Southwestern Athletic Conference (1920).

## "THE IDEA MAY SEEM REVOLUTIONARY, AS INDEED IT IS."

**IN ITS FORMATIVE YEARS**, the Southern Conference created a constitution with bylaws, regulations, resolutions, and all other manner of infrastructure. Some have lasted 100 years. Other concepts never received the traction their advocates hoped for.

In March of 1924, a resolution was proposed that would eliminate full-time coaches from guiding varsity teams. Instead, student-athletes would schedule, organize, and operate their own squads.

The resolution, not attributed to any individual person in the minutes, read in part:

> After a term of years (say, after 1928) the duties of all paid coaches at Conference institutions shall be confined to the development of mass athletics for the entire student body. All teams engaging in intercollegiate contests shall be coached by students alone, the coaching staff to consist of the Captain of each team together with a corps of strategists and assistants made up of players and other students familiar with the sport.
>
> The idea may seem revolutionary, as indeed it is.
>
> High priced and efficient (coaching) talent would be employed in improving the physique of the youth of the nation. The coach would no longer be at the mercy

*Tie games no longer exist in college football, but back in the 1920s they were fairly common. In 1923, four of Georgia Tech's five SoCon games ended in a draw, and Auburn played three ties. In all, there were ten tie games in league play that season, roughly 20 percent of all results. In fact, it was not until 1936 that a Southern Conference football season finished without a league game ending in a tie. The last tie game in SoCon history came on November 18, 1989, when VMI and Chattanooga played to a 14–14 deadlock.*

*Cross country became a Southern Conference sport in 1926. The first championship meet was held on the University of Georgia campus in Athens and featured six programs—Auburn, Clemson, Georgia, Georgia Tech, North Carolina, and Virginia Tech. UNC easily won the inaugural championship, led by individual winner GALEN ELLIOT. Nicknamed "the Dixie Flyer," Elliot won the conference championship again in 1927 and earned All-America honors in the mile run in outdoor track. He missed qualifying for the 1928 Olympic mile by two-tenths of a second in the US trials. He was later ordained into the Presbyterian ministry and served as a pastor and interim minister until the age of 90.*

of the Alumni and others who measure his success and usefulness by the number of major games won or lost. . . . If some practical plan can be derived from this idea, he will become a teacher and his life will be the stable and peaceful one of any other member of the faculty.

At present, there is no real undergraduate competition. The hired coach furnishes the brain, the wits, the skill, the discipline. The team becomes a mere machine under the control of an expert.

The minutes make no further reference to this resolution, which apparently died a quiet death. But if coaches were to lead varsity teams, at least the membership might persuade them to avoid that most undignified of practices—recruiting.

The following resolution, proposed by Dr. Steadman Sanford of Georgia, was adopted, but soon enough ignored and then rescinded.

The Southern Conference at this annual meeting desires to go on record as disapproving and condemning the practice of any member of the coaching staff, directly or indirectly, soliciting, visiting or recruiting students for athletic teams. The Conference believes that dignity and honor will be reflected on the institution, the coaching staff, and the alumni association if such practices are discontinued.

A 1924 proposal "that baseball be eliminated as a college sport" was initially tabled, and never successfully acted upon.

The growing popularity of radio also concerned administrators convening in Nashville in December of 1928. "The question of radio broadcasting of college football games was

*One of the most successful athletes during the Southern Conference's first decade was ROSS O'DELL (pictured) of Clemson. A native of Liberty, South Carolina, who dreamed of attending Clemson as his father did, O'Dell became one of the premier pole-vaulters in America. As a sophomore in the 1926 conference championship meet, he set a record in winning the event. He subsequently repeated as champion in both his junior and senior years, each time establishing record heights. His winning vault of thirteen feet, three inches in 1928 stood as a conference record for thirty years. That same year, O'Dell placed second in the Penn Relays, fourth in the NCAA championships, and sixth in the Olympic Trials at Harvard Stadium. He earned his degree from Clemson in agriculture, served as a county agent and schoolteacher, and later saw his son, Billy, become the third generation of O'Dells to attend Clemson. (Clemson University Athletics)*

discussed informally," read the minutes written by secretary William D. Funkhouser, dean of the Department of Zoology at the University of Kentucky.

"It seemed to be the opinion of the committee that the broadcasting was very detrimental to gate receipts. It was agreed that members would look with disfavor on institutions that violate the spirit of this opinion."

Another conference concept that ran counter to modern thinking was restricting members from playing in any post-season football game. In each of the first five New Year's Day bowl games played by Southern Conference members, a waiver had to be approved to permit that participation. The waiver was granted on each occasion. (This would become a crucial issue in the early 1950s and ultimately contribute to a membership split that led to the creation of the Atlantic Coast Conference.)

One concept that *was* ahead of its time was the creation in 1926 of a Central Board of Officials for football. Only officials accredited by the board could work in a Southern Conference game. The league started this practice in coordination with the Southwest Conference, Western Conference (i.e., Big Ten), and Missouri Valley Conference. Today, almost all conferences are members of officiating consortiums.

*Fencing could have become a Southern Conference sport at the tail end of the decade. In March of 1929, the executive committee received a letter from W. R. REESE, president of the Southern Fencing Conference, a loose organization of institutions promoting the sport. The letter requested consideration as a full championship sport under the Southern Conference umbrella. The committee had no objections to its members participating in the other organization, but deferred taking any action other than drafting a letter to Mr. Reese stating that the matter would have to be placed before the conference at the annual meeting in December. The minutes reveal no further serious discussions of adding fencing.*

# THE
# 1930S

By 1930, the Southern Conference had ballooned to a fairly unmanageable twenty-three-member entity, stretching from Gainesville, Florida, north to College Park, Maryland, west to Nashville, Tennessee, and south to Baton Rouge, Louisiana. Team travel was hard, either by train or with buses operating on narrow, poorly paved roads in an era before the current interstate highway system. The result was regional scheduling in all sports, with teams playing different numbers of league games all under the SoCon umbrella.

Like the dance marathons being staged as inexpensive entertainment during the Great Depression, the Southern Conference basketball tournament was a long-running event in the early years of the decade. Sixteen teams participated, with fifteen games played over the course of five days. This included the marathon first round, featuring eight games in a single day. Play began in the morning and concluded late in the evening. Games were usually scheduled for one-hour intervals, with the next game's teams expected to warm up during halftime of the preceding game.

A result of the wear and tear occurred in the 1931 tournament ultimately won by Maryland, 29–27, over Kentucky. The basketball court at the Atlanta Municipal Auditorium took such a pounding on the opening day that three planks of the hardwood under one basket

The Atlanta Municipal Auditorium was the site of the Southern Conference's postseason basketball tournament from 1921 to 1932. (Kenan Research Center at the Atlanta History Center)

*A Proud Athletic History: 100 Years of the Southern Conference*

*Tulane spent ten years in the Southern Conference (1922–32). Perhaps its greatest performer during that time was DON ZIMMERMAN, a superb athlete from Lake Charles, Louisiana. Dubbed "The Flying Dutchman," Zimmerman was a triple-threat back for Green Wave football teams that went undefeated in league play from 1929–31. He also was a conference champion pole-vaulter and held the US national junior record. A brief feature in the September 22, 1931, edition of the* Gettysburg Times *was headlined "Don Zimmerman Is Tulane's Greatest." Discussing his abilities in baseball, basketball, and other sports, the article concluded, "He also plays tennis and handball in the off season for exercise and spends much time in gymnastics."*

*An assistant football coach with the unlikely name of ELLIS PRUITT (DUMPY) HAGLER forged a remarkable stint as golf coach at Duke. The 22-year-old Hagler followed Wallace Wade from Alabama to Durham and was subsequently handed the reins to the Blue Devil golf program. Duke won the Southern Conference championship in 1933, finished seven strokes behind Washington & Lee the next year, then reeled off eight straight titles until World War II interrupted the sport in 1942. After serving in the armed forces, Hagler returned to coach until 1973. In all, he produced eighteen conference championship teams.*

*Despite the many hardships caused by the decade's harsh economic times, intercollegiate athletics continued on. Said one Penn State historian, "The Great Depression failed to dampen the students' enthusiasm for athletics. During the lean years of the 1930s, athletics offered inexpensive recreation, whether students participated in intramurals or attended intercollegiate athletics as spectators." As trying financial realities intervened, students improvised. When the University of Washington considered canceling the remainder of its baseball season, the eighteen players on the squad piled into six borrowed cars and traveled from Seattle as far away as Idaho to play games and complete their season.*

Dr. Steadman V. Sanford of Georgia was voted the first president of the Southern Conference. (Edward Taylor Newton, Hargrett Rare Book and Manuscript Library, University of Georgia Libraries)

caved in, necessitating a delay so that repairs could be made. "As one might expect," reported the *Atlanta Journal*, "the carpenter was given an ovation."

The inability to regularly compete against all conference members, combined with the wide range of institutional philosophies concerning scholarships, recruiting, even the proper amount of coverage by the media, led some presidents to seek another solution. On December 9, 1932, at the annual league meetings in Knoxville, Tennessee, the first fissure in Southern Conference membership occurred. Shortly after the meeting was called to order, Dr. Steadman Sanford, president of the University of Georgia, announced that his program and twelve others would be departing immediately to form a new league—the Southeastern Conference.

University of Florida president Dr. John T. Tigert was quoted in the next day's *Atlanta Journal*, saying, "In our judgment, the time has arrived for a more compact organization for the administration of athletics. It seems wise for a division of the Southern Conference to be made solely on geographical lines."

The departing institutions included Alabama, Auburn, Florida, Georgia, Georgia Tech, Kentucky, LSU, Mississippi, Mississippi State, Sewanee (the University of the South), Tennessee, Tulane, and Vanderbilt. They formed the original thirteen-member SEC.

The ten remaining members of the SoCon—Clemson, Duke, Maryland, North Carolina, North Carolina State, South Carolina, Virginia, VMI, Virginia Tech, and Washington & Lee—accepted the decision and moved on. But the desire to become bigger and more powerful led administrators to continually look at potential membership options—just as most conferences would do some eighty years later.

| Remaining in the Southern Conference | Leaving to form the Southeastern Conference |
|---|---|
| Clemson | Alabama |
| Duke | Auburn |
| Maryland | Florida |
| North Carolina | Georgia |
| North Carolina State | Georgia Tech |
| South Carolina | Kentucky |
| Virginia | LSU |
| VMI | Mississippi |
| Virginia Tech | Mississippi State |
| Washington and Lee | Sewanee |
| | Tennessee |
| | Tulane |
| | Vanderbilt |

The SEC had its start when thirteen members of the Southern Conference announced their departure in December of 1932. (Graphic by Emily Fulton, Southern Conference)

By 1936, the Southern Conference was bitten by the expansion bug and admitted six new members. Joining the league were the Citadel, Davidson, Furman, Richmond, Wake Forest, and William & Mary. The expansion diversified the membership by adding four more private institutions to go along with Washington & Lee and brought the league's total to sixteen members. But only temporarily.

Frustrated with escalating expenses associated with athletics while the country was in the midst of terrible financial circumstances, Virginia withdrew from the SoCon in the summer of 1937. Until it became a charter member of the Atlantic Coast Conference in 1953, UVA competed as an independent, although it still scheduled Southern Conference opponents in many sports. Four years later, the conference added George Washington University to get back to sixteen members.

Among the conference's premier athletes during the 1930s were football players Ace Parker of Duke, a three-time All-SoCon back, and George Stirnweiss of North Carolina, twice an All-Conference back and later a starting second baseman for the World War II-era New York Yankees. Another star was Banks McFadden of Clemson, who in 1939 led the Tigers to a 9-1 football season that included a 6–3 Cotton Bowl victory over eleventh-ranked Boston College. It was the first bowl appearance in Clemson history.

The best-known coach in the Southern Conference was still Wallace Wade. After guiding Alabama to its third national championship with a perfect season in 1930, Wade stunned the sports world by resigning to accept a similar appointment at Duke. Wade was the Blue Devils' head coach from 1931 to 1950, losing several seasons to military service. His 1938 Blue Devils did not allow a point until a 7–3 loss to Southern California in the final minute of play at the '39 Rose Bowl.

The decade saw Washington & Lee win its only two Southern Conference men's basketball tournament championships, defeating Duke in 1934 and North Carolina in '37.

*An All-America basketball player, Duke's Billy Werber played eleven years in the major leagues and was a member of the 1940 world champion Cincinnati Reds. (Duke University Athletics)*

*Duke's Ace Parker was an All-Southern Conference back in the 1930s. He later played professionally in both the NFL and major league baseball. (Duke University Athletics)*

*VMI's Dick Strickler was a three-time Southern Conference shot put champion. (The Bomb 1939 Yearbook, VMI archives)*

North Carolina captured six outdoor track championships in the thirties. The Tar Heels also produced five consecutive individual tennis champions from 1935 through '39. Duke dominated men's golf, winning six of the seven championships held in the decade.

One program not having success was baseball at Tulane. "Baseball died a violent death in its last season on a Tulane diamond, dropping every game of fourteen they played," reported the somewhat dramatic 1931 *Jambalaya*, the university's yearbook. Tulane's athletic and student councils both voted to discontinue the sport due to "the shocking [lack of] support received at Tulane and the general unpopularity of college amateur baseball." With the move to the SEC, however, Tulane's administration had a change of heart and restored the program to varsity status in 1933.

## WITHDRAWAL LEADS TO THE SEC

AT 2:15 P.M. ON FRIDAY, DECEMBER 9, 1932, Virginia Tech's Clarence (Sally) Miles, president of the conference, called the afternoon session of the annual meeting to order at Knoxville's Farragut Hotel. The first speaker was Dr. Steadman V. Sanford, president of the University of Georgia.

Sanford confirmed what had become a growing rumor—that thirteen member institutions would be withdrawing from the Southern Conference to form a new league called the Southeastern Conference. Those departing were Kentucky, Tennessee, Vanderbilt, the University of the South (Sewanee), Georgia, Georgia Tech, Alabama, Auburn, Mississippi, Mississippi State, Louisiana State, Tulane, and Florida.

Sanford told his colleagues that this division was being made for geographical reasons of the "more closely associated institutions." He hoped that this would help both leagues address athletic problems and lead to better solutions for each group. He stressed that the

*One of Dumpy Hagler's premier golfers at Duke was STEWART (SKIP) ALEXANDER, (pictured) a Durham native who captured back-to-back Southern Conference medalist honors in 1938 and '39, the latter coming on Pinehurst's famed No. 2 course. Alexander became a PGA pro and won twice on the tour in 1948. In September of 1950, he was the lone survivor of the crash of a civil air patrol plane in Evansville, Indiana, and suffered burns over 70 percent of his body. After numerous skin grafts, he had surgeons permanently fuse his pinky fingers to be able to wrap them around the grip of a golf club.*

*Although suffering constant pain and occasional bleeding of the hands while playing, he recovered enough to be named to the 1951 US Ryder Cup team. Playing at the same Pinehurst No. 2 where he won the SoCon championship twelve years earlier, Alexander set a then-record victory margin, beating Great Britain's JOHN PANTON, 8 and 7. He later spent three decades as the head pro at the St. Petersburg Country Club in Florida before passing away in 1997. (Duke University Athletics)*

departure was not a criticism of those left behind. Those leaving would not participate in any Southern Conference championships in the spring of 1933. The withdrawal was immediate.

Despite the jolting news, the attendees more or less continued working on the day's agenda until adjourning to attend a 6:30 dinner hosted by the University of Tennessee at the nearby Andrew Johnson Hotel. The representatives reconvened at 8:30 P.M.

Dr. Allan Hobbs of North Carolina, speaking on behalf of the ten conference members remaining, made it clear that all should recognize that "there are now two separate organizations." After a few awkward moments, Dr. John Tigert, president of the University of Florida, rose to formally tender the resignation of the departing thirteen. Tigert later told observers the conference had "just grown too large."

The official minutes stated, "It was moved and carried that the resignation be accepted."

In retrospect, it seems obvious that divisive issues such as restrictions on participating in football bowl games, discouraging radio broadcasts and out-of-market promotions for football, the lack of consistent in-league scheduling, and the resulting disputes as to who truly was the league champion would lead to cracks in the Southern Conference's foundation.

The SEC began life in the fall of 1933. The league did not appoint a commissioner until former Mississippi governor Martin S. Conner took the position seven years later. Sewanee, Georgia Tech, and Tulane all would eventually leave the SEC.

The remaining ten Southern Conference members carried on their business and almost immediately began sizing up potential expansion candidates. They would take action within three years.

# ANATOMY OF AN EXPANSION

**ENTERING THE 193536 ACADEMIC YEAR,** the Southern Conference was a ten-member organization. It had been almost four years since the mass departure of thirteen institutions to form the Southeastern Conference. Athletic directors and other administrators were interested in growing the league.

South Carolina and Clemson wanted more competition closer to home. Likewise, VMI, Washington & Lee, and, to a lesser extent, Virginia were interested in the same thing. Duke and Washington & Lee wanted a greater presence of private institutions.

There was no shortage of interested candidates—at least eight institutions indicated they would be receptive to joining the Southern Conference if invited. All shared similar traits. The candidates were all either private or military institutions. The league minutes do not reflect any desire to create separate divisions of large state institutions and private ones. The conference was simply eager to add programs that would provide more depth of competition.

Expansion talks first took place at the annual Southern Conference meeting in December of 1934. It was decided that the optimal number of members was sixteen. Two years later, the conference met at the John Marshall Hotel in Richmond on February 7, 1936, with intentions to act. The names of eight potential members were written on a chalkboard. President Forest Fletcher of Washington & Lee conducted a formal vote, with a minimum of six "yes" votes per institution necessary for acceptance.

The eight institutions were The Citadel, Furman University, Centre College, Davidson College, College of William & Mary, University of Richmond, Wake Forest College, and Presbyterian College

Davidson and Richmond each received nine votes. William & Mary, Furman, and the Citadel received seven apiece. Wake Forest received the minimum amount of six votes. There were two votes for Presbyterian and zero for Centre.

Invitations were extended to the six new members who would begin competition in the Southern Conference on September 1, 1936. The geographic balance of the expansion could not have been much better. There were two new members from North Carolina, South Carolina, and Virginia. The conference had become stronger and deeper.

---

*The North Carolina tennis program dominated the thirties, capturing seven SoCon titles in the decade. Named the first coach in UNC tennis history, JOHN KENFIELD joined the program in 1928 and remained through 1955. Among those he coached were All-Americans BITSY GRANT and VIC SEIXAS, the latter a 2011 inductee to the Southern Conference Hall of Fame. Before entering the world of collegiate tennis, Kenfield worked for the Curtiss Candy Company and was a primary participant in the naming of the Baby Ruth candy bar. His coaching record at UNC was 452-32 and included ten undefeated seasons and fifteen conference championships.*

*In 1939, PRESTON B. (HOBY) HOLTZENDORFF III won the 50- and 100-meter freestyle events to lead Clemson to its only Southern Conference swimming championship. The Tigers' were coached by his father, Preston B. Holtzendorff Jr. Two years later, upon graduation, the younger Holtzendorff enlisted in the Army Air Corps and became a fighter pilot with the renowned Flying Tigers squadron. He flew numerous missions in China, eventually earning the rank of lieutenant colonel. Holtzendorff returned to the US as a director for the YMCA in South Carolina and was an air combat consultant to the United Nations. He died in 2002 at the age of 82.*

*On August 26, 1939, using only an overhead camera and one perched down the third base line, station W2XBS in New York City—eventually to become WNBC—carried the majors' first televised game between the Cincinnati Reds and the Brooklyn Dodgers from Ebbets Field. The leadoff hitter for the Reds was Bill Werber, former Duke shortstop. Werber graduated from Duke in 1930 after hitting above .400 in each his three varsity seasons and was also a starter for the basketball team. His ten points led all Blue Devil scorers in a 31–24 loss to Alabama in the 1930 Southern Conference Basketball Championship game.*

The good feelings that existed among administrators lasted all of ten months.

In a December meeting at the same Richmond hotel, faculty representative Norton Pritchett of the University of Virginia was recognized and read a prepared statement composed by the Rector and Visitors—essentially, the university's board of trustees—tendering the resignation of UVA from the Southern Conference. The minutes, recorded by VMI's William Couper, grimly noted, "The communication was laid on the table for the time being."

Two days later, the membership passed a resolution urging Virginia to reconsider. But the UVA administration had made its final decision and formally left the conference in the spring of 1937. Perhaps concerned that Virginia's absence would lead to more expansion talk, Clemson proposed a regulation to limit the Southern Conference to institutions from the states of Virginia, North Carolina, and South Carolina. The motion was defeated, 9–6.

As things turned out, the 1936 expansion would be the last mega-expansion for the Southern Conference. The league added only two new members between 1937 and 1963 (George Washington in 1941 and West Virginia in 1950). And it never again added more than three new members at a time.

From that '36 expansion, only the Citadel and Furman remain affiliated to this day. September 1, 2021, represents their eighty-fifth anniversaries as Southern Conference members.

*Tragedy ended the lives of two Southern Conference boxing champions from the early part of the decade. JAMES (RED) WATTS of South Carolina won the 1932 lightweight title, defeating Duke's LeRoy Sides in the final. Watts, who was elected vice president of his freshman law class at USC, later became a prominent attorney in Darlington, South Carolina. On April 3, 1952, Watts was shot to death as he drove home from work. Two men were charged but were subsequently acquitted. The case became the subject of a 2015 book by Beverly Spears titled* Unsolved: A Murder in the Solid South.

*At the 1933 boxing championship, Virginia's TOM FISHBURNE scored an upset in the final of the welterweight class, outpointing defending champion Charlie Garner of North Carolina. Just five weeks later, Fishburne's body was discovered by a morning housekeeper outside a UVA residence hall. After being hospitalized, he died later that evening. An obituary in the Staunton, Virginia,* News-Leader *stated, "At just what time young Fishburne fell was not known. Supposedly he had fallen from the window while sleep walking."*

# THE
# 1940s

A ny historical account of the 1940s has to begin with the staggering implications of World War II. College athletics in the US were as deeply affected as all other parts of American life. Thousands of potential college students served in the armed forces, and those who attended institutions of higher education realized that the work force they would enter afterwards would be irrevocably altered. College admissions declined, arrangements were made to accommodate veterans, and colleges and universities coped with rationing and supply shortages like any other American industry.

Nevertheless, competition on ball fields, in gymnasiums, on running tracks, golf courses, and tennis courts continued. Surprisingly, the membership of the Southern Conference remained steady throughout the decade.

Duke was the preeminent football program in the conference, winning four championships in a five-year period and playing in the 1942 Rose Bowl and 1945 Sugar Bowl. The '42 Rose Bowl was played at Duke Stadium because of concerns the West Coast might still be a target for the Japanese following the attack on Pearl Harbor less than a month earlier. Despite the home-field advantage, the Blue Devils were defeated by Oregon State, 20–16.

Only one SoCon football team went undefeated during the forties. That was the Clemson Tigers in 1948. Coached by Frank Howard, the Tigers blanked the Citadel, 20–0, in Johnson Hagood Stadium to complete a perfect 10-0 season, thereby earning an invitation to the Gator Bowl in Jacksonville. On New Year's Day, Clemson edged Missouri, 24–23, to complete a perfect season. The biggest player on the Tiger roster was tackle Luke Deanhardt, who was listed at six-foot-three, 230 pounds.

Fuel restrictions and other hardships associated with wartime travel led conference administrators to cancel a number of league championships in the middle of the decade. These included golf, wrestling, indoor and outdoor track and field, and tennis. Only the basketball tournament continued uninterrupted (as it has since 1921).

College basketball in the 1940s took on a different aura with the emerging popularity of two postseason tournaments. The NCAA launched its national championship in 1939, with Oregon winning an inaugural tournament that featured eight teams. More popular was the National Invitation Tournament

*Frank Howard was the Southern Conference Coach of the Year after guiding Clemson to an undefeated season in 1948. (Clemson University Athletics)*

*After a long, stirring touchdown run by a North Carolina tailback, a naval officer watching from the press box told a nearby sports writer, "Look at that guy run! He looks like a runaway train. We ought to call him Choo Choo." Thus was born one of the more colorful nicknames in Southern Conference history. CHARLIE (CHOO CHOO) JUSTICE (pictured) attended UNC Chapel Hill and was twice voted the SoCon's Player of the Year (1948 and '49). Both times he finished runner-up in the balloting for the Heisman Trophy. The Asheville native ran or threw for sixty-four touchdowns in his career and compiled a total of 4,883 total yards. He led UNC to SoCon championships in 1946 and '49. In 1950, Justice was drafted by the Washington Redskins and was the MVP of that year's College All-Star game. In 1961, he was inducted into the College Football Hall of Fame. (University of North Carolina Athletics)*

(NIT), held exclusively in New York's Madison Square Garden, which began a year earlier. Although consistent participants in both tournaments, the Southern Conference never saw one of its members win either event.

North Carolina did manage to reach the championship game of the NCAA tournament in 1946. Coached by Ben Carnevale, the Tar Heels were narrowly beaten by Oklahoma A&M (now Oklahoma State), 43–40. One of the starters for UNC was a skinny six-foot-six forward named Horace (Bones) McKinney, who would ultimately carve out twenty-plus years as a basketball coach, most notably at Wake Forest.

The unwieldy nature of a sixteen-team conference during wartime was perfectly captured by the final league standings for the 1944–45 basketball season. South Carolina was declared the league champion with a 9-0 conference record. Richmond was also undefeated in the league—but played only two SoCon games. Other conference game totals—Duke (7), North Carolina (14), Clemson (8), VMI (5)—reflect the hodge-podge nature of conference scheduling. In fact, it would not be until the 1980–81 season, the SoCon's sixtieth basketball season, that all members would play the same number of league games.

North Carolina earned six outdoor track and field titles, five of them coming on their home track in Chapel Hill. The Tar Heels also won all four indoor championships contested during the 1940s.

Washington & Lee had more success in wrestling than any other Southern Conference sport. Of the first thirteen championships conducted by the SoCon, the Generals won seven times, including a three-peat from 1948 to 1950. Owing to the popularity and success of the sport for both Washington & Lee and VMI, the wrestling tournament was commonly held in Lexington, Virginia, through the late 1950s.

Swimming and diving was a sport heavily impacted by the war. At the beginning of the decade, seven programs participated in the annual March conference meet. By 1943 the depleted ranks of male students combined with gasoline rationing and travel restrictions led to only four teams competing—North Carolina, Duke, VMI, and Virginia Tech. The league's swimming committee recommended suspending the championship for the duration of the war. Indeed, the meet would not be brought back until 1947.

*Only one baseball program has ever represented the Southern Conference in the championship game of the College World Series. It came in 1949 when Wake Forest faced Texas in Wichita, Kansas. (Note: The CWS moved to Omaha a year later and remains there today.) The Demon Deacons knocked off some heavyweights to reach the championship round, beating Kentucky, Mississippi State, Notre Dame, and Southern Cal. Wake Forest was led by second baseman CHARLIE TEAGUE, a .353 hitter that season and an eventual SoCon Hall of Famer.*

*In the semifinal round against Southern California, Teague's triple in the bottom of the twelfth inning scored GENE HOOKS (pictured) with the winning run in a 2–1 victory. Hooks would go on to serve as Wake Forest's director of athletics for twenty-eight years. In the championship game, Coach LEE GOOCH'S Deacons fell to the Texas Longhorns, 10–3. Six years later, Wake Forest won the CWS as a member of the Atlantic Coast Conference (Wake Forest University Athletics)*

The UNC Tar Heels easily won all seven swimming championships contested in the decade. The Heels' best showing nationally was a seventh-place finish in the 1946 NCAA championships at Yale University.

As the fifties approached, the Southern Conference seemed serene and stable on the surface. But factors were at work that would once more lead to massive upheaval. The next set of conference realignment issues would challenge the league's leadership to keep the SoCon relevant in the world of college athletics. And once again, that leadership would respond.

## THE QUESTION OF FRESHMAN ELIGIBILITY

**PERIODICALLY SINCE THE FORMATION OF THE NCAA** in 1906, colleges and universities have struggled with the question of whether freshmen student-athletes should be eligible to compete in varsity athletics. Opponents of the rule decry the difficulties all freshmen students face in adjusting to college life, believing athletes should have a full year to establish themselves academically and socially before competing. Proponents generally cite the better reward on the recruiting investment of having a student-athlete compete for four seasons and reduced turnover in roster management.

In the early twentieth century, freshmen were ineligible to compete. But the American entry into World War I in 1917 thinned the ranks of college men. Most institutions permitted freshmen to compete. The Southern Conference, however, had prohibited freshmen from varsity competition since its inception in 1921. The entrance of the United States into World War II led the NCAA to pass regulations again declaring freshmen eligible beginning in 1943. The Southern Conference abided by this change.

During the war, participation regulations were generally relaxed. But when the war ended, young men were now returning to college on the GI Bill in large numbers. Most conferences felt that the prohibition on freshman eligibility needed to be restored. With the Big Ten Conference leading the way, the vast majority of institutions agreed to honor a rule

When the attack on Pearl Harbor triggered American involvement in the Second World War, Southern Conference administrators quickly realized collegiate athletics would be severely impacted. Domestic rationing of supplies and goods, restrictions on transportation, and other wartime factors led to playing schedules being reduced and, in some cases, eliminated. Football and basketball suffered some effects, but golf, tennis, wrestling, track and field, cross country, and swimming and diving all experienced conference tournament cancelations between 1942 and 1945.

On December 12, 1941, just four days after Congress authorized the United States to enter the war, Southern Conference administrators met in Richmond for the league's annual meeting. The conference budget—which included annual dues of $50 per member—was quickly approved. There followed some rambling discussions on relatively insignificant pieces of legislation. Finally, Virginia Tech's CLARENCE (SALLY) MILES addressed what was, no doubt, on all minds when he moved that the executive committee be empowered to call a special meeting to consider "any question which the Executive Committee deems necessary as a result of the present war emergency." The group approved the motion unanimously. These discussions were conducted the following August and centered primarily on certification matters for those in the armed forces as well as the intricacies of competition versus noncollegiate athletic squads.

making freshmen ineligible effective New Year's Day of 1947. The NCAA would follow the same guideline in adjudicating eligibility for its championships.

The Southern Conference, however, did not go along with the others.

At its annual winter meeting in December of 1945, some four months after the war's end, Southern Conference delegates debated the timing of freshman ineligibility. Most of the representatives in attendance—which included Maryland football coach Paul (Bear) Bryant—favored making the cutoff one year later than the Big Ten's date. Subsequent advocacy by William & Mary faculty representative Sharvy Umbeck and Duke's Wallace Wade convinced the group to adopt July 1, 1948, as the beginning of freshman ineligibility. The revised date was unanimously approved by the sixteen member institutions and all seemed fine.

Fast forward to the end of the 1950–51 basketball season.

Everett Case's North Carolina State Wolfpack won the league championship with a 13-1 record and withstood a thirty-one-point barrage from Dick Groat to outlast Duke in the final of the conference basketball tournament, 67–63. But shortly before the conference tournament, Athletic Director Roy Clogston was notified that three of his senior stars had been declared ineligible by the NCAA.

The three—Sammy Ranzino, Vic Bubas, and Paul Horvath—had competed as freshmen in 1947–48. Therefore, participation in the 1951 NCAA Tournament would represent their fourth year of varsity eligibility, a violation of the relatively new NCAA rule. Case and his administrators were stunned. The trio were starters and All-Conference performers.

*During the years 1943, '44, and '45, six conference members suspended their football programs due to decreased wartime male enrollment. They included the Citadel, Furman, Davidson, George Washington, Virginia Tech, and Washington & Lee. All returned to gridiron competition in the 1946 season. Duke won the regular-season title in three of the four wartime years (1942–45) and defeated Alabama, 29–26, in the Rose Bowl on New Year's Day in 1945.*

In those days, teams could compete in both the NCAA and NIT tournaments. NC State traveled to Madison Square Garden as the No. 2 seed in the 1951 NIT. Playing with their complete roster for the final time that season, State dropped a 71–59 decision to Seton Hall.

The NCAA regional would be held on the Wolfpack's home court of Reynolds Coliseum. Playing without Ranzino, Bubas, and Horvath, Case rallied the undermanned Wolfpack to a 67–62 victory over Villanova before losing to Illinois in the regional semifinals.

*A Proud Athletic History: 100 Years of the Southern Conference*

Case's team finished the year 30–7, becoming only the second Southern Conference basketball team to win thirty games in a season. But the eligibility snafu became a *cause celebre* in Raleigh for years.

Freshmen were permitted eligibility by the NCAA in 1950 and '51 during the Korean War. After that, they were again banned from competing on varsity teams. Freshman teams became the norm in select sports. Perhaps the most famous example of a freshman team was the 1965–66 UCLA men's basketball squad that included Lew Alcindor (later known as Kareem Abdul-Jabbar), Lucious Allen, and Lynn Shackleford. The three led the Bruins' frosh to a resounding win over the two-time defending NCAA champion Bruins' varsity in the first game ever played at Pauley Pavilion.

In 1968, the NCAA repealed freshman ineligibility in all sports except football and basketball. Four years later, citing efforts to reduce expenses, collegiate administrators declared freshmen eligible in all varsity sports, a status that remains to this day.

## MEMORABLE MOMENTS

### MAY 8, 1948

### PALMER CAPTURES SOCON CHAMPIONSHIP

Competing for Wake Forest, Arnold Palmer earned the first of his two Southern Conference golf championships at the league's tournament in Pinehurst, North Carolina. Playing on the famed No. 2 course, the freshman from Latrobe, Pennsylvania, shot 145 during the two rounds to edge North Carolina's Harvie Ward by a stroke. Ward's approach shot on the last hole missed going in by about three or four inches. "It was a great shot that scared me to death," Palmer later recalled. A year later,

*Arnold Palmer (left) shows his putting stroke to a pair of teammates. (Wake Forest University Athletics)*

Palmer repeated as conference champion with a blistering 136 score, a thirty-six-hole record that stood until the early 1970s.

# THE
# 1950s

On January 1, 1951, as SoCon members Washington & Lee and Clemson played in New Year's Day bowl games, Wallace Wade officially became the first commissioner in Southern Conference history. He soon established a small office in the Carolina Theatre Building in his hometown of Durham, North Carolina, hired a secretary at an annual salary of $2,700 to handle his correspondence, and began the task of supervising conference business.

His duties were multifaceted—setting up league meetings, maintaining minutes from those meetings, visiting the campuses to chat with administrators and coaches, determining championship sites, and, increasingly, conducting discussions related to athletes' eligibility and scholarships. Wade used his knowledge as a widely respected coach to craft rules and regulations designed to improve the Southern Conference.

But he had figuratively stepped into a minefield and the inevitable explosion was only a matter of time.

The large state universities in the seventeen-member SoCon—the league had added West Virginia in 1950—wanted more flexibility, more structure in their scheduling, and more opportunities to compete nationally rather than regionally. They wanted to promote their athletic programs and increase their exposure. Maryland and North Carolina, in particular, began thinking the Southern Conference was no longer a solution for their athletic goals.

These feelings crystallized later in 1951 when SoCon presidents voted 14–3 to eliminate spring football practice and no longer participate in bowl games. This would, essentially, downgrade football as a Southern Conference sport. After an undefeated regular season on the gridiron, Maryland announced it would accept an invitation to play Tennessee in the

*JOHNNY MAPP (pictured with coach John McKenna, center, and teammate George Ramer) established himself as one of the finest two-sport athletes in VMI history. In his three years of varsity track and field competition, the Portsmouth, Virginia, native was a champion in the sprints and hurdles. His four individual victories in 1954 led VMI to its first-ever outdoor track championship. On the football field, Mapp used his great speed as both a defensive back and halfback. As a junior, he intercepted a SoCon-record ten passes for the Keydets. In his senior year, he played both offense and defense, scored thirteen touchdowns, and averaged almost six yards per carry. Beginning in 1957, the Keydets won four Southern Conference championships in six years.*

*He was subsequently voted the conference's Athlete of the Year and was drafted by the Cleveland Browns, but opted to attend medical school and later became a physician in the state of Virginia. He is a member of the VMI Hall of Fame. (Virginia Military Institute Athletics)*

Sugar Bowl. "Never before has a Southern Conference team failed to receive the league's blessings to play in a bowl game," said Maryland head coach Jim Tatum. "I think the individual school should make its own decision on such matters."

Clemson, too, decided to play in the Gator Bowl, even after asking and being denied permission by the other members. Both programs were put on probation by the conference presidents for the 1952 season and prohibited from playing any Southern Conference members. At a March meeting in Chapel Hill, Maryland president Harry (Curley) Byrd, a former football coach for the Terrapins, was mostly conciliatory in his remarks.

"We did not feel the action of the Presidents group was legal," he said, reading a prepared statement. "But Maryland violated a Southern Conference regulation when we played in the Sugar Bowl. Disciplinary action was proper toward both institutions. We look forward to continuing our Conference relationships."

Jim Tatum coached Maryland to a pair of bowl game victories while the Terrapins were Southern Conference members. (University of Maryland Athletics)

Despite sanctions limiting them to only three home games in 1952, the Terrapins still finished 7-2. But they could not play in a postseason game. The fuse was set, waiting only for the match to be lit. A growing resentment had been introduced and soon led to a serious membership rift.

Talk of the league breaking apart followed for months. Finally, on May 8, 1953, at a conference meeting at the Sedgefield Inn in Greensboro, seven members announced their intentions to separate from the Southern Conference and immediately form a new alliance. They would soon name it the Atlantic Coast Conference.

The new ACC would include North Carolina, South Carolina, Duke, North Carolina State, Maryland, Wake Forest, and Clemson. In a move that would never happen today, Commissioner Wade was asked to serve in the same role for the new conference in its first year. This he did from his office in Durham before turning over the ACC reins to Wake Forest athletic director Jim Weaver a year later.

"It was a complete surprise to me and I thought I knew Duke about as well as anybody," recalled Wade years later. "I knew there was interest in it, and I knew they were talking about it, but I had no idea they had developed a program to the extent that they had when they sprang it in Greensboro that day.

"I personally hoped that it wouldn't come," he added. "We had a pretty homogeneous group and we were doing pretty well."

Colonel David S. McAlister, faculty representative for the Citadel and a member of the Class of 1924, had been on the scene since the Citadel joined the Southern Conference in 1936. He later remembered, "The size of the league had made the basketball tournament awkward at a time when the tournament had become a major source of income."

Before the ACC split, Southern Conference basketball was starting to receive more respect from opponents, the media, and the increasing number of fans following the sport. Newspapers and magazine articles trumpeted the accomplishments of star players competing across the conference.

*Begun as a conference sport in the 1955–56 academic year, rifle was initially dominated by Virginia Tech. The Hokies won the first three championships, all hosted by West Virginia in Morgantown. But in 1959, the Citadel climbed to the top and earned its first championship behind the sharpshooting of ROBERT METSKER, who led all participants with 289 points. Metsker subsequently became the first rifle All-America selection in the Citadel's history. The triumph in '59 signaled the beginning of a highly successful stretch for the Bulldogs. The Citadel captured ten rifle championships in sixteen years through the early 1970s.*

At Duke, a two-sport athlete named Dick Groat earned All-SoCon selection as a basketball guard in 1950–51 and 1951–52. Groat also attracted the attention of major league baseball scouts and wound up signing with the Pittsburgh Pirates, for whom he would become an All-Star shortstop and the National League's Most Valuable Player in 1960. He would ultimately be the first Duke basketball player to have his jersey (No. 10) retired.

Sammy Ranzino and Paul Horvath, members of coach Everett Case's Indiana/Illinois pipeline, led the Wolfpack of North Carolina State to NCAA tournament appearances in 1950 and 1951. Case's teams, which captured six consecutive SoCon basketball tournaments, became the first program to celebrate a championship by getting a ladder and a pair of scissors to cut down the nets from each goal.

At Furman, a slender six-foot-three guard from Corbin, Kentucky, caught the attention of the entire sports world in 1954. Frank Selvy had led the nation in scoring as a junior and was well on his way to being named All-America for a third consecutive year. On February 13, 1954, Selvy scored 100 points in a Furman rout of Newberry College, setting an NCAA single game record that stands to this day. The first college basketball player in the NCAA to score 1,000 points in a season, Selvy was the No. 1 overall pick in the '54 NBA draft.

Up in Morgantown, West Virginia, coach Fred Schaus was building a dynasty with the West Virginia Mountaineers. His foundation included a pair of high-scoring players with very different styles. Rod Hundley, nicknamed "Hot Rod," combined great skills with a playful, irreverent attitude on the court. Schaus's other star, Jerry West, was a deadly serious competitor who could score, rebound, and pass as well as any player in the country. Upon joining the conference, West Virginia placed first or second in the league in all but two years during the

*Left, Paul Horvath was one of three key North Carolina State players ruled ineligible for the 1951 NCAA Tournament because of Southern Conference freshman eligibility policies in the 1940s. Right, the Wolfpack of NC State captured the 1950 Southern Conference Basketball Tournament. Future Duke head coach and Sun Belt Conference commissioner Vic Bubas is third from the right, top row. (North Carolina State University Athletics)*

1950s and finished the decade with a Southern Conference-record forty-four-straight league victories.

The high-water mark for West Virginia was the 1959 NCAA Tournament. Four wins put the Mountaineers in the championship game against All-America center Darrell Imhoff and the University of California. After leading by double digits in the first half, West Virginia lost when Imhoff tipped in a rebound with seventeen seconds to play, giving Cal a 71–70 victory. It remains the only time a SoCon team has played for the national championship.

Frank Selvy (far right) on a backyard court in his hometown of Corbin, KY. Selvy's 100-point game in February of 1954 drew national attention. (Furman University Athletics)

Under head coach John McKenna, VMI launched its greatest football era, earning the Southern Conference championship in 1957, '59, '60, and '62. In a six-year stretch, the Keydets were 27-5-2 in league play. The undefeated 1957 team, quarterbacked by future NFL head coach Bobby Ross, finished thirteenth in the final poll of the Associated Press.

A memorable season ended with a 14–6 Thanksgiving Day triumph over rival Virginia Tech. Much to McKenna's eventual regret, he put the decision whether to accept an invitation to the Sun Bowl to the members of his team in the winning locker room. By a 2-to-1 margin, the team voted to decline the invitation, preferring to have an uninterrupted Christmas vacation.

It was a devastating decision for the VMI coaching staff and administration, which saw its one and only chance to play in a bowl game evaporate. "They sure fooled me," McKenna told the press as he relayed the outcome.

Tom Joynes, VMI's director of sports information, recalled speaking with McKenna the night of the vote. "He told me that he should have let the starters do the voting," Joynes remembered. "The coaches wanted to go, and it hurt them that the players didn't want to go."

One casualty of the latest conference realignment was the SoCon baseball tournament. With the sport dominated by the members of the new ACC, the tournament, initiated in 1950, was discontinued in 1954 to reduce expenses. It would be thirty years before it would be reinstated.

In 1954, an academic cheating scandal in the football program at Washington & Lee led the institution's board of trustees to eliminate athletic scholarships. Already among the smallest

Nicknamed "The Cadillac" as much for his elegant style on the field as for the way it rhymed with his last name, STEVE WADIAK (pictured) was a legendary figure in the history of South Carolina football. After serving in the navy in World War II, Wadiak immediately made an impact with the Gamecocks, rushing for 420 yards as a freshman. In 1950, he broke CHARLIE JUSTICE'S Southern Conference record by gaining 998 yards and was named Player of the Year.

Following his senior season, Wadiak was drafted by the Pittsburgh Steelers in the third round. Tragically, he was the only fatality in the crash of a vehicle with six passengers near Aiken, South Carolina, on March 9, 1952. Thrown from the car, he suffered a broken neck, was rushed to a hospital in Augusta, and died later that day. He was 24 years old. Wadiak's No. 37 jersey was eventually retired by South Carolina. (University of South Carolina Athletics)

A Washington & Lee wrestler works to pin his opponent in a 1948 match. W&L won the conference tournament that year, the first of three in a row for the program. (Washington & Lee University archives)

members in terms of enrollment, the board's decision led Washington & Lee to leave the Southern Conference in 1958. W&L departed having won SoCon championships across four decades in football, basketball, indoor track, golf, swimming, and wrestling.

Midway through the decade, conference administrators introduced a new sport. The first rifle championship took place in Morgantown in 1956 and saw Virginia Tech emerge as the team champion, with the Citadel's D. H. Smith posting the high individual score. Rifle became the tenth championship sport sanctioned by the Southern Conference. It would take a full ten years for the next new men's sport—soccer—to be introduced.

## ANOTHER SPLIT AND THE ACC IS BORN

ON MAY 8, 1953, the Southern Conference convened its annual league meetings at the Sedgefield Inn in Greensboro. President Max Farrington of George Washington University called the meeting to order shortly after 10:00 A.M. He then recognized Dr. James T. Penney, a biology professor at the University of South Carolina, who read the following resolution:

> As most of you know, for some time there has been under consideration a possibility of forming a new and smaller playing conference. These ideas were crystallized at a meeting last night in which Clemson College, Duke University, the University of North Carolina, the University of South Carolina, Wake Forest University, North Carolina State College, and the University of Maryland decided that they should notify the Southern Conference that they propose to organize a new intercollegiate athletic conference.

Dr. Penney continued by expressing his group's hope that this action would prove best for all parties concerned and that a committee of departing members would work with the remaining institutions to iron out all obligations. Dr. Farrington quickly suggested a recess be declared with the remaining ten institutions staying put in the meeting room. The departing seven—who would soon become part of the Atlantic Coast Conference—left to go sit in patio chairs by the pool.

"We knew it was going to happen unless lightning struck," recalled Irwin Smallwood, a reporter covering the meetings for the *Greensboro Daily News*. "Reflecting on it," the 91-year-old Smallwood told Barry Jacobs of the *Charlotte Observer* in 2017, "the culture of the haves and have nots had really come to play a role."

Several factors played a part in the fissure that launched the ACC. Scheduling, particularly in football and basketball, had become a serious concern. The size and geography of the seventeen-member league made true round-robin scheduling impossible. Teams could arrange to play whomever they chose in the conference. "You could win the Southern Conference football championship and never play anybody," recalled Smallwood.

Another sticking point was the question of freshman eligibility for varsity sports. The league had not restored eligibility for freshmen after the war as other conferences did, thereby rendering star players ineligible for postseason competition. The conference's basketball tournament was making significant revenue but being largely supported by fans of the departing seven programs. The final straw likely was the vote to prohibit teams from playing in bowl games. A majority of the presidents and faculty representatives did not want seasons extended, thereby causing students to miss additional class. Both Maryland and Clemson ignored the ban in 1951 and were placed on probation by the Southern Conference.

The departing institutions all had similar lofty ambitions for their athletic programs and had been the most successful in the conference. They no longer wanted to be restricted by some of the less ambitious athletic programs.

In the evening session at the Sedgefield Inn, the seven departing institutions met with the remaining ten to discuss specific terms of the split. Both conferences would use the services of Commissioner Wallace Wade's office for an undetermined period of time. The scheduling of spring sports would continue intact through the end of the semester. The ACC group would begin its own competition in the fall. Financial assets would remain with the Southern. The remainder of the May agenda would be postponed until the next scheduled meeting.

---

## MEMORABLE MOMENTS

### FEBRUARY 13, 1954
### SELVY SCORES 100 POINTS

More than sixty-five years later, the NCAA Division I basketball record for most points in a game by one player remains the 100 scored by Furman's Frank Selvy in a 149–95 victory over visiting Newberry College at Greenville's Textile Hall. Selvy, who would go on to play nine seasons in the NBA, made forty-one field goals in sixty-six attempts and was eighteen for twenty-two at the foul line. Sitting on ninety-eight points with time about to expire, he took a pass and swished a flying one-hander from about thirty feet out on the left side to reach 100. His teammates proceeded to carry him off the court on their shoulders as the crowd rushed onto the court.

Selvy, whose family traveled from Corbin, Kentucky, to watch him play at Furman for the first time, accomplished the feat without benefit of the three-point shot which was still twenty-six years away.

Before President Farrington could gavel the session to adjournment, Dr. George Modlin, president of the University of Richmond, said he hoped he was speaking for all parties when he said he "appreciated the fine spirit in which the separation of the conferences was taking place."

The ACC immediately established itself as one of the premier conferences in the nation. Now free to play in a bowl game whenever it received an invitation, Maryland won the mythical 1953 football national championship by completing an undefeated regular season, before losing, 7–0, to Oklahoma in the Orange Bowl.

Ironically, at the December league meeting, Southern Conference representatives who just two years earlier had banned bowl appearances now passed a resolution congratulating the football programs at both Maryland and West Virginia (which had represented the SoCon in the Sugar Bowl) on their successful seasons.

*The 1957 Southern Conference Basketball Tournament in Richmond featured eight teams playing seven games over three consecutive days. Only five officials shared those fourteen total assignments, sometimes working an afternoon game followed by one in the evening. This was standard operating procedure for the conference during this era. In 1964, only four officials worked the entire tournament.*

*One of the group at both the 1957 and '64 tournaments was LOU BELLO, a long-time SoCon official with a reputation as a skilled referee who might do or say anything.*

*"Lou was all referee and part clown," said Wake Forest coach BONES MCKINNEY. "But he had as good a judgment as anybody refereeing during my time." Bello once instructed a booing crowd tossing pennies at him to start throwing half dollars instead. In a one-sided game, he'd kid with, but never embarrass, the losing coach and players. His personality and quick wit led to a post-officiating career as a TV and radio basketball commentator in the Carolinas before his death in 1991.*

# THE
# 1960s

January 1, 1960, began a new year, a new decade, and, with the election in November of John F. Kennedy, a new era in America. It also ushered in a new era in the Southern Conference, one that would include continuing realignment, the end of segregation on many team rosters, and the addition of new championship sports. Like America, the SoCon also boasted a new leader.

After nine years of steering the conference through the ACC split, 67-year-old Wallace Wade decided to step down as commissioner in December of 1959. His replacement was Lloyd Jordan, a slightly younger contemporary of Wade's.

Jordan, whose snow-white hair parted in the middle gave him the look of a college professor, had enjoyed football and basketball coaching success at little Amherst College in the 1930s and forties. His football coaching career ended in 1956 following a nondescript seven-year stint at Harvard. Born in Punxsutawney, Pennsylvania, and educated at the University of Pittsburgh, where he played football for legendary coach Pop Warner, Jordan would serve as commissioner for fourteen years.

Aside from secretarial help with his correspondence and travel, the only full-time assistance Jordan had was J. Dallas Shirley, who started in 1967 as assistant to the commissioner and coordinator of officials. Until his retirement in 1988 at the age of 74, the silver-haired Shirley's responsibilities ranged from assigning football and basketball officials, to overseeing league championships, to securing advertisements for the basketball tournament program, to publishing media guides and generally coordinating events requiring the commissioner's presence.

He did all this while working out of an office in Reston, Virginia. His contact with the commissioner was limited to either a long-distance phone call in an era before cell phones, or, if it wasn't as crucial a matter, a typed letter dropped in the mail.

Shirley had been one of the premier basketball officials in the eastern half of the United States. He began calling games in the Southern Conference in 1937 and also worked in the

*Southern Conference football teams made thirty-six appearances in bowl games between 1926 and 1971. Seven of those came in the Tangerine Bowl. At a time when there were less than a dozen bowl games played in college football, the Tangerine Bowl was a significant event.*

*The game had its origins in 1947 when local organizers and tourism officials looked for a way to bring fans from other parts of the country to warm, sunny Orlando in the dead of winter. The game was generally played shortly after Christmas while students were on break. The logistics certainly appealed to Southern Conference fans from Virginia and the Carolinas.*

*With his roots in football as a player and coach, Commissioner LLOYD JORDAN made it a priority to align the Southern Conference with the Tangerine Bowl. He met with bowl officials repeatedly to work out a tie-in. At the time, the SEC was aligned with the Sugar Bowl, the Big Eight with the Orange Bowl, the Big Ten and Pac 8 with the Rose Bowl, and the Southwest Conference with the Cotton Bowl. By the late 1960s, the same league tie-in was in place at the Tangerine Bowl between the SoCon and the Mid-American Conference.*

*In a twelve-year span, SoCon teams appeared in the game seven times, winning four. From 1968 to 1971, the game pitted the SoCon champion versus the MAC champ. The conference's last appearance—and last bowl game—was Richmond's 28–3 loss to Toledo in 1971. The Tangerine Bowl was renamed the Citrus Bowl in 1982.*

ACC, officiating more than 2,000 games in a three-decade career. He worked the 1959 Pan American Games and the 1960 Olympics in Rome.

Shirley kept meticulous records and meeting minutes in carefully organized three-ring binders. He expected his officials to fully follow all mechanics and regulations. And he guarded the league's money as if it were his own.

"I was scheduled to work the first game in the new Ramsey Center in 1986, North Carolina State and Western Carolina," recalled Mike Wood, longtime SoCon basketball official who was named the conference's officiating coordinator in 2011. "When we get to the locker room, my partners and I find three other officials. I called Mr. Shirley immediately.

"I hear him shuffling through papers. Then he says, 'Mr. Wood, there's been a mistake. It's an ACC assignment. You can go home.' Well, I've now driven 120 miles, eaten a pre-game meal, have another 120 miles to get home and have lost a date where I could have worked. So I ask him if there's any compensation coming.

"He says, 'Mr. Wood, would you have me take it out of my own pocket?' The idea that the Conference would cover some of the crew's costs for his error never entered his mind."

Shirley, who passed away in 1994, also had a dry sense of humor. As he always did, he was responsible for taking minutes at the 1973 spring meeting at Myrtle Beach. When a lengthy session of the athletic directors ran almost to midnight, it was decided that the meeting's secretary would type up the minutes and distribute them to the ADs before the next day's 8:00 A.M. start.

Wrote Shirley, "The secretary uttered a few dirty words and went to bed."

As the decade began, one resurgent athletic program for the now nine-member SoCon was the Citadel. The Bulldogs captured their first-ever football championship in 1961 led by All-Conference running back Early Eastburn and quarterback Bill Whaley, who led the league in total offense. The basketball team posted back-to-back records of 15-8 and 17-8, reaching the SoCon Tournament semifinals in 1961. The baseball team, too, was a league co-champion in 1960 paced by the conference's leading batter, Henry Mura, who hit a cool .478.

At George Washington, history was made in 1964 when Garry Lyle, a sophomore quarterback from the suburbs of Pittsburgh, became the first African-American football player to earn All-Southern Conference recognition.

"Lyle, sophomore dazzler of the GW backfield, is the first Negro to be accorded all-conference honors in a league that until last year had no Negro players at all," wrote Ed Young of the Associated Press. "Lyle's selection for the All-Southern backfield is one of two signs of the times implicit in this year's team. For the first time in a decade, it's a two-platoon squad with offensive and defensive units."

Lyle was eventually drafted in the third round as a defensive back by the Chicago Bears and played seven seasons in the NFL. George Washington discontinued its football program following the 1966 season.

Midway through the decade Virginia Tech became the last charter member to depart the Southern Conference after forty-four years. From the "1964–65 Report of the President of Virginia Polytechnic Institute" came the following explanation: "The decision had not been unexpected. It was apparent with the increasing momentum of the athletic program at V.P.I., and the outstanding physical facilities being made available, that the University would seek to schedule games with more comparable institutions—particularly the state universities of the region."

*Garry Lyle spent seven seasons with the Chicago Bears after earning All-Conference honors at George Washington. (Gelman Special Collections, the George Washington University Libraries)*

The report also expressed the institution's serious desire to become a member of the ACC, a wish that would not be granted until 2003.

Meanwhile, another Virginia-based SoCon member was building its own dynasty in track and field. Beginning in 1966, William & Mary put together ten consecutive years of winning both the indoor and outdoor championships. W&M Hall of Famers Jim Johnson (mile) and Juris Luzins (880-yard run) were among those capturing three conference titles during their careers in the mid-1960s at a time when freshmen were ineligible for varsity competition.

While William & Mary dominated the decade in track and field, the sixties saw increasing parity in the conference's most visible sport—football. Nine different programs earned at least a share of the championship from 1960–69. This included East Carolina, which shared the title in 1966 with William & Mary. The Pirates were competing in only their third season as a Southern Conference member.

*VMI's swimming and diving championship in 1962 was its fifth straight Southern Conference title. It was also the second consecutive year that the Keydets edged Virginia Tech by two points. One of the linchpins of the VMI program was senior GEORGE COLLINS (pictured).*

*The West Haven, Connecticut, native won the 220-, 400-, and 1,500-meter freestyle events in the '62 championship meet. Collins's achievements in the pool led to his induction into the VMI Hall of Fame in 1973.*

*He went on to carve out a truly impressive professional career. After serving in the US Air Force, Collins entered the world of financial investments, eventually becoming the CEO of T. Rowe Price & Associates. Later he was managing partner of Collins Capital Investors Trust in Florida. He earned numerous community and civic awards and served on several boards. In July of 2012 he was appointed to the VMI Board of Visitors. (Virginia Military Institute Archives)*

As the decade drew to a close, Davidson completed what would be the Wildcats' lone SoCon title as it finished 5-1 in the league, earning co-champion honors with Richmond. Davidson quarterback Gordon Slade was the conference's Player of the Year, guiding the 7-4 Wildcats to an appearance in the 1969 Tangerine Bowl. Davidson's Homer Smith parlayed his Coach of the Year success to subsequent head coaching positions at the University of the Pacific and Army.

But as exciting as a share of the football championship may have been for Davidson fans, what was occurring in basketball carried far more national significance.

In the spring of 1960, the Davidson administration reached out to a highly successful high school basketball coach from Newport News High in Virginia. His name was Charles (Lefty) Driesell. Inheriting a team that went 0-10 in the SoCon, Driesell had the Wildcats contending for the conference championship within three years. By his fourth season (1963–64), the Wildcats were the class of the league and among the nation's top programs.

Davidson had stars in rugged forward Fred Hetzel and smooth-shooting guard Dick Snyder. Hetzel, a member of the SoCon's Hall of Fame, would eventually become the No. 1 overall pick in the 1965 NBA draft.

In 1964–65, Davidson went unbeaten in league play, but was upset by West Virginia in overtime in the semifinals of the Southern Conference Tournament at Charlotte. In those days, only one team per conference qualified for the NCAAs. Wrote Joe Jares in *Sports Illustrated*: "The tiny Presbyterian school . . . was the obvious choice to represent the Conference against Providence in Philadelphia on March 8. But few things are logical in the Southern Conference, a strange assortment of public, private and military schools that has changed borders more often than Czechoslovakia."

The next year, Davidson followed up another league championship by winning the conference tournament and made its first-ever NCAA tournament appearance. Driesell led the Wildcats to a pair of NCAA appearances in 1968 and 1969, losing in the regional final both times to Dean Smith and North Carolina by a combined total of six points. Driesell, a

*Coach Lefty Driesell accepts the championship trophy after his Wildcats won the 1968 Charlotte Invitational by beating Maryland and Texas. (Davidson College Athletics)*

member of the SoCon's Hall of Fame, left Davidson in 1969 to start a legendary career as head coach of the Maryland Terrapins.

Davidson's archrival for basketball supremacy in the SoCon was undoubtedly West Virginia. From 1961 through 1969, one or the other shared or won outright the league regular-season title. But West Virginia's administration decided it wanted more competition versus larger public schools—where had conference members heard that before?—and left the league in the spring of 1968.

For Commissioner Jordan, the once-sprawling Southern Conference of twenty-three members had been whittled down to eight. And as the turbulent 1960s gave way to the seventies, the realignment cycle showed no signs of stopping.

"We had a very compatible league, although we did have some changes in membership," Jordan would later reminisce with writer Bob Spear of the *Columbia* (SC) *State*. "I considered it this way—when one door closes, look for another that opens."

# MISS SOUTHERN CONFERENCE

**TO RAISE AWARENESS OF THE 100TH ANNIVERSARY** of the first college football game, the NCAA partnered with one of its leading television sponsors, Chevrolet, to conduct a national contest to select a college football queen for 1969. Conferences were asked to select a candidate to participate. Each contestant filled out a basic application form, supplied black-and-white photos, and completed a short essay entitled "What I Like Most About College Football."

Working with school administrators, Assistant to the Commissioner J. Dallas Shirley handled all the arrangements for the Southern Conference. In November of 1968, seven contestants were introduced to the crowd at halftime of the Citadel-William & Mary game at Williamsburg, Virginia. Following a parade that featured the women riding in open Chevy cars in school colors, Grace Roselli, a junior majoring in Spanish at William & Mary, was crowned Miss Southern Conference.

"It was all pretty much a whirlwind," she recalled five decades later from her home in Princeton, New Jersey. "At the time I was a little self-conscious about it. I didn't really do anything to win it."

Roselli had been entered in the contest by previously being chosen "Miss William & Mary." The contest's judge was popular actor Steve McQueen. "She is a vivacious brunette . . . with a long, bouncing hairdo," wrote Marcia Brewster in the *Newport News Daily Press*. The game program describing each of the finalists commented, "Grace is a northerner with that Southern charm." She was a member of the Pi Beta Phi sorority and a William & Mary majorette. "It was so much fun performing and going to the football games," she said.

Chevrolet flew fourteen finalists representing different conferences to Los Angeles for a busy schedule of appearances. The women were photographed for an article in *Life* magazine. They were introduced on television's *Joey Bishop Show*. They ate dinner at the famous Brown Derby restaurant. Accompanied by their female chaperones (Roselli's mother joined her on the trip), the contestants danced at several of LA's hottest night clubs. And they were introduced as a group during halftime of the Notre Dame-Southern Cal game at the Los Angeles Coliseum.

"I distinctly remember that we stayed at the Century Plaza Hotel, which was very nice," recalled Roselli. "And we got tickets to *The Tonight Show*, although Johnny Carson was not there that night. I do remember Della Reese was one of the guests."

"It was just such a fun and innocent experience," she said. "When I got back from the trip I received maybe 15 letters from boys. Nice letters. They said things like 'You're so pretty.' And a group of servicemen from a missile base in Maryland saw me and named me Miss Delta Battery. I remember that. I thought that was kind of sweet."

*Grace Roselli, a junior at William & Mary, was voted "Miss Southern Conference" in a 1968 league-wide contest. (Thomas L. Williams for Southern Conference)*

The eventual winner, crowned College Football Centennial Queen, was Barbara Specht of Texas Tech, representing the Southwest Conference.

Roselli graduated from William & Mary in 1970 and later earned an MBA from Rutgers. She taught Spanish Language and Literature at Middlebury College then had subsequent careers in management consulting and information technology in her native New Jersey.

"Thinking about that experience brings back some very nice memories," she said.

## FROM FIELDS AND COURTS TO THE MICROPHONE

**AS THE GOLDEN AGE OF TELEVISION EMERGED** in the decades following World War II, a select number of ex-Southern Conference student-athletes decided to try a broadcasting career to enjoy the benefits of staying connected with their love of sports. A few in particular enjoyed great success and longevity in their new professions.

**Al DeRogatis** was an All-SoCon tackle at Duke in 1946 who played professionally with the New York Giants until a knee injury ended his career. He went to work in the insurance industry before being hired as a radio analyst for Giants' games on powerful New York radio station WNEW-AM. He worked with legendary broadcaster Marty Glickman on Giants' broadcasts before moving on to NBC Sports in 1966, where he became part of the American Football League's leading broadcast team with Curt Gowdy. He was highly regarded for his succinct observations and superior knowledge of both player and team tendencies. DeRogatis worked three Super Bowls for NBC before retiring in 1977.

**Jay Randolph** parlayed golf in the Southern Conference into a broadcasting career that spanned more than fifty years. Winner of the 1957 SoCon Golf Championship as a student at George Washington, the West Virginia native used his college connections to earn play-by-play assignments doing high school and college sports before his career truly took off. Randolph called the action in the 1960s and seventies for the NFL, the PGA Tour, the Olympics, the PBA Tour, and ultimately became the lead baseball announcer for the St. Louis Cardinals. He was inducted into the Missouri Sports Hall of Fame in 2008.

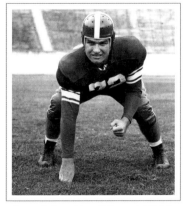 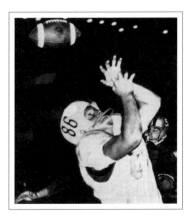 

*Former SoCon athletes (left to right) Al DeRogatis (Duke), Paul Maguire (the Citadel), and Sam Wyche (Furman) all became prominent television and radio football analysts. (Duke University Athletics, the Citadel Athletics, Furman University Athletics)*

George Washington University's twenty-nine-year stint in the Southern Conference produced basketball and baseball championship teams in the 1950s. But the closest thing to a dynasty the Colonials enjoyed came in men's tennis. From 1956 to 1964, GW reigned as the conference champion. The Colonials had the advantage of hosting all but one of those conference tournaments on their home courts in Washington, DC.

JAMES TARR (pictured) of the Colonials won three consecutive championships playing at No. 1 singles. He also captured the No. 1 doubles titles two years in a row playing with older brother Jack. In 1965, Davidson nipped George Washington by a point, 28–27, ending the Colonials' dominance. George Washington would not win another tennis championship before leaving the Southern Conference in 1970. (Leah Richardson, Gelman Special Collections, George Washington University Libraries)

The nation's leader in touchdown receptions in 1959 with ten, the Citadel's **Paul Maguire** became a familiar voice to football fans in his role as an analyst on both television and radio. Before that, he enjoyed a stellar career as a linebacker and punter with the Chargers and Bills of the American Football League, retiring as the AFL's all-time leader in total punts (795) and punting yardage (33,137).

Maguire emerged as a premier football analyst, calling two Super Bowls, numerous NFL playoffs, and college football bowl games. Combining detailed preparation, color-coded lineup charts, and a heavy dose of natural wit, Maguire carved out a forty-six-year career as an analyst. In 2013 he returned to the Southern Conference to broadcast games for the league's weekly ESPN3 football package.

It seemed only natural for **Hot Rod Hundley** to move into broadcasting after his basketball career ended. The former West Virginia and Los Angeles Laker star was always quick with an observation about the sport he loved. "Rod was such an outgoing personality going back to his playing days and everything," said longtime Phoenix Suns' broadcast partner Al McCoy upon Hundley's death in 2015. "I think that just normally came out in his broadcasts."

Beginning as an analyst with the Suns and Lakers, Hundley eventually became the original play-by-play announcer for the New Orleans Jazz, accompanying the franchise when it moved to Utah in 1979. He endeared himself to his listeners with stock phrases such as "yo-yo dribble" and "leapin' leaners." He was eventually inducted into the Basketball Hall of Fame as a broadcaster. In 2010 Hundley entered the Southern Conference Hall of Fame and characteristically gave a lengthy acceptance speech filled with humorous anecdotes and stories from an illustrious basketball life.

**Sam Wyche** was an outstanding quarterback at Furman, a starter with the expansion Cincinnati Bengals, and had a lengthy run as both an assistant and head coach in both the college ranks and the NFL. As head coach of the Bengals, he utilized a then-radical no-huddle offense to bring Cincinnati within a late Joe Montana touchdown pass of winning Super Bowl XXIII. In all, Wyche coached the Bengals for eight seasons and the Tampa Bay Buccaneers for four.

So what led him into broadcasting? "I got fired," said Wyche of his 1996 dismissal at Tampa Bay.

"But right after that, NBC and CBS sent me letters and bouquets of flowers asking me to become an NFL analyst. They were both recruiting me." Act Two of Wyche's football career came behind a microphone. He quickly was paired with Marv Albert doing American Football Conference games for NBC and later worked on the network's studio show. "I preferred calling the games on site," recalled Wyche. "It made me feel like I was more part of the game."

Moving to CBS as a game analyst, Wyche's broadcasting career was disrupted for two years by a biopsy surgery that inadvertently cut a nerve to one of his vocal cords and left him with a thin, raspy voice. Wyche overcame that setback through different breathing exercises and resumed his career. He joined Westwood One radio calling Monday Night Football before accepting analyst positions on broadcast packages for the Southern Conference and Furman University.

*NBA teams drafted nineteen Southern Conference athletes during the 1960s. The most illustrious was West Virginia's JERRY WEST (pictured). West, two-time SoCon Player of the Year, chosen in the first round by the Minneapolis Lakers in 1960. The franchise moved to Los Angeles in the spring of 1960, so West never played for the Minneapolis Lakers.*

*Two Davidson products enjoyed stellar pro careers. DICK SNYDER used a deadly jump shot to score more than 11,000 points in thirteen years for four NBA clubs. FRED HETZEL, the No. 1 pick in the 1965 draft, played six seasons professionally before becoming successful in real estate development.*

*Another SoCon product who had an impact in the NBA was ROD THORN of West Virginia. Thorn played eight years in the NBA as a smart, reliable guard who could score (10.8 points-per-game career average) and play strong defense. But Thorn left his mark on pro basketball in many other ways. He coached in the ABA and spent one season as interim head coach of the Chicago Bulls in the pre-MICHAEL JORDAN era. His forte, however, was working in the front office, and he had terms as general manager of the Bulls, Nets, and 76ers. In 2013, Thorn was named Director of Basketball Operations for the NBA, with responsibilities for disciplinary measures and on-court matters. He was elected to the Naismith Basketball Hall of Fame in September of 2018 as a special contributor to the game. (West Virginia University Athletics)*

# THE
# 1970s

In 1970, the NCAA passed legislation permitting football teams to schedule eleven games during the regular season instead of ten. The Southern Conference champions that year were the Indians (now the Tribe) of William & Mary, who traveled an unusual path to the league title.

By the end of October, William & Mary was limping along with a 2-6 overall record and had split its only two conference games. But W&M rallied to win three straight, including a pair of one-point decisions on the road at Davidson and Richmond, to finish 3-1 in the SoCon and 5-6 overall. Their .750 winning percentage gave them the conference title, and with it, a berth in the Tangerine Bowl, where they were hammered by Toledo, 40–12. Even with only eight football members, the SoCon played a true round-robin schedule just once in the 1970s.

William & Mary also had the SoCon's best track and field program in the first half of the decade. The Indians took six consecutive indoor and outdoor titles from 1970 to 1975. Another elite sports program was Furman golf. The Paladins won five championships in the seventies and missed out on an eighth by a single stroke. Furman's Ken Ezell was a three-time Southern Conference tournament medalist in the latter part of the decade, a three-time Collegiate All-America Golf Team selection, and later became a successful golf course architect.

When Lefty Driesell parlayed his basketball success at Davidson into the head-coaching position at Maryland, there was little doubt as to who would replace him at the picturesque college north of Charlotte. Terry Holland had been a captain for Driesell and became an assistant coach after graduating in 1964. Just 27 years old when given the reins of the Wildcats,

*The conference's Male Athlete of the Year award was inaugurated in 1948. The first football player to win the award in consecutive years was the Citadel's BRIAN RUFF in 1976 and '77. Ruff was a ferocious linebacker who earned Associated Press All-America honors as a senior in 1976. He was a three-time All-Conference selection and was chosen in the eleventh round by the Baltimore Colts in the 1977 NFL draft. He became the first athlete at the Citadel to have his jersey (No. 51) retired. He was inducted into both the Citadel's and the state of South Carolina's Hall of Fame.*

Holland kept the program humming, earning three consecutive Coach of the Year awards on his way to four straight league titles. After a second-place finish to Furman, Holland left his alma mater in 1974 to become the winningest head coach in the history of the University of Virginia.

Another young coach—the youngest in America at the time of his hire in 1975—also achieved Southern Conference success. Bobby Cremins, a native of the Bronx who played for Frank McGuire on several outstanding South Carolina teams, took an Appalachian State program that finished 3-23 and within three years guided it to back-to-back league championships and a berth in the 1979 NCAA Tournament.

One sport that did not see a single dominant team was baseball. Always one of the conference's leading sports, with the lure of warm playing weather, the SoCon had a number of high-quality baseball players in the seventies.

Appalachian State shortstop Mike Ramsey was a three-time All-Conference performer and was selected in the third round of the major league draft by the St. Louis Cardinals. He played seven years in the majors and was a member of the Cardinals' 1982 World Series champion team. Another All-SoCon shortstop, Wayne Tolleson, also played wide receiver for the Western Carolina football team. Tolleson spent ten years in the majors playing six different positions for the Rangers, White Sox, and Yankees.

Left-hander Atlee Hammaker of ETSU was the first Southern Conference product to be taken in the first round of the MLB draft. The Kansas City Royals drafted Hammaker, but he achieved his greatest success with the San Francisco Giants. In 1983, he led the National League in earned run average and was the NL's starting pitcher in the All-Star Game.

Randy Ingle of Appalachian State never reached the majors, but he carved out a remarkable baseball career for himself. In 1979, Ingle earned Player of the Year and ABCA All-America honors by hitting a SoCon-leading .477 for the Mountaineers. After nine years in the minors, Ingle retired as a player and moved into the coaching ranks. In 1990, the Atlanta Braves asked him to manage their Rookie League farm club at Pulaski, Virginia.

He remained a Braves minor league skipper for twenty-six seasons, grooming such future Atlanta stars as Steve Avery, Kevin Millwood, Brian Hunter, and Brian McCann. "Patience is the most important thing I've learned," he told the *Rome* (GA) *News Tribune* in 2017. "This game is filled with times you do not succeed, so you cannot be afraid to make a mistake."

East Carolina's football team had its best stretch in the SoCon in the early part of the decade. The Pirates, coached by former NFL receiver Sonny Randle, went undefeated in league play in both 1972 and '73. The Furman Paladins enjoyed their most successful run on the basketball court, winning six conference tournament championships, led by versatile forwards Clyde Mayes and Jonathan Moore.

Conference realignment once again paid multiple visits to the Southern Conference in the 1970s. The first rumble came when George Washington University departed in 1970 after twenty-nine years of membership. A year later, at a league meeting on

*Bobby Cremins (center) is flanked by assistant coaches Kevin Cantwell (left) and Gene Littles as the new staff takes over at Appalachian State in 1975. Cremins was 27, the youngest head basketball coach in Division I. (Appalachian State University Athletics)*

*Wayne Tolleson was an All-SoCon wide receiver at Western Carolina who went on to play ten years as an infielder in the major leagues. (Western Carolina University Athletics)*

*Left-hander Atlee Hammaker of ETSU was a first-round draft pick of the Kansas City Royals in 1979. (East Tennessee State University Athletics)*

*In its relatively brief time in the Southern Conference (thirteen years), East Carolina had its greatest success in the sport of wrestling. ECU won five conference tournament championships in a row starting in 1972. The 1974 team set a tournament record with 171 points, winning at seven of the ten weight classes.*

*During the decade, the Pirates had nine different wrestlers win their respective weight classes in two or more consecutive seasons. That list is headed by BILL HILL, (pictured) who captured first-place honors at 177 pounds in all four years he competed. A member of ECU's Hall of Fame, Hill finished with a career record of 122-15-1 and placed fifth in the NCAA national championship in 1974. That same year the media voted him the finest wrestler in the state of North Carolina. (East Carolina University Athletics)*

the VMI campus, Commissioner Lloyd Jordan announced the addition of Appalachian State University to take GW's place.

"We went after the Southern Conference more than they approached us," recalled Jim Jones, ASU's business manager for athletics at the time and later the athletic director there. "They were down to seven schools, they needed a replacement, and their schools were in our region."

To show how different the process of expansion was in the 1970s, Jones recalled that the two men working to gain Appalachian's admission to the conference—he and Roy Clogston—negotiated mostly through intermediaries at East Carolina and other league members who supported App State. They had precious little contact with Commissioner Jordan in Richmond. There is some doubt as to whether Jordan ever visited the campus prior to the announcement inviting them. The process pretty much played out with minimal involvement by the league office.

"Before any of this, I doubt Lloyd Jordan had ever heard of Appalachian State," chuckled Jones. "Hell, I'm not sure he could pronounce our name."

By the middle of the decade, significant changes were on the horizon for the NCAA in both flagship sports of football and basketball.

In 1973, the NCAA voted to organize collegiate competition into three distinct categories. There was Division I, representing a high level of athletically related aid; Division II, representing lower levels of athletically related aid, and Division III, representing institutions awarding no aid based on a student's athletic ability. Regulations were established to encourage the vast bulk of competition would occur within each division.

But the large state universities that played football before 60,000 fans on any given Saturday were frustrated by the NCAA's governance policy of "one institution, one vote." Inevitably, decisions to increase football scholarships or coaching personnel or playing schedules or TV opportunities were being stifled by the smaller state and private institutions with more modest ambitions.

Penn State coach Joe Paterno, a graduate of Brown, used his alma mater's affiliation when expressing his irritation for the status quo. "The Ivy League is in another world all by their own. They are in another world. I'm in the real world."

At the 1978 NCAA Convention at Atlanta's Peachtree Plaza, Division I delegates approved the creation of two subdivisions. Division I-A would include the larger members with bowl game aspirations. Division I-AA would include other football-playing members who awarded fewer scholarships. The latter group would play for an NCAA-sponsored championship. The

inaugural 1978 contest was a victory for Florida A&M, 35–28, over Massachusetts before 13,604 in Wichita Falls, Texas.

In time, members of the Southern Conference would dominate this championship. Initially, the SoCon made the choice to meet I-A budgetary and attendance qualifications and stay at the highest classification.

Progress was taking place in basketball as well. The popularity of the NCAA basketball tournament, and particularly the Final Four, had skyrocketed following the decision to move the championship contest to a prime-time Monday evening TV slot in 1973. The tournament soon thereafter expanded to thirty-two teams and created more automatic qualifying slots for conference champions. This put independent programs with no postseason conference tournament in real danger of being excluded from the field.

Seeing this need, the Eastern Collegiate Athletic Conference (ECAC), a loosely configured federation of Northeast and mid-Atlantic institutions, organized a set of basketball-only conferences to produce a champion and receive automatic bids to the NCAAs. There was an ECAC Metro (New York City area), ECAC South, ECAC New England, etc. But soon enough, discussions took place among athletic directors about multi-sport affiliations that would serve the same purpose. In the Northeast, this led to the creation of two new basketball-centric multi-sport conferences—the Eastern Athletic Association, nicknamed the "Eastern Eight," in 1975, and the Big East Conference in 1979. The Eastern Eight officially became the Atlantic Ten Conference in 1982.

In the mid-Atlantic region, a group of institutions from Virginia, Maryland, and North Carolina began sifting through blueprints for a new conference. This group included several SoCon members. In 1976, Richmond pulled the trigger and departed. The exits of East Carolina and William & Mary came one year later. The three would eventually join with others to form what is now known as the Colonial Athletic Association.

Ken Germann, who replaced Lloyd Jordan as commissioner in January of 1974, had been closely monitoring these developments. Working behind the scenes, he began identifying potential expansion candidates. Eventually, he announced that the Southern Conference would add the University of Tennessee at Chattanooga, Marshall University, and Western Carolina University as new members for 1976.

The constant upheaval within the SoCon's membership hardly went unnoticed. "The saying 'the old grey mare ain't what she used to be' can be applied to the Southern," wrote columnist Stubby Currence in the *Bluefield* (WV) *Daily Telegraph*. "There is even one rumor that the NCAA will withdraw its automatic bid to the SC basketball winner for the NCAA playoffs." Let the record show that such a move never occurred and that VMI advanced to within one game of the Final Four the very same year (1976) the three new members were admitted.

Two years later, East Tennessee State University accepted an invitation to join, bringing the league's membership to nine institutions spread across five states. All of the members played football, but Davidson did not compete in the Southern Conference, having decided in 1973 to award scholarships to football student-athletes exclusively on a need-based basis.

*The top Southern Conference men's soccer program in the 1970s was Appalachian State. The Mountaineers thoroughly dominated their league competition, winning seven of the decade's ten regular-season championships. In all but one of those years, ASU did not lose a Southern Conference match. In fact, from 1973 through 1981, App State's conference record was 50-1-3, the lone defeat coming at East Carolina in 1976.*

*The Mountaineers' dominance resulted in five Player of the Year awards in the 1970s. The most notable was THOMPSON USIYAN (pictured), who earned the honor three straight years beginning in 1978. When he completed his eligibility, Usiyan held NCAA records for the most goals in a season (forty-six in 1980), most goals in a career (109), most points in a season (108 in 1980), and most points in a career (255). On November 12, 1978, he netted seven goals and an assist in a 9–3 NCAA tournament victory over George Washington.*

*A year later, Usiyan and the Mountaineers played in the first live collegiate soccer match broadcast by a startup cable network called ESPN. ASU blanked visiting Western Carolina, 3–0.*

*Usiyan enjoyed a long postgraduate career playing professional soccer. He led the United Soccer League in goals in 1984 and played for teams in the North American Soccer League and the Major Indoor Soccer League. He represented his native country of Nigeria in international and FIFA competitions. He is a member of ASU's Hall of Fame. (Appalachian State University Athletics)*

## BUILDING A PROGRAM IN BOONE

ON A DAY OFF FROM HIS DUTIES as a graduate assistant basketball coach at the University of South Carolina, Bobby Cremins was enjoying a game of tennis with USC tennis coach Ron Smarr in the spring of 1975.

"Ron told me he had played college tennis for Jim Jones at Appalachian State, and that Jim was now the athletic director there," Cremins recalled. "He said he'd told Jim that I was the person they should hire as their next basketball coach."

The Mountaineers had gone 3-23 in their third year as a Division I program and were looking for a new coach to replace Press Maravich. An interview was quickly arranged. "We were looking for a guy who knew how to recruit talent," remembered Jones. "Cremins was a real salesman, he was selling himself. In a way, he was recruiting us. And he did a helluva job."

Jones offered him the position and Cremins accepted. He was 27 years old and would start the season as the youngest Division I coach in the nation.

"I didn't have any idea what Appalachian State was about, but I knew two things," said Cremins, who grew up in the Bronx, New York, and played his college ball for legendary coach Frank McGuire at South Carolina. "I knew it was a Division I program and it was located in the South. And I had fallen in love with living in the South."

Cremins soon realized that Boone, North Carolina, was indeed a scenic location, but that attracting recruits from the Tar Heel state would be a challenge. "I started calling some kids from North Carolina and they weren't interested," said Cremins. "No one wanted to play for a losing program. I may have been too dumb to realize what I had gotten into."

Instead, he utilized his New York contacts and recruited athletes from the big city. His efforts quickly paid off with the signing of six-eight center Mel Hubbard from the Bronx and Darryl Robinson, a wily six-four guard from Brooklyn who averaged fifteen points per game as a freshman, was the MVP of the 1979 Southern Conference Tournament, and finished his career with 1,631 points. "I'll probably get in trouble for this, but I think Darryl Robinson was the greatest player in App State history," said Cremins.

In Cremins's first season, the Mountaineers improved from eighth place in an eight-team league to a tie for third. He was voted Coach of the Year by the conference media. By his second season, App State was a perennial SoCon contender, winning the conference regular-season championship in 1977–78, 1978–79, and 1980–81.

"I was young, I basically coached by the seat of my pants," Cremins recalled. "But I hired a good assistant, Kevin Cantwell. We had some success. That's when I really fell in love with coaching, during my time in Boone."

Like Lefty Driesell and Terry Holland before him, Cremins used his success in the Southern Conference to land a coaching job in the prestigious ACC. He moved to Georgia Tech in 1981 and led the program to ten NCAA tournament appearances and the school's first Final Four appearance. The playing court at Alexander Coliseum is named in his honor.

After six years in retirement, Cremins returned to the Southern Conference in 2006 as the head coach at the College of Charleston. He finished his NCAA coaching career with 579 victories.

# THE
# 1980S

I n previewing the league's sixtieth anniversary, the 1980–81 Southern Conference basketball media guide drew on a historical analogy when discussing the conference's evolution. "In the same way that countries and kingdoms have disappeared or experienced drastic alterations of borders on the map of Europe, so too has the form of the Southern Conference changed," the piece stated. "No longer does the venerable league, established in 1921, blanket the nation from the Chesapeake Bay to the mouth of the Mississippi."

Ironically, the decade of the 1980s would be one of the most tranquil for the SoCon when it came to membership changes. No new institutions were added between 1979 and 1990. The only departure came in 1988 when Davidson left after fifty-two years of Southern Conference affiliation.

The Davidson decision—like the vast majority of conference realignment throughout the NCAA's history—was driven by football. The college had made the fiscal choice in the 1970s to cease awarding athletic aid in a number of sports and go to a need-based financial aid system. Efforts were made to force Davidson to continue to play a league schedule despite

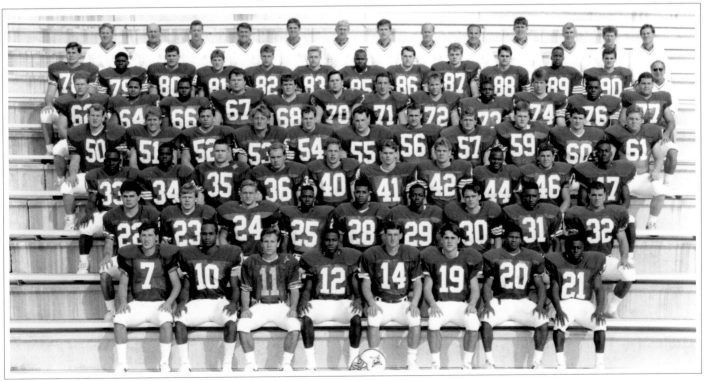

*The 1988 Furman Paladins were the NCAA champions in Division I-AA football. (Furman University Athletics)*

*When the 1953 membership split resulted in the birth of the Atlantic Coast Conference, Southern Conference administrators were forced to look at some difficult issues. One of these was the four-year-old conference baseball tournament which had been played exclusively in what was now ACC territory—Winston-Salem and Raleigh.*

*Washington & Lee representative R. A. SMITH addressed the matter at the 1953 annual December meeting in Richmond. "The result of the tournament was very disappointing," reported Smith. "The Baseball Committee wishes to recommend there be no baseball tournament this spring. The Conference standings will determine the champion."*

*His report was adopted unanimously. There would be no baseball tournament in 1954. And as the league's membership and geography fluctuated through the next thirty years, restoration of the event never met with sufficient support.*

*Finally, after years of digesting research on improving the conference's baseball pedigree prepared by Citadel head coach Chal Port, the conference voted to try again. In 1984, Western Carolina played host to a four-team championship. The tournament was won by Appalachian State, which defeated the Citadel, 6–1, in the championship game.*

*Within three years, the tournament would be moved to a neutral setting at Asheville's McCormick Field. In 1997, Charleston's Joe Riley Park became the site for sixteen of the next nineteen championships. In 2016, the membership elected to establish an ongoing relationship with Fluor Field, the replica-Fenway Park home of the Greenville (South Carolina) Drive minor league team.*

the lack of scholarship athletes. From 1983 through 1986, the Wildcats were winless in twenty-two conference football games and looking for other options.

Opportunity knocked in 1986 when the Colonial League—soon to be renamed the Patriot League—announced its formation as a Division I-AA group patterned after the Ivy League model. No scholarships would be awarded based upon athletic ability. Davidson announced it would transfer to the new conference in 1988 for football only, joining Bucknell, Colgate, Holy Cross, Lafayette, and Lehigh.

"This is the choice we felt we had to make," said the president, John Kuykendall. "It's going to be difficult and expensive."

Needing a home for the rest of its athletic programs, Davidson withdrew from the SoCon in June of 1988 and joined the Big South Conference the following month. Following a four-year run in the Big South, Davidson was granted readmission to the Southern Conference in 1992.

On the field and on the court, the conference had a lot of highlights to point to.

Chattanooga and Marshall established a terrific men's basketball rivalry. The Mocs captured five regular-season titles while Marshall's Thundering Herd earned three. Their conference tournament battles for the automatic bid to the NCAAs led to the increasing popularity of the league's championship, which moved to Asheville in 1984. Buoyed by the work of the ticket-selling Junior League of Asheville, the event flourished. For four straight years, the championship game never produced less than a 6,000-plus near-capacity crowd.

UTC was led by the duo of Gerald Wilkins and Willie White. The younger brother of NBA star Dominique Wilkins, Gerald was a two-time All-Conference selection who went on to forge a quality pro career of his own, primarily with the New York Knicks. White, a six-foot-three guard from Memphis, was the conference's Player of the Year as a junior. He opted to leave UTC and enter the NBA draft and spent two undistinguished seasons with the Denver Nuggets.

James (Skip) Henderson of Marshall was the Southern Conference's all-time leading scorer until surpassed by Stephen Curry in 2009. A four-time All-Conference selection, Henderson was the 1987–88 Player of the Year and helped the Thundering Herd advance to a pair of NCAA tournaments. Sadly, his post-college days evolved into a string of convictions and incarceration for various felony crimes.

On the gridiron, Furman dominated the decade under the tutelage of head coaches Dick Sheridan (1978–85) and Jimmy Satterfield (1986–93). The Paladins took seven championships

*Willie White was a key component of the Chattanooga basketball teams that won multiple championships in the early 1980s. (University of Tennessee at Chattanooga Athletics)*

*The Citadel's Stump Mitchell was the 1980 Player of the Year after rushing for a then-league record 1,647 yards and fourteen touchdowns. (The Citadel Athletics)*

in the decade, peaking in 1988. One of three Southern Conference teams to earn a slot in that year's sixteen-team Division I-AA postseason field, Furman knocked off Delaware, league rival Marshall, and Idaho to reach the NCAA Division I-AA championship game.

Playing in a domed stadium in Pocatello, Idaho, against future league rival Georgia Southern, the Paladin defense held the Eagles to less than 200 total yards and forced three turnovers to win the national championship, 17–12. Furman linebacker Jeff Blankenship intercepted two passes, the second coming with 35 seconds remaining, to choke off Georgia Southern's last chance.

Among the league's stars during the eighties were future NFL standouts Stanford Jennings (Furman), Stump Mitchell (the Citadel), Dino Hackett (Appalachian State), and Clyde Simmons (Western Carolina).

Furman and ETSU consistently matched up to see which men's golf program was the best. ETSU won the conference tournament five consecutive years led by All-American and 1980 SoCon Player of the Year Mike Hulbert, later a multiple winner on the PGA Tour. Another stellar performer was Steve Munson, a two-time runner-up for conference medalist honors before winning the 1982 SoCon Tournament. When the Bucs' streak ended in 1984, it was Furman that captured four of the next five titles.

The Paladins' best player was Brad Faxon, a New Jersey-born player with an outstanding putting stroke on the greens. After losing the individual championship in a playoff in 1982, Faxon won medalist honors in '83 at Raintree Country Club in Charlotte by a whopping eleven strokes. He would eventually go on to a successful career as a PGA player, earning several awards as the tour's top putter. Later a golf TV commentator, he was elected to the Southern Conference Hall of Fame in 2016.

Both indoor and outdoor track and field saw a changing of the guard. VMI entered the 1980s as the dominant program under head coach Wade Williams, a six-time Coach of the Year selection. In 1984, the Keydets were overtaken by Appalachian State. The Mountaineers used superior depth to win conference titles, both indoor and outdoor, in 1984, '85, '86, and '87.

But perhaps the most important development in the decade took place when the Southern Conference, like the rest of the NCAA, began sponsoring women's athletics beginning in 1983. Just as it had done for more than sixty years with men's sports, the conference office would arrange league schedules, assign officials, and run championships for female student-athletes.

At an April 1983 meeting, faculty representatives Charles Clark of ETSU and Dorothy Hicks of Marshall presented a report to the executive committee detailing the need for, and structure of, women's athletics under the SoCon umbrella. The conference had experimented with volleyball tournaments and loosely arranged scheduling in basketball but had not yet embraced women's athletics in the same manner as the men.

The membership agreed the time had come. The three sports selected for Southern Conference championship status in 1983–84 were volleyball, basketball, and tennis.

Only five programs sponsored volleyball in 1983, and no regular-season contests were considered league matches. The first official Southern Conference-sanctioned women's contest was Appalachian State's straight-set victory over Furman on November 18 in the first conference volleyball tournament.

Western Carolina's Trish Howell became the first women's Coach of the Year in Southern Conference history as she led the Catamount volleyball squad to the championship with a 3-sets-to-1 victory over host ETSU. Chattanooga captured both the women's basketball and tennis championships.

For his advocacy of women's athletics, Ken Germann was honored by the membership in a lasting manner. The trophy awarded to the women's program having the greatest all-around success during the year was christened the Germann Cup. Germann's successors, Dave Hart and Wright Waters, continued the trend. In all, seven additional women's championships were added to the original three—cross country (1985), outdoor track (1987), indoor track (1988), golf (1994), soccer (1994), softball (1994), and lacrosse (2018). Rifle, a coed sport, was introduced in 2016.

By the 2018–19 academic year, more than 1,400 female student-athletes would compete for Southern Conference championships, All-Conference awards, and NCAA postseason invitations.

## THE FIRST TREY

**WITH THE BLESSING OF THE NCAA**, the Southern Conference was given approval to experiment in the 1980–81 basketball season with a radical departure in the playing rules. The league would award three points instead of two for a field goal made behind an arc drawn twenty-two feet from the center of the basket. The American Basketball Association (ABA) had used a three-point shot throughout its nine-year history, but the shot had not been employed in the college game.

Part of the Southern Conference's interest in the experimentation was creating what today would be referred to as "brand awareness." Said Furman head coach Eddie Holbrook, "There's no question that exposure's one of the paramount reasons we're doing this. When you're in the location we're in you have to fight for all the publicity you can get."

*Once women's athletics came under the Southern Conference umbrella, basketball coaches had more leverage to attract highly skilled players. Three of the conference's all-time finest played in the early era.*

*REGINA KIRK (pictured) was an All-Conference performer at Chattanooga in each of her four seasons. She led the Mocs to regular-season titles in 1984–85 and 1985–86 and was the Player of the Year in 1985–86. A versatile forward, she finished her career with 2,376 points and 1,086 rebounds.*

*At Marshall, KAREN PELPHREY established eye-popping statistics in her four-year career. Pelphrey's first year at Marshall was not a part of the Southern Conference. Nevertheless, the sharp-shooting backcourt player tallied 2,163 points in her final three years, all without benefit of the three-point shot. As a senior, Pelphrey was named Player of the Year, averaging 26.1 points per game.*

*VALORIE WHITESIDE started at Appalachian State in 1984. By the time she concluded her four-year career, Whiteside was the leading all-time scorer in Southern Conference basketball history—men or women. The five-eleven Whiteside powered the Mountaineers to a pair of conference tournament titles. She finished with 2,944 points and 1,369 career rebounds.*

*Kirk, Pelphrey, and Whiteside all won conference championships. All rank among the top four women's scorers in SoCon history. All three posted individual high games of forty-five or more points. And all three are enshrined in the conference's Hall of Fame. (University of Tennessee at Chattanooga Athletics)*

The NCAA would count all three-point baskets as two points for individual SoCon player statistics. Each game was to be charted and the data turned over to the NCAA. The basketball rules committee was charged with conducting a postseason evaluation. "I'm not sure one season would be enough time to swing it through," said coordinator of officials J. Dallas Shirley when asked about the likelihood of immediate approval.

Most conference head coaches, thinking about the poor percentages likely to result from long range, figured they'd use the three-point shot simply as a device to come from behind late in a game. Strategies had to change as well. Three-point leads in the final seconds previously meant a defending team was in good shape as long as it didn't commit a foul. Now, that math was irrevocably altered.

On November 29, 1980, Western Carolina hosted Middle Tennessee State in Reid Gym on the WCU campus. Western Carolina sports information director Steve White, anticipating an historic occasion, had convinced the athletic department to move up the tip-off by thirty minutes to try and get in the record books. Chattanooga was hosting a game at 7:30, so Western moved its start to 7:00 P.M. "We knew we had a great three-point shooter," recalled White years later for Steve Megargee of Rivals.com. "So we decided to start the game earlier to get a jump on everybody else.

With a little more than sixteen minutes remaining in the first half, Ronnie Carr, a six-three sophomore guard for Western Carolina, took a pass from Larry Caldwell and launched a shot from the left corner. Carr was about one foot behind the twenty-two-foot line when he released the ball. The result was the first three-point basket in college basketball history.

White quickly noted the actual time (7:06 P.M.) and called his colleagues around the league to confirm that Carr's shot was the first. The game was halted while administrators retrieved the basketball and snapped a photo of Carr, both of which were sent off to the Basketball Hall of Fame in Springfield, Massachusetts, by the Southern Conference office. A subsequent article in *Sports Illustrated* bore the headline, "IN THE SC 22 WILL GET YOU THREE."

"I was accustomed to shooting that distance," Carr subsequently said. "It was just a matter of them putting that line on the floor."

The Catamounts sank thirty-six three-pointers all season. Caldwell, not Carr, wound up the team

*Play was halted in the first half on November 29, 1980, to recognize Ronnie Carr after the Western Carolina guard made the first three-point basket in NCAA history. (Western Carolina University Athletics)*

leader with nineteen in forty-two attempts, a very respectable 46 percent figure. Carr finished with fifteen treys in thirty-nine attempts.

Over the next five seasons, the NCAA rules committee let all conferences experiment with the three-point shot and set their own distances. The ACC voted in the shortest distance (seventeen feet, nine inches), using an arc that intersected below the top of the circle near the free-throw line. After studying all the data, the rules committee in 1986 approved a three-point line at nineteen feet, nine inches for all NCAA men's games. It was subsequently moved back on two separate occasions.

## ETSU NEARLY TAKES DOWN A NO. 1 SEED

**AS THE 1980S WERE SOON TO BECOME THE 1990S,** the premier basketball program in the Southern Conference was the Buccaneers of East Tennessee State University. From the 1988–89 season to 1991–92, ETSU won or shared three regular-season championships and captured four straight SoCon basketball tournament titles. The Bucs represented the SoCon in the NCAA tournament in each of those seasons.

In 1992, ETSU knocked off No. 3-seed Arizona in the NCAA's first round, 87–80, before losing to Michigan's Fab Five squad that reached the national championship game. And the Buccaneers had come close the year before, dropping a tight three-point game to Iowa. But it was ETSU's 1989 NCAA appearance, its first in twenty-one years, that truly put the program on the map.

The coach was Les Robinson, in his fourth year since taking over in Johnson City. The team, 14-15 the year before, had finished in the middle of the Southern Conference pack at 7-7. But it had shown flashes of excellence. During the season, the Bucs beat Mississippi State and Wake Forest and lost a close game at Virginia Tech.

The team had a pair of standouts in Greg Dennis and Keith (Mister) Jennings. Dennis was a six-eleven center from Robinson's hometown of Charleston, West Virginia. "He must have grown five inches alone in his senior year in high school," recalled Robinson many years later. "On my recruiting visit to his home, his mother and I were talking about my being from Charleston and I happened to mention the hospital where I was born.

"She said, 'I'm a nurse there!' I thought that was a good omen that we had a chance to sign him."

At five-seven, 160 pounds, Jennings was nicknamed "Mister" because he earned respect from his opponents despite his size. He was good enough from the outside to shoot almost 50 percent from three-point range but didn't mind driving to the basket when the opportunity presented itself.

ETSU entered the Southern Conference Tournament in Asheville having lost five of its last eight games. But the Bucs took full advantage of the second chance afforded by the tournament. After edging the Citadel, 93–89, ETSU won a semifinal squeaker over top-seeded

Chattanooga, 76–73. Facing Marshall in the championship game, the Bucs broke open a two-point game at the half to win going away, 96–73.

They would enter the NCAA tournament as a No. 16 seed against No. 1-seed Oklahoma at Vanderbilt's Memorial Gymnasium. Robinson remembered the practice session the Bucs had the day before the game.

"I was pointing out the unusual architecture of the arena and how the benches were on the baselines and not on the sidelines," he recalled. "I said there were more scoreboards in that building than anywhere I'd ever been because of all the odd angles.

"Then I said, 'So tomorrow when CBS is showing this game across the nation and the scoreboard says Oklahoma 23, ETSU 4, think about how they're going to feel back in your hometown.'"

Robinson's psychological ploy worked. "They had a good practice and I could tell they were ready to play," he said.

OU, with a 28-5 record, was led by two All-America players, forward Stacey King and guard Mookie Blaylock. Unfazed by the circumstances, ETSU came out the aggressor and dominated play against the bigger Sooners. Eventually, ETSU built a seventeen-point advantage. The crowd of 12,226 did what NCAA tournament crowds always do—it began cheering loudly for the underdog. The Bucs went into the locker room at halftime ahead 39–31.

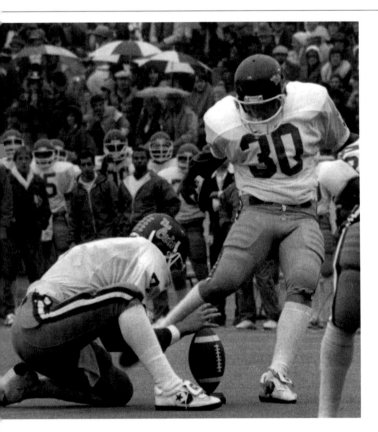

*As straight-on football placekickers disappeared from the scene, no Southern Conference program benefitted from the power and accuracy of the soccer-style kickers as much as Western Carolina.*

*Beginning in 1980, coach BOB WATERS relied on DEAN BIASUCCI (pictured) as a source of points for the Catamounts. Biasucci kicked fifty-four field goals in his career at Western, including five in one game as a junior. He earned All-Conference honors in 1982 and '83.*

*Undrafted by the NFL, Biasucci impressed during a 1984 camp tryout with the Indianapolis Colts. He earned the kicking job and remained a fixture in Indianapolis for ten years, earning Pro Bowl honors before winding up his career with the St. Louis Rams. He was successful on 71 percent of his career field goals.*

*When Biasucci left Western, his replacement went about wiping out all his school records. KIRK ROACH came to WCU from suburban Atlanta and was a four-time All-Conference selection and three-time All-American. In one season, he made a then NCAA-record seven field goals from fifty yards or longer.*

*At Western, he connected on seventy-one FGs and eighty-nine of ninety extra points. He twice hit from fifty-seven yards away, the existing Southern Conference record. Said Waters, "I cannot believe there is a better all-around kicking specialist in the nation on any level. Kirk is everything a coach is looking for in a kicker."*

*He was drafted in the fifth round by Buffalo to challenge SCOTT NORWOOD, but Roach suffered an injury in preseason camp and spent a year on injured reserve. He never attempted a kick in the NFL. Western Carolina retired his No. 14 jersey in 2006. (Western Carolina University Athletics)*

ETSU came out in the second half and picked up where it left off. With just over seventeen minutes remaining, the lead grew to 48–33. All over the country, fans became aware that a No. 16 seed might finally upset a No. 1. It had not happened since the tournament bracket was expanded to sixty-four teams in 1985.

But Blaylock and forward William Davis led an Oklahoma comeback and the Sooners steadily chipped away at the deficit. With less than four minutes remaining, Jennings was whistled for a reach-in foul, his fifth. "If Mister doesn't foul out, we win the game," Robinson said. "He controlled the pace of that game for us and when he left we were just trying to hang on."

Oklahoma took its first lead of the game on a tip-in by Davis with 1:55 to play. With eight seconds left, and the Sooners up 72–71, Blaylock missed the front end of a one-and-one. ETSU rebounded and called a timeout. There were four seconds left.

After Oklahoma coach Billy Tubbs called two consecutive timeouts, ETSU inbounded to guard Alvin West, who was double-teamed as he dribbled across midcourt. Forced to take a long, desperation jumper, West's shot from about thirty-five feet was partially blocked by Oklahoma's Mike Bell and never came close to the basket. The horn sounded as King tossed the ball high in the air. The Bucs had come excruciatingly close.

"I don't think this was a fluke game, I really don't," Robinson told the media afterwards. ETSU had handled the pressure of an NCAA appearance remarkably well, making nineteen of twenty-two from the foul line and committing only nine turnovers.

Years later, as head coach at North Carolina State, Robinson stepped on a hotel elevator at the Final Four and noticed a solitary passenger—Billy Tubbs. He introduced himself.

"I know who you are," Tubbs cried. "You gave me one of the worst damn days of my life!"

It would be twenty-nine years before a No. 1 seed would lose in the first round of the tournament. On March 16, 2018, UMBC exacted revenge for the '89 Bucs and all the other vanquished No. 16 seeds by beating No. 1-seeded Virginia, 74–54.

# THE
# 1990s

I n the 1990s, the Southern Conference firmly cemented its reputation as one of the premier Division I-AA conferences in football. (Note: I-AA was the forerunner of the present Football Championship Subdivision, or FCS.) In a stretch of seventeen seasons (1991–2007), the conference placed a team in the NCAA's championship game eleven times. The run started in 1991 with the first of three consecutive title games between Marshall of the Southern Conference and Youngstown State, a Division I-AA independent at the time.

Youngstown State won the first meeting, 25–17, at Georgia Southern's Paulson Stadium. A year later, Marshall's Willy Merrick booted a twenty-two-yard field goal with ten seconds to play, giving the Thundering Herd revenge, 31–28. The rubber match in 1993 saw Marshall fall, 17–5. In its last year as a Southern Conference member (1997), Marshall won its second national championship by routing Montana, 49–29.

During the early nineties, Marshall's top performer was its quarterback, Michael Payton, a remarkably accurate passer from Harrisburg, Pennsylvania. He was a two-time Southern Conference Player of the Year, a two-time conference Male Athlete of the Year selection, and won the 1992 Walter Payton Award as the nation's top offensive player. As a junior, he connected on 64 percent of his attempts. In his final two seasons with the Thundering Herd, Payton threw fifty-seven touchdown passes, including a then-SoCon record thirty-one as a senior.

Marshall's absence was quickly filled by Georgia Southern. Coached by Paul Johnson, the Eagles from Statesboro, Georgia, won four SoCon championships during the decade. Beginning in '98 they were led by a marvelous running back named Adrian Peterson. A two-time SoCon Player of the Year and the 1999 winner of the Walter Payton Award, the five-ten native of Gainesville, Florida, combined superior speed with raw power.

In the 1999 Division I-AA championship game against Youngstown State, Peterson ran for 247 yards and three touchdowns in a 59–24 triumph. Included was an electrifying fifty-eight-yard burst through the defense that saw him break six tackles, which became forevermore known in Statesboro—and on YouTube—as "The Run." A year later, the Eagles would again win the national championship, one of six the program amassed.

Women's basketball emerged as one of the conference's most competitive sports. No less than seven different programs claimed regular-season or tournament titles in the 1990s. One of those was Appalachian State in 1995–96. The Mountaineers

*Adrian Peterson dodges tacklers on "The Run" during Georgia Southern's 1999 NCAA Championship Game win over Youngstown State. (Georgia Southern University Athletics)*

completed the first undefeated season (14-0) in league history. In the conference tournament championship game, ASU squeaked past Marshall, 77–75, to reach NCAA postseason play.

On the men's side, the Mocs of Chattanooga reached the tournament championship game five times in six years, winning four titles. The most memorable year was 1997. Led by forwards Johnny Taylor and Chris Mims, the Mocs needed overtime to defeat Marshall, 71–70. Sent to the NCAA tournament's Southeast region in Charlotte, the No. 14-seeded Mocs stunned Georgia, 73–70, and Illinois, 75–63, to reach the NCAA's Sweet Sixteen.

Pitted against No. 10-seed Providence College in Birmingham, Chattanooga lost by six points. It would be more than a decade before another Southern Conference men's basketball team won a game in the NCAA Tournament.

From a membership perspective, the 1990s were a good decade for the Southern Conference. The lone departure was Marshall, a program intent on playing for bowl game invitations in Division I-A. Expansion strengthened the SoCon on three different occasions.

In January of 1991, Georgia Southern accepted an invitation to join the league, a process that wasn't truly completed until two years later. "We want them to be a full-fledged conference member as soon as possible, but it may take some time to work out a master football schedule with them," announced Commissioner Dave Hart. Indeed, GSU did not play a league men's basketball schedule until 1992–93 and was not part of the football standings until the 1993 season.

With Wright Waters at the helm, the SoCon expanded again in 1997 when it added two programs that had undergone years of transition to move up to Division I. UNC Greensboro had been a Division II program until 1991, primarily known for the national success of its men's soccer program. Wofford, which became the smallest Division I program in the nation by enrollment, had been in the National Association of Intercollegiate Athletics as recently as ten years before. That left the conference with an uneven number of members, but that concern was addressed a year later when the College of Charleston became the twelfth member of the SoCon.

The Southern Conference was now one of the most diverse in the nation. It consisted of both public and private institutions, had two military colleges, and three institutions that did not play football. League members embraced the diversity. "I always thought that was a great strength of the Southern Conference," said former commissioner Danny Morrison. "I loved the mix of schools, the way it mirrored higher education in America."

*Chattanooga's 1996–97 team reached the NCAA Tournament's Sweet Sixteen after winning the Southern Conference Championship. (University of Tennessee at Chattanooga Athletics)*

The latter part of the decade saw unprecedented growth in the size of NCAA postseason brackets, particularly on the women's side. This led to an increasingly greater emphasis on conference championships, most of which now came with automatic qualifier (AQ) status to the postseason.

The first SoCon team to compete in the NCAA's volleyball tournament was Appalachian State in 1993. In 1997, the first SoCon representative in an NCAA women's soccer tournament, UNCG, upset Duke in double overtime. Three years later, Chattanooga became the first SoCon team to play in the NCAA softball tournament.

As the membership prepared for the arrival of a new century in 2000, a rather amazing winning streak began amid little notice. On March 28, 1998, Furman University's women's tennis team blanked Davidson, 9–0. The victory would be the first in the longest string of success in Southern Conference history. The Paladins would win 100 consecutive Southern Conference regular-season matches, the longest winning streak in the first century of the conference in any team sport. Their next regular-season league loss would not come until 2010.

## THE CITADEL HEADS TO OMAHA

**ON THE MORNING OF JUNE 2, 1990,** head baseball coach Chal Port of the Citadel was preparing to lead his team against LSU in the College World Series. He may have been as surprised to be in that position as anyone. "When we looked at the calendar last fall," he told reporter William Rhoden of the *New York Times*, "our goal for June was to make sure the kids turned in all their equipment."

The Bulldogs' historic route to Omaha was certainly a memorable one.

To begin the academic year, the coaches and players had to deal with all the material and psychological effects of Hurricane Hugo, which tore through Charleston in September of '89 and devastated the city, including College Park, the Citadel's practice and game facility.

"The stadium's lights had been knocked down, the press box was completely removed, and the outfield fence was destroyed as well as both dugouts," recalled third baseman Tony Skole, who was named head coach at the Citadel in 2017. "We ended up finishing our last couple of weeks practicing in a grass parking lot outside the football stadium that was turned into a baseball diamond. If you could field ground balls on that surface, you could field them anywhere."

In a preseason poll, the Bulldogs were picked sixth in a seven-team Southern Conference. But they broke from the gate in blistering fashion, winning twenty-seven of their first twenty-eight games. Included was a twenty-six-game winning streak, the longest in the NCAA that season. The Citadel finished 13-1 in Southern Conference play to capture the regular-season title.

*ETSU's SEAMUS POWER belongs to the exclusive club of student-athletes who took first place in their competition in all four years of their collegiate career. But Power did it in three different sports. A native of Ireland, he won Southern Conference cross country championships in each of his four tries. Power remains the only runner in conference history to do so. His best time was 24:23 in 1991 at a course in the mountain town of Blowing Rock, North Carolina. In outdoor track, he was four-for-four in the conference's 5,000-meter run. Indoors, he was perfect in the mile run from 1991–94. Power won five All-America honors during his career. "ETSU carved me into not only the runner I became, but the man I became," Power later told the* Johnson City Press. *"It was a great opportunity and experience for a farmer's son from the West of Ireland to head off to America."*

*Ironically, the ETSU Athletic Department would feature another successful young man from Ireland with the same name the following decade. That SEAMUS POWER played golf for the Bucs and eventually went on to compete on the PGA Tour.*

*Women's golf has always been a pillar of excellence in the foundation of Furman University athletics. A program that featured future pro stars BETSY KING, BETH DANIEL, and DOTTIE PEPPER established its dominance immediately upon the sport being recognized by the Southern Conference in 1994. The Paladins captured the first nine SoCon championships and eighteen of twenty-six through 2019. In the middle of the decade, Furman's CAROLINE PEEK stood out as the program's top golfer. A two-time Player of the Year selection, she won the inaugural '94 championship with a fifty-four-hole total of 216 and was a three-time All-America selection. Gaining her LPGA card after graduation, Peek led the tour in average driving distance in 1998. She was voted into the Furman Hall of Fame in 2000.*

*Third baseman Tony Skole of the Citadel slides safely into second base during the Bulldogs' 9–5 victory in the 1990 championship game against Western Carolina. (The Citadel Athletics)*

Outfielder Anthony (A. J.) Jenkins batted .397 and led the SoCon in hits, runs scored, and runs batted in. Second baseman Dan McDonnell stole thirty-eight bases to lead the conference. Starters Ken Britt (10-2, 2.45 ERA) and Richard Shirer (8-1, three shutouts) led a pitching staff fortified by reliever Hank Kraft (4-1, seven saves).

At the conference tournament, played at a refurbished College Park, the Citadel tore through four opponents without a loss to earn a trip to the NCAAs. The Bulldogs were the No. 5 seed in the six-team Atlantic regional at Coral Gables, Florida, home of traditional power and No. 1-seed Miami.

"Miami was college baseball royalty back then, so we were excited to be in their regional," said Skole. "But mostly we were just excited that we still had baseball left to play after the SoCon Tournament."

The Bulldogs pounded North Carolina State, 11–3, before edging East Carolina, 8–5, to set up a winner's bracket meeting with Miami. A two-run single by first baseman Chris Coker highlighted a four-run third inning, and Shirer tossed a complete game, allowing two runs and seven hits in a 6–2 Bulldog victory.

"I doubt any of us will get any sleep tonight," Port told the *Charleston Post & Courier*, with his team one win away from Omaha. "We're on unchartered ground and we don't know how to behave."

The next day, Brad Stowell and Kraft combined to limit the Hurricanes to four hits and one run in a 4–1 victory. The offensive star for the Bulldogs was Skole, who had three hits, including a homer, scored twice, and drove in a run. "I was fortunate to be seeing the ball well that day and got some good pitches to hit," he remembered. "The home run I hit was the biggest of my career. It gave us a little cushion going into the later innings."

The Citadel was the first Southern Conference team to reach the College World Series in thirty-seven years. In their first contest at Rosenblatt Stadium in Omaha, the Bulldogs suffered an 8–2 loss to LSU and future major league right-hander Paul Byrd.

Two days later, the Bulldogs survived a seven-error, extra-inning slugfest with Cal State-Fullerton, winning 8–7 to stay alive. The winning run scored on a twelfth-inning single by Skole.

"I got lucky," he said. "Our best player, Anthony Jenkins, made a wonderful slide at home to give us the lead."

Facing LSU again the following day, the Bulldogs couldn't get much going before a crowd of 14,614, the largest to ever watch a Citadel baseball game. LSU won, 6–1, to send the Bulldogs home with an overall record of 46-14. Said LSU coach Skip Bertman, "They're America's team—touched by Abner Doubleday himself. A real field of dreams."

Bulldog teammates Skole (ETSU, the Citadel), McDonnell (Louisville), and Chris Lemonis (Indiana, Mississippi State) would all go on to become Division I head coaches.

"This team was special," Skole said. "No one thought we could do it. It truly was an amazing journey."

*The first Southern Conference softball championship took place on the Furman campus in May of 1994, and the host team convincingly proved itself the league's best. Entering as the No. 1 seed, the Paladins swept the four-team, double-elimination tournament by yielding only a single run in three games. Pitcher KIM CURRIER (pictured) was the star for Furman. She allowed one run in the opener against Marshall, then tossed two shutouts against Georgia Southern, striking out twelve in one game. Currier finished her career with sixty-one victories, twenty-two shutouts, four no-hitters, and 640 strikeouts. (Furman University Athletics)*

# THE

# 2000S

A t the 2000 Southern Conference men's outdoor track and field championships VMI outdistanced the ten-team field to capture its fourteenth title in the sport. It would be the last time any program other than Appalachian State or Western Carolina won the event for fourteen years.

Under head coaches John Weaver (ASU) and Danny Williamson (WCU), the two programs routinely competed for championships during the decade, both on the men's and women's sides. Weaver's Mountaineers were generally more successful. Between 2000 and 2009, the ASU men had a 6–3 edge in outdoor championships and a 5–3 margin indoors. The tally on the women's side was 8–2 indoors and 6–3 outdoors in favor of App State.

During the middle of the decade, the conference moved its indoor championship to the field house at Clemson University when membership changes made the Minidome on the East Tennessee State campus no longer a viable site. That was one ramification of ETSU's decision to drop its football program effective with the 2004 season. The decision, a controversial one in the Johnson City community, led to the membership's vote to remove ETSU from the conference at the end of the 2004–05 academic year.

A few years earlier, VMI announced that it would leave the SoCon primarily due to concerns with its football scheduling. VMI joined the Big South Conference in 2003, ending an affiliation with the SoCon that extended for eighty years. Both ETSU and VMI would subsequently accept invitations to rejoin the Southern Conference beginning in 2014. ETSU's return included the restoration of its football program.

The conference bolstered its ranks during this period by expanding on two occasions. In 2003, Elon University gave the league its fifth member in the state of North Carolina. Five years later, the membership climbed back to twelve with the addition of Samford University, a move that brought the Southern Conference its first presence in the state of Alabama since the departure of ex-members Auburn and Alabama in 1932.

The league's basketball tournament continued to move around during the decade. Sites included Greenville (South Carolina), North Charleston, Chattanooga, and Charlotte. The latter had not hosted a SoCon basketball championship in thirty-nine years when the membership voted to award the 2010 tournament to the Queen City as a way to minimize travel issues for member institutions seeking to reduce expenses during the decade's economic recession. The first two rounds of the combined men's and women's championships were played in Bojangles Coliseum, the new name for the original Charlotte Coliseum. The semifinals and championship games were played at Time Warner Arena, home of the NBA's Charlotte Bobcats (now Hornets).

No matter where the tournament was played, Davidson remained the premier Southern Conference program during this period. Coach Bob McKillop's Wildcats won tournament championships in 2002, '05, '06, '07, and '08. The Wildcats typically played competitive games in the NCAA tournament but had no wins to show for their efforts until 2008. That postseason truly introduced the basketball world to Stephen Curry, the smooth-shooting, baby-faced guard from Charlotte who had not received any Division I scholarship offers out of high school except for Davidson.

The Wildcats knocked off three straight higher-seeded teams—Gonzaga, Georgetown, and Wisconsin—before falling, 59–57, to Kansas with a trip to the Final Four on the line. The following year, Davidson routinely sold out Southern Conference arenas as Curry, a junior, led the nation in scoring. But the Wildcats were upset in the 2009 conference tournament by the College of Charleston. On April 23, Curry announced his intentions to enter the NBA draft and was a first-round selection by the Golden State Warriors.

Chattanooga also had basketball success in the first decade of the new century. The men's program won tournament championships in 2005 and 2009. The women's program set a remarkable standard, earning eleven consecutive regular-season championships and nine SoCon tournament crowns starting in 2000.

Perhaps the most famous sporting event involving a Southern Conference team came in the 2007 football season opener at Ann Arbor, Michigan. Appalachian State, in the midst of the best stretch in the program's history, stunned the football world by beating No. 5-ranked Michigan, 34–32. Corey Lynch's block of a Michigan field goal attempt as time expired sealed the deal, but the exploits of All-America quarterback Armanti Edwards were the real story. The left-hander connected on seventeen of twenty-three passes for 227 yards and three touchdowns, and ran for sixty-two yards and another touchdown.

Edwards, a rail-thin sophomore from Greenwood, South Carolina, had already proven his coolness under fire countless times before facing the Wolverines. As a freshman, he guided the Mountaineers to the 2006 national championship. After the triumph at Michigan, Edwards led ASU to another NCAA championship, routing Delaware and future NFL Pro Bowl quarterback Joe Flacco in the title game, 49–21.

*When Wofford's football program was added in 1997 to replace outgoing national champion Marshall, critics said the Southern Conference had not made a wise decision. Wofford had only been a Division I program for two years. Indeed, the Terriers struggled during their first two seasons in the SoCon, finishing with losing records.*

*But beginning with a second-place finish in 2002, Coach MIKE AYERS'S team served notice it would be a contender. Wofford went a perfect 8-0 in SoCon play the following year and advanced to the national semifinals of the Division I-AA championship. The Terriers followed up with another league championship and two more playoff appearances during the decade. The Wofford formula was a triple-option attack that routinely ranked among the nation's leaders in rushing and a bend-but-don't-break defense. The Terriers' success quieted all concerns about the program's ability to adapt to a higher level of competition.*

*Wofford's Eric Breitenstein finished his career with 5,734 yards rushing, including 321 in a 2012 game against Elon, a Southern Conference record. (Wofford College Athletics)*

Armanti Edwards threw for three touchdowns and ran for another in Appalachian State's 34–32 upset of fifth-ranked Michigan in 2007. (Appalachian State University Athletics)

By the time Edwards's career was over, he had become the first Division I player to amass 10,000 yards passing and 4,000 rushing. He twice was voted the Walter Payton Award as the top offensive performer in the FCS ranks. He would go on to a four-year NFL career with the Carolina Panthers and Cleveland Browns as a wide receiver and return specialist.

Edwards may have been the linchpin, but the success of the Mountaineer football program could be attributed to many others. Quarterback Richie Williams, the SoCon's Offensive Player of the Year, guided App State to the 2005 national championship before Edwards's arrival. Running back Kevin Richardson was an integral part of the ASU attack, rushing for more than 4,000 yards in his career and scoring a season-record thirty touchdowns rushing in 2006. Lineman Marques Murrell, safety Corey Lynch, and linebacker Jacque Roman were consecutive recipients of the league's Defensive Player of the Year awards.

One of the most prolific Southern Conference passing combinations in history was the Elon connection of quarterback Scott Riddle and wide receiver Terrell Hudgins. Riddle, who was also an infielder for the baseball team, threw for a then-league record 13,264 yards in his four years as a starter. His favorite target was Hudgins, who established NCAA records for career receptions (395) and yards receiving (5,250). Riddle and Hudgins led the Phoenix to a 17-6 league mark over a three-year stretch beginning in 2007.

During the decade, the conference found a sprinkling of NCAA postseason success in its women's sports. Playing on its home court at McKenzie Arena, No. 10-seed Chattanooga defeated No. 7-seed Rutgers, 74–69, in the first round of the 2004 NCAA Basketball Tournament. In soccer, the UNCG Spartans' women's team shut out Memphis, 1–0, in the first round of the 2007 NCAA Tournament.

**MEMORABLE MOMENTS**

SEPTEMBER 1, 2007

### APP STATE STUNS NO. 5 MICHIGAN

Appalachian State opened the 2007 football season with what a subsequent *Sports Illustrated* cover would label the "Alltime Upset." Taking the lead on a twenty-four-yard field goal by Julian Rauch with 26 seconds remaining in the fourth quarter, the Mountaineers still needed a blocked field goal by Corey Lynch on the game's last play to defeat fifth-ranked Michigan, 34–32. "We're still sort of shocked," said head coach Jerry Moore after his team built a 28–17 halftime lead then came from behind to register a stunning victory in the first live event carried by the Big Ten Network.

Another consistently successful women's team was the volleyball program at the College of Charleston. The Cougars won the championship tournament in 2002, lost in the finals a year later, then reeled off four consecutive titles. Middle blocker Tiffany Blum became the only SoCon volleyball player to be named Most Outstanding Player in three consecutive conference tournaments (2005–07). In 2005, C of C knocked off North Carolina, 3-sets-to-1, in the opening round of the NCAA Tournament.

A number of student-athletes destined for professional careers first gave indications of their superior abilities while playing in the Southern Conference during the decade. Wofford's William McGirt won the 2001 men's golf championship in a sudden-death playoff with ETSU's Pat Beste. McGirt went on to a successful career on the PGA Tour.

Brett Gardner was a two-time All-SoCon outfielder for the College of Charleston who once led the conference in hits and stolen bases. Drafted in the third round by the New York Yankees, Gardner enjoyed a long career in the Yankee outfield, winning the World Series in 2009. Another SoCon product, pitcher Greg Holland from Western Carolina was a three-time All-Star reliever who registered thirty-two saves for the 2015 champion Kansas City Royals.

Wide receiver Andre Roberts of the Citadel tied a conference record by returning three punts for touchdowns during the 2008 season. A two-time All-Conference selection, Roberts earned NFL Pro Bowl honors with the New York Jets in 2018.

However, the most famous pro sports SoCon alum during the 2000s had to be Steph Curry. As good as Curry was at Davidson (conference's all-time leading scorer, nation's leading scorer as a junior, first-team All-America honors), he developed into a bigger star with the Golden State Warriors. On his way to multiple Most Valuable Player Awards, Curry spearheaded a complete turnaround for a previously moribund franchise and became one of the leading faces of the NBA alongside LeBron James.

*Tiffany Blum, a middle blocker for the College of Charleston, earned three consecutive Most Outstanding Player awards at the SoCon Volleyball Tournament. (College of Charleston Athletics)*

*Former Western Carolina right-hander Greg Holland led the 2015 world champion Kansas City Royals in saves. (Western Carolina University Athletics)*

*Stephen Curry averaged thirty-two points per game in leading Davidson to the Elite Eight round of the 2008 NCAA Basketball Tournament. (Tim Cowie, Tim Cowie Photography)*

# THE LOGO THROUGH THE YEARS

"CREATING YOUR BRAND" became a marketing buzzword as America entered the twenty-first century. The use of marks and logos were deemed critical ingredients as businesses sold their products and services. But nobody thought this a critical concept in the first thirty-plus years of the Southern Conference.

The conference had no official mark or logo until Wallace Wade received membership approval on a design in time for the 1958–59 year. It featured the words "Southern Conference" at the top of an inner band in a circle, with "1921" at the bottom of the band. Centered in the circle were the letters "SC," surrounded by smaller circles containing the names or abbreviations of the nine members, along with the year each joined.*

The conference was able to use the new mark for six years before membership changes made it obsolete. The new logo, rolled out in 1964, made no reference to individual members. Instead, it positioned the "SC" in the center and the words "Southern Conference" in the circle's inner band more prominently. Again, the 1921 reference was listed at the bottom.

This mark, although not terribly interesting, was at least impervious to membership changes and served ably for more than three decades. At the time, media members routinely abbreviated Southern Conference to "SC" in headlines, newspaper articles, and the like. But "SC" could refer to lots of things. As an example, ESPN used giant "SC" lettering to brand its signature news show, *SportsCenter*.

Eventually the acronym "SoCon" was used with greater frequency and became the abbreviation of choice.

When Alfred White became commissioner in May of 1998, he hired the Exeter Group consulting firm to appraise the league and recommend action to best position the Southern Conference for the new century on the horizon. One of the strategies involved creation of a new logo.

"I recall strategic planning discussions centering around how "SC" was used by Southern Cal, South Carolina, and Santa Clara," remembered White. "And we thought promotion of the nickname would bring positive attention to the Conference."

Exeter's new mark again had a circular shape. The word "SOUTHERN" was at the top of an inner band and "CONFERENCE" was centered at the bottom. Above the band was "1921." But the biggest change was use of "SoCon" boldly displayed horizontally across the center of the circle. The logo was done in red, white, and blue and designed to permit members to use it in their own colors. Only the letters SoCon had to be consistently the same color (white).

Exeter's notes on the benefits of the new logo include that it "communicates the Conference's longevity; captures its heritage; and features SoCon with unmistakable and easily-readable boldness." The conference soon began using the letters S-o-C-o-n as its secondary mark for applications when the full logo wasn't practical.

*The Chattanooga Mocs were the dominant softball program during the 2000s, capturing seven Southern Conference tournaments. The Mocs' best postseason showing in their seven NCAA tournament appearances came in 2002 when UTC lost a 1–0 heartbreaker in extra innings to Florida State in the regional final.*

*One of Chattanooga's most prolific players during the decade was pitcher LACEY SWARTHOUT. A right-hander who grew up pitching to her father after school in their Orlando backyard, Swarthout threw a conference-record 333 innings in 2004, striking out 331. She compiled a 1.81 earned run average and won fifty-eight games over her two-year career for the Mocs. She was twice voted the league's Pitcher of the Year. After graduation, she became a collegiate pitching coach.*

One result of the new design was to validate, perhaps encourage, the use of "SoCon" as the league's identity. This didn't sit well with everyone.

"I keep hearing people call it SoCon, SoCon," Hall of Fame coach Lefty Driesell once mildly rebuked Commissioner John Iamarino. "Don't they know the name is the Southern Conference?"

To commemorate its centennial anniversary, the conference office created a new mark to use during the 2020–21 academic year.

The Southern Conference logo today.

*The VMI circle in the original logo lists the date of 1924. But minutes from the December 8, 1922, annual league meeting state that the Committee on Colleges made a resolution "that the Virginia Military Institute be admitted to membership in the Southern Intercollegiate Conference, said membership to date from September 1, 1923." This followed a written request for membership submitted on December 5, 1922, by R. B. Poague, chairman of the administrative committee on athletics at VMI. "It is therefore earnestly hoped," concluded Poague's letter, "that your action on this application will be favorable."*

*The committee's resolution to admit VMI was adopted by the membership, and the Keydets are listed in the conference's 1923 football standings. Additionally, there are references in the 1924 VMI yearbook to the league's ban on freshman eligibility affecting the 1923–24 Keydet track roster. Yet somehow the error persisted in league records right up until research was conducted for this book.*

Entering the final three games of the 2005 Southern Conference baseball season, the Furman Paladins had lost seven of their last eight games. They faced the daunting challenge of having to sweep a series at Davidson just to qualify for the conference tournament. The Paladins won the opener, 9–5, erasing a one-run deficit by scoring four times in the top of the ninth. They won the second game, then captured a 5–4 squeaker on the final day to earn a trip to the tournament. Shortstop A. J. DAVIDIUK'S eighth-inning single drove in what proved to be the deciding run.

But the magic for coach RON SMITH'S squad didn't end there. The eighth-seeded Paladins outslugged top seed College of Charleston, 9–7, then took down Elon, 6–3. In a winner's bracket showdown with Georgia Southern, Furman posted a 4–1 victory to advance to the championship round.

Once again facing Georgia Southern, Furman completed the remarkable turnaround by beating the Eagles, 5–4, with the winning run scoring on a passed ball in the bottom of the seventh. Right-handed reliever NICK HOLLSTEGGE recorded saves in all four victories to clinch the Walt Nadzak Most Outstanding Player award. The Paladins earned the automatic bid to the NCAAs and headed to Atlanta sporting one of the tournament's more modest overall records (30-27). Furman did not go easily, dropping a 5–4 decision to host Georgia Tech in ten innings before being eliminated by Michigan, 6-3.

Two years later, a similar improbable story was written at the baseball tournament when No. 9-seed Wofford won five consecutive games at Joe Riley Park in Charleston to win the championship. The big bat for the Terriers was third baseman BRANDON WARING, who smacked fourteen hits, including five homers, and drove in sixteen runs on his way to MOP honors.

# "FOLKS, WE GOT A STAR HERE!"

**COMING DOWN ON A FAST BREAK**, Davidson's Stephen Curry took a pass at the three-point line and gave a ball fake to a trailing Wisconsin defender who flew past him. With nobody near him, Curry raised up and swished the three-pointer.

"Folks, we got a star here!" exclaimed CBS play-by-play announcer Gus Johnson after another one of Curry's other-worldly moves.

Indeed, Davidson's 2008 run to within one shot of reaching the Final Four not only introduced Curry's super talents to America, but was a rewarding validation of the consistent excellence of the Davidson basketball program under head coach Bob McKillop. The Wildcats had won their sixth SoCon divisional title in seven years, finishing a perfect 20-0 in league play. A sixteen-point Southern Conference Tournament Championship Game victory over Elon landed Davidson in the NCAA tournament as a No. 10 seed.

"We played North Carolina and Duke during the opening weeks of the '07–'08 season," recalled McKillop. "We lost both games, but in both games we were a few possessions away from victory. It was incredibly uplifting to the team's confidence that we could compete so well against Top 10 teams."

Facing Gonzaga in a first-round game in nearby Raleigh, Davidson fell behind by ten points in the second half before Curry heated up. The sophomore guard scored thirty of his game-high forty points in the second half, and the Wildcats had earned the SoCon's first win in the tournament in eleven years.

The second-round contest against No. 2 Georgetown saw Davidson climb out of an even deeper second-half hole. With just under eighteen minutes to play, Georgetown led 46–29. But Curry (thirty points) and backcourt mate Jason Richards (twenty) helped the 'Cats chip away, and Curry's layup with 3:51 to play gave Davidson a lead it would not relinquish. When it was over, Davidson had a 74–70 victory and a trip to Detroit's Ford Field for a Sweet Sixteen date with No. 3 Wisconsin.

*In April of 2006, the Citadel called a press conference to name ED CONROY their new head basketball coach. Conroy, cousin of famous writer Pat Conroy, had been a captain on the basketball team and a lieutenant colonel in the corps of cadets as a student at the Citadel. He inherited a program that lost fourteen of fifteen SoCon games.*

*The Bulldogs were just slightly better in Conroy's first year. But a quality recruiting class began to pay dividends. Among the thirteen freshmen on the roster in 2007–08 were guards CAMERON WELLS and ZACH URBANUS and forward AUSTIN DAHN. The trio remained together for four years, all becoming double-figure scorers. Wells was a four-time selection on All-Conference teams.*

*As sophomores, the trio led the Citadel to their best season in thirty years. The Bulldogs caught fire in the second half of the campaign, finishing with a 15-5 league mark that included an eleven-game winning streak. The streak featured a pair of victories over cross-town rival College of Charleston and an eighteen-point walloping of regular-season champion Davidson.*

*Following a disappointing ouster in the quarterfinals of the Southern Conference Tournament, the Citadel made the first postseason tournament appearance in the program's history. Facing Old Dominion in the CollegeInsider.com Tournament, the Bulldogs fell, 67–59, to conclude an outstanding season at 20-13.*

Against the Big Ten champion Badgers, Richards contributed thirteen assists as the Wildcats broke a 36–36 halftime deadlock and won going away, scoring seventy-three points against a Wisconsin team that led the nation in scoring defense with fifty-three points per game. Curry finished with thirty-three.

"I distinctly remember sitting on press row next to [Davidson athletic director] Jim Murphy in the second half," said SoCon commissioner John Iamarino. "A few rows behind us, LeBron James is leading cheers for Davidson. There's all this noise from 40,000 or so fans in this massive stadium. And it's becoming obvious that Davidson is going to win.

"I looked at Jim and said, 'This is just surreal,' and all he could do was nod."

Curry deservedly received most of the attention, but the quality play of forward Andrew Lovedale and point guard Richards played a big role throughout Davidson's tournament success. The latter wound up leading the nation in assists. "I kept my head down, I did my job," Richards told Mike Lopresti of NCAA.com some ten years later.

Against No. 1-seeded Kansas, with a trip to the Final Four at stake, Curry struggled through a nine-for-twenty-five shooting day. But the Wildcats got unexpected scoring from their bench and hung around as the lead went back and forth. When Curry hit his last three-pointer of the night off an offensive rebound, Davidson trailed 59–57. Kansas missed a shot at the other end, and the Wildcats had seventeen seconds to tie or win it. But with Curry tightly double-teamed, he was forced to pass to Richards whose long three-point attempt banged off the backboard ending the game.

"It was an open look," Richards would recall. "Yeah, it was deep. Obviously I missed it, but I would take it again if I had the opportunity."

The Wildcats had become America's darling underdogs over a two-week stretch. Their accomplishments led to sellout crowds just about everywhere they played the following year. The team went 18-2 in conference play but was upset in the semifinals of the Southern

*From 2004 to 2008, the premier low post basketball player in the Southern Conference was KYLE HINES (pictured) of UNC Greensboro. The six-six, 230-pound New Jersey native graduated as the conference's all-time leader in blocked shots and finished as one of only six NCAA players to record 2,000 points, 1,000 rebounds, and 300 blocks. He was a first-team All-Conference selection in each of his four years with the Spartans. During the two seasons they competed against each other, Hines and Davidson's STEPHEN CURRY were the only two SoCon athletes selected as the Player of the Month (seven for Curry, three for Hines).*

*Hines went on to enjoy a long career playing professionally in Europe and Russia. He was the Most Valuable Player in a league in Italy and played on a EuroLeague champion team in Greece. In 2018 he told his regional hometown newspaper, the Camden (NJ) Courier Post, "I lived in Athens, Greece, for two years and my apartment was literally 50 feet from the beach.*

*I lived in Italy and was 30 minutes from Rome. I got the chance to drive by the Colosseum every day. I'm happy to accomplish my dream of playing professional basketball." (University of North Carolina at Greensboro Athletics)*

Conference Tournament by the College of Charleston, 59–52. Playing in the NIT, the Wildcats knocked off South Carolina before falling to St. Mary's to finish the season 27-8.

Reflecting on the 2008 NCAA Tournament run years later, McKillop said, "It changed my life. It changed the life of Davidson basketball. It changed the life of the coaching staff and all the players who were part of that roster. They can take that memory for the rest of their lives, it will be so cherished and so treasured."

# CELEBRATING 25 YEARS OF WOMEN'S ATHLETICS

**THROUGHOUT THE 2007-08 ACADEMIC YEAR**, the Southern Conference celebrated twenty-five years of sanctioning intercollegiate athletics for women. The first championship for women took place in November of 1983 when Appalachian State hosted the inaugural SoCon Volleyball Tournament.

The year-long festivities reflected on the NCAA's landmark 1982 decision to sponsor women's intercollegiate championships. The Southern Conference was among the first Division I conferences to conduct championships for women. Volleyball and basketball began in 1983. Tennis followed a year later, followed by cross country in 1985. By 1994, the SoCon was sponsoring nine women's championships. A tenth—lacrosse—began in 2018.

Preparations for the silver anniversary celebration started in 2006 when a committee was selected to determine appropriate methods to honor the early pioneers and contributors in each sport. Special anniversary teams were chosen in each sport by a panel of administrators and coaches. A special twenty-fifth-anniversary logo was designed and used on printed materials, websites, gifts, and lapel pins throughout the year.

Website features highlighted student-athletes from each of the then-eleven members. A special category, "25 of Distinction," honored twenty-five administrators, faculty representatives, coaches, and student-athletes who made special contributions to the growth of women's athletics. A twenty-sixth person, Sue Arakas of the Southern Conference office, was later added to the list by acclamation of the membership in May of 2008.

A traveling exhibit featuring a video slideshow, stand-up banners with highlights and timelines, and an extensive photo gallery was created and displayed on each campus at league championships. The year-long activities culminated with a twenty-fifth-anniversary brunch on March 9, 2008, in conjunction with the Southern Conference Basketball Tournament in North Charleston, South Carolina. Members of the special sports anniversary teams attended, and the keynote speaker was Jennifer Alley, executive director of the National Association of Collegiate Women Athletic Administrators (NACWAA).

*Going back to its pre-Division I days, UNCG has boasted consistently strong soccer programs. The men won five Division III national championships in the 1980s. In 2004, the Spartans were ranked No. 1 in the nation for eleven weeks. But the women's program has made its mark in the Southern Conference as well.*

*From 2000 through 2007, UNCG women earned four regular-season conference titles and made four trips to the NCAAs. During that time, three different Spartans were voted Player of the Year in the SoCon—LYNSEY MCLEAN (2001), AMY CARNELL (2004), and SHANNON DONOVAN (2006). The Spartans also enjoyed success in the NCAA tournament, winning their first-round match in 2000, 2003, and 2007. As of this writing, UNCG remains the only SoCon women's soccer team to win a match in NCAA postseason play.*

# "25 OF DISTINCTION"

| NAME | INSTITUTION | ROLE |
|---|---|---|
| Lynne Agee | UNC Greensboro | Basketball Coach |
| Elaine Baker | Furman | Administrator |
| Janie Brown | Elon | Faculty Representative |
| Brenda Carter | Georgia Southern | Administrator |
| Judy Clarke | Appalachian State | Administrator/ Multi-Sport Coach |
| Beth Daniel & Betsy King | Furman | Golf Student-Athletes/ Benefactors |
| Tom Davis | VMI | Faculty Representative |
| Sherry Dunbar | College of Charleston | Volleyball Coach |
| Kellie Harper | Western Carolina | Basketball Coach |
| Dorothy Hicks | Marshall | Faculty Representative |
| Amy Kiah | Wofford | Soccer Coach |
| Laura Lageman | College of Charleston | Administrator |
| Terri Lewitt | Wofford | Administrator |
| Kerry Messersmith | Georgia Southern | Volleyball Coach |
| Betty Peele | Western Carolina | Multi-Sport Coach |
| Caroline Price | Davidson | Tennis Coach |
| Cathy Roberts | UNC Greensboro | Administrator |
| Jerry & Jeanne Robertson | Elon | Benefactors |
| Linda Robinson | Appalachian State | Basketball Coach |
| Janice Shelton | ETSU | Administrator |
| Kelly Simpson | The Citadel | Administrator |
| Ed Steers | The Citadel | Administrator |
| Rebecca Stimson | Davidson | Tennis Student-Athlete |
| Alice Luthy Tym | Chattanooga | Faculty Representative |
| Shannon Wommack | Chattanooga | Track Student-Athlete |

*Subsequently added to the list by membership acclaim:*

| | | |
|---|---|---|
| Sue Arakas | Southern Conference | Administrator |

# THE

# 2010s

A s the new decade began, there emerged some serious challenges to the Southern Conference dominance established by the Chattanooga women's basketball program under head coach Wes Moore. The Mocs' 72–67 victory over Samford in 2010 represented UTC's eighth SoCon tournament championship in a ten-year stretch. But Chattanooga was knocked out in the semifinals in each of the next two years.

Samford and Appalachian State met in both the 2011 and 2012 women's basketball championship games. A tight defense and a controlled, Princeton-style offense helped coach Mike Morris's Samford team to consecutive titles, the first coming on Paige Anderson's three-pointer with sixteen seconds remaining. Chattanooga regained its stride and added five straight tournament championships beginning in 2013, the last four under Hall of Fame coach Jim Foster.

This string was snapped in 2018 when coach Susie Gardner's Mercer Bears blew through the league in dominant fashion. Mercer went undefeated in the conference, enjoyed three lopsided victories to win the SoCon Tournament, and rode a twenty-seven-game winning streak into the NCAAs. The Bears fell to Georgia in a first-round game at Athens, 68–63.

The following year, Mercer repeated its undefeated conference season and narrowly defeated Furman in the tournament championship game, 66–63. Both Amanda Thompson (coaches) and KeKe Calloway (media) received Player of the Year honors, giving the Bears five straight seasons with the league's Player of the Year.

Mercer had officially joined the conference on July 1, 2014, in conjunction with the readmission of former members ETSU and VMI. With its main campus in Macon, Georgia, and another in Atlanta, Mercer brought a desirable location to the conference's footprint. It also boasted a sterling national reputation for academics, excellent facilities, and an athletic program with a strong competitive nature. When the university and conference confirmed mutual interest during a series of preliminary discussions, Mercer's invitation for membership became the proverbial slam dunk.

"They will be a great addition and could become one of our best overall programs," commented one member of the conference's search committee after visiting the Mercer campus. "In

*To his coach and teammates, DEVLIN HODGES was known as "Duck" for his uncanny proficiency at duck calls. But to football opponents of the Samford quarterback, he was known as nothing but trouble. The native of Kimberly, Alabama, rewrote the Samford, SoCon, and FCS record books in a stellar four-year career. Hodges finished with 14,584 passing yards, breaking the existing FCS mark held by former NFL quarterback Steve McNair. As a senior in 2018, Hodges put up video game numbers, completing 70.5 percent of his passes for 4,283 yards and thirty-two touchdowns. He left Samford holding twenty-three school records.*

*A two-time All-America selection and three-time offensive Player of the Year pick in the SoCon, Hodges became the seventh Walter Payton Award winner in Southern Conference history. He became a starter for the Pittsburgh Steelers in 2019.*

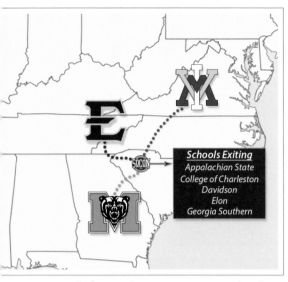

*Conference realignment was a major issue throughout the NCAA in the early years of the decade beginning in 2010. The additions of ETSU, Mercer, and VMI solidified the SoCon membership at ten institutions. (Graphic by Emily Fulton, Southern Conference)*

fact," he added, tongue-in-cheek, "the more I think about it, I'm not sure I want to bring them in. They may be *too* good."

Based upon postseason success, a case could be built that baseball challenged football as the premier team sport in the SoCon during the decade. Conference teams came tantalizingly close to advancing to the NCAA super regional round, losing in the title game of regional play on four separate occasions. In 2012, the conference sent three teams—Samford, Appalachian State, and the College of Charleston—to the NCAA Tournament.

Since 2009, the annual baseball tournament had been rotating between South Carolina locations in Charleston and Greenville before the membership pursued a long-range strategy in Greenville. The venue, Fluor Field, was a smaller replica of Boston's Fenway Park, complete with a "green monster" left field wall and a hand-operated scoreboard.

A pair of long-distance runners representing Southern Conference programs captured national honors. UNCG's Paul Chelimo became the first US runner since 1964 to take home a medal in the Olympic 5,000 meters when he earned a silver medal in the 2014 Games at Rio de Janeiro. Chelimo subsequently won the 5,000 meters at the US national outdoor meet. A recipient of multiple academic scholarships at UNCG, Chelimo was a multiple SoCon champion in indoor and outdoor track, as well as a three-time individual winner in cross country.

Samford's Karisa Nelson, a native of tiny Brewton, Alabama, became her institution's first NCAA champion when she captured the mile run at the 2017 NCAA indoor championships at College Station, Texas. She entered the race ranked twelfth among the field but turned in a sizzling time of 4:31.24 to win.

"Samford is such a great program and I wanted to show everyone what it did for me as an athlete," Nelson told Johanna Gretschel of flotrack.org. "You don't have to go to a huge name school to be a national champion. You just have to be motivated and have good coaches."

Chattanooga's 2011 softball team became the third SoCon program to reach the championship game of an NCAA regional tournament after a dramatic 2–1 victory over Memphis. From 2010–18, six different programs represented the SoCon in NCAA softball tournament play, illustrative of the growing interest being placed on the sport nationally.

In football, SoCon teams reached the national semifinals of the NCAA playoffs three straight years at the beginning of the decade. But after all the conference realignment, the league had to recover from the loss of three programs, including two (Appalachian State and Georgia Southern) that had combined for nine national championships. Southern Conference coaches rose to the challenge, however, and in 2016 the league sent its all-time high of four teams to the FCS playoffs.

The league was blessed with a myriad of highly skilled gridiron performers during the decade. Samford's Devlin Hodges obliterated league and NCAA records at the quarterback position, winning the 2018 Walter Payton Award. Chattanooga's Jacob Huesman was a three-time selection to the All-Southern Conference first team, combining accurate passing

UNCG's Paul Chelimo earned a silver medal in the 5,000 meters at the 2014 Olympic Games in Rio de Janeiro. (University of North Carolina at Greensboro Athletics)

Samford's Karisa Nelson was an NCAA national champion in the indoor mile. (Samford University Athletics)

with the ability to run like a halfback. Huesman played a significant role in the resurgence of the Mocs' football program and guided Chattanooga to the first two of three consecutive appearances in the FCS playoffs.

Jaquiski Tartt was an All-Conference safety in all four of his years at Samford. He was drafted in the second round by the San Francisco 49ers and became a starting defensive back. Georgia Southern running back Jerick McKinnon became a starter for the Minnesota Vikings before being signed by the 49ers. Furman's Dakota Dozier, an All-America offensive lineman, became a starting guard for the New York Jets. Dozier was the recipient of the 2013 Jacobs Blocking Trophy, awarded to the top offensive lineman in the Southern Conference.

On the basketball court, Wofford firmly established itself as a men's program to reckon with. The Terriers had previously enjoyed precious little success (5-11 record) in Southern Conference tournaments. That all changed beginning in 2010. Under long-time head coach Mike Young, Wofford rolled to its first championship game. Playing in Time Warner Arena in Charlotte, the Terriers used tenacious defense to build a 33–18 halftime lead and held off Appalachian State, 56–51, to earn their first trip to the NCAA Division I Tournament. Wofford then nearly upset No. 4-seeded Wisconsin, falling 53–49.

Wofford won the SoCon Tournament again the following year, then put together back-to-back titles again in 2014 and '15. Along the way was another near miss in the NCAAs when the Terriers lost 56–53 to No. 5-seed Arkansas in 2015. By the end of the decade, Wofford was playing in its new, upscale Richardson Indoor Stadium, had a pair of victories over North Carolina on its resume, and had won an NCAA tournament game versus Seton Hall. The Terriers had become one of the nation's foremost mid-major programs to watch.

The same could be said for ETSU. Hired as head coach in 2015–16, Steve Forbes led the Buccaneers to four consecutive appearances in the SoCon Tournament's championship game. The Bucs captured the 2017 championship and made the program's first appearance in the NCAA tournament in thirteen years. ETSU followed that with seasons of twenty-five and twenty-four victories.

*Wofford fans celebrate on the court following the Terriers' 70–58 victory over UNCG in the championship game of the 2019 conference basketball tournament in Asheville. (Todd Drexler, SoCon Photos)*

Basketball revivals also took place at UNC Greensboro and Furman. After eight straight losing seasons, coach Wes Miller guided UNCG to consecutive regular-season championships and a berth in the 2018 NCAAs, where the Spartans nearly upset Gonzaga. Led by sharpshooting guard Francis Alonso in 2018–19, UNCG finished 29–7, winning its first-ever postseason game in the NIT and narrowly missing an at-large berth to the NCAA tournament.

At Furman, players such as Devin Sibley and Matt Rafferty brought excitement and large crowds to Timmons Arena as the Paladins strung together seasons of nineteen, twenty-three, twenty-three, and twenty-five victories. Included were three postseason tournament appearances.

The biggest noise in basketball postseason play during the decade came from Mercer in its last season before joining the Southern Conference. The 14th-seeded Bears busted a lot of NCAA brackets and became a household name when they played a skilled, poised game to upset the Duke Blue Devils, 78–71, in a 2014 NCAA Tournament game at Raleigh.

The decade also saw the introduction of two new sports to the Southern Conference—and the revival of a third.

Following another round of conference realignment, the SoCon introduced men's lacrosse as a championship sport with seven participating institutions. Full-time members Furman, Mercer, and VMI were joined by associates Bellarmine, High Point, Jacksonville, and Richmond. One year later, the United States Air Force Academy, seeking a conference home, applied and was accepted as an eighth member.

The first championship tournament was won by High Point, 9–8, on a goal by midfielder Sean Harrison in double overtime against the host Richmond Spiders. Air Force captured the next two titles before Richmond rewarded its home fans in 2018 with a thrilling 11–10 overtime victory in the final against Jacksonville on a goal by the Spiders' Teddy Hatfield.

In a similar fashion, the conference utilized associate members to sanction women's lacrosse for the 2018 season. The inaugural regular-season championship was shared by Central Michigan and Detroit Mercy, but it was Mercer, playing at home in Five Star Stadium, that won the first SoCon Women's Lacrosse Tournament and advanced to the NCAAs. The Bears defeated Furman, 18–8, for the conference title, with tournament Most Outstanding Player Kelly Hagerty (five) and Kate Leone (four) combining for half the Mercer goals. The Bears repeated as tournament champions the following year.

Rifle was a Southern Conference sport for thirty-nine years beginning in 1956. When Western Carolina dropped the sport in June of '85, it left the membership with only four programs. "Our Constitution requires that at least five institutions must have a sport in order for the Conference to hold a championship," wrote Commissioner Ken Germann in a 1985 memo to the rifle coaches. "At the recent meeting of the Athletic Directors, rifle was officially dropped from the list of Southern Conference sponsored championships."

VMI's return to the conference in 2014 meant three full-time members offered rifle as a varsity sport. The league office was able to identify three associate members looking for a conference affiliation (UAB, Georgia Southern, and North Georgia), and Southern Conference rifle was reinstated in the spring of 2016.

The University of North Georgia won the first two championships after the sport's return. UNG's Ruthanne Conner earned consecutive Pinnacle Awards in 2017 and '18. She was also the small-bore rifle champion at the 2017 tournament. UAB, whose program was discontinued for a time before being reinstated, captured the 2019 championship. That same year, Georgia Southern's Rosemary Kramer earned All-America honors by placing third in the air rifle competition at the NCAA championships in Morgantown, West Virginia.

In keeping with its commitment to support the overall missions of its member institutions, the conference initiated the SoCon Academic Exchange in 2014, a collaborative effort of all ten institutions designed to create learning opportunities and benefits for students and faculty outside the realm of intercollegiate athletics.

Organized by the chief academic officers and/or provosts at each institution, the Exchange created the SoCon Undergraduate Research Forum (SURF); operated a faculty-oriented Leadership, Education, and Development program (LEAD); approved creation of the Pinnacle Award, to be presented to the student-athlete with the highest cumulative grade point average as a member of the SoCon championship-winning team in each sport; and launched recognition

## MEMORABLE MOMENTS

### NOVEMBER 26, 2014

### CHATTANOOGA WOMEN KNOCK OFF NO. 4 TENNESSEE

Tied at 63–63 with less than a minute to play, UTC's Keiana Gilbert blocked a breakaway layup attempt and the Chattanooga Mocs converted free throws down the stretch to upend No. 4-ranked Tennessee, 67–63, before 4,160 at McKenzie Arena. It was the first victory against a Top Ten opponent in UTC women's basketball history. Gilbert, who scored twenty-seven points, earned national player of the week honors from ESPN. "I think we were just aggressive enough," said Chattanooga coach Jim Foster, whose team made 53 percent of its field goal attempts. The Mocs would put together a twenty-five-game winning streak and reach No. 17 in the polls before their season ended with a loss to Pittsburgh in the NCAA Tournament.

for faculty and staff members via an All-Southern Conference awards program.

At the annual honors dinner held in conjunction with the league's 2019 spring meetings, the Southern Conference introduced the ten recipients for its graduate scholarship awards. Since the program's inception in 1991, the conference had honored 176 student-athletes who went on to continue their studies at the graduate level. More than $350,000 in scholarships dollars had been distributed by the conference to assist the families of those students.

*Chattanooga's Emily Boring discusses her research project at the 2017 SoCon Undergraduate Research Forum (SURF). (Mark S. Olencki, Wofford College)*

In March of 2020, collegiate athletics—indeed, ordinary life worldwide—was interrupted by the coronavirus pandemic. Just days after East Tennessee State and Samford, respectively, captured the SoCon men's and women's basketball tournament championships, all competition was cancelled for the remainder of the season as colleges and universities sent students home to avoid spreading the highly contagious virus.

And so a league founded just two years after the 1918-19 Spanish flu epidemic now confronted the challenges associated with another deadly outbreak as the Southern Conference approached its centennial.

## REALIGNMENT WARS

**WHILE SPEAKING WITH MEMBERS OF THE MEDIA** in late 2009, Big Ten Conference commissioner Jim Delany mentioned that his eleven-member league was open to the possibility of expanding its membership. It was the proverbial shot across the bow to virtually every other Division I conference.

His comments triggered discussions, detailed studies, campus visits, and ultimately decisive action. The Big Ten's additions of Nebraska in 2010 and Maryland and Rutgers in 2014 typified a frantic wave of conference realignment throughout Division I. The shuffling of members, done primarily to improve TV/media contracts or, in some cases, to replace lost members, meant the end to decades-long conference rivalries such as Kansas-Nebraska, Pittsburgh-West Virginia, and Texas-Texas A&M and completely altered the landscape of college athletics.

The changes occurred in a somewhat orderly progression, starting with the so-called Power Five conferences, moving to other members of the Football Bowl Subdivision (FBS), and eventually tagging most mid-major conferences whether they played football or not.

The prestigious Big East Conference, founded in 1979 as a basketball-dominant league that finally embraced football in a big way, toppled from the sheer weight of sixteen members. For a short period, the league included Boise State, whose campus was more than 2,600 miles and two time zones from the conference headquarters in Providence, Rhode Island. The Big East's football-playing members formed a new league, the American Athletic Conference, while the remaining members, initially called the "Catholic 7," kept the Big East name and reformed as an organization of ten basketball-oriented programs.

The Southern Conference was among the most impacted conferences hit by the realignment wars. The first tremor occurred when the College of Charleston hired a consultant in 2012 to consider membership in the Colonial Athletic Association (CAA). At a vote of its board of trustees in November, the institution announced its departure from the SoCon at the conclusion of the academic year.

In March of the following year, Appalachian State and Georgia Southern, two institutions with long-stated goals of placing their athletic programs in an FBS conference, were invited to join the Sun Belt Conference. The SoCon was down to only nine members.

"Membership issues preoccupied my time," remembered Commissioner John Iamarino. "It didn't matter what I was doing. Eating dinner, driving to a game, mowing my lawn. It's all I thought about.

"One time, my wife, Mary Ann, mentioned to me how bad it would be if I was the guy in charge when a league that had been around since the 1920s disbanded. That was a disturbing thought."

To remind himself to avoid such a disaster, Iamarino made the famous 1937 photo of the Hindenburg bursting into flames the wallpaper on his office computer screen.

In May of 2013, Davidson suddenly announced it was joining the Atlantic 10 Conference in 2014, thereby becoming the only institution in history to leave the Southern Conference twice (it previously joined the Big South in 1988 before returning in '92). Weeks later, Elon followed suit, heading to the CAA. There were now seven institutions left.

The league's non-departing athletic directors held an ADs-only teleconference to pledge their loyalty to the conference and each other. Iamarino had been actively considering possible replacements and holding clandestine talks with a sizeable number of interested parties. "I've spoken to enough schools to start a brand-new conference all by itself," he told one sports writer.

In the end, the conference stabilized itself by adding two former members eager to return (ETSU and VMI) and an aggressive program (Mercer) looking to align itself with more like-institutions. One of the first steps taken by the presidents and chancellors of the new ten-member Southern Conference was to significantly raise the exit fee for leaving the league. "I took that as a very good sign for the future," recalled Iamarino.

*Few runners have made their mark on an athletic program quite like ALLIE BUCHALSKI (pictured) did at Furman. She became the program's first female All-American in cross country, indoor track, and outdoor track. She won conference individual honors in all three sports and was a consistent member of the league's all-academic team while completing a double major in business and art. She placed fourth in the NCAA indoor track championships in the 5,000 meters as a junior and was sixth in the same event outdoors.*

*She was runner-up in her first Southern Conference cross country championship, but then won that event in each of her three succeeding years to help lead the Paladins to victory each time. In June of 2018, Buchalski finished second in the 5,000-meter run at the NCAA outdoor championship meet in Eugene, Oregon. Shortly thereafter, she announced her intentions to train with a professional coach in Seattle to set her sights on the 2020 Olympic Games in Tokyo. "Without question," said Furman assistant coach Rita Gary, "Allie is by far the best runner Furman has ever seen." (Furman University Athletics)*

The new configuration would begin play in the fall of 2014. On the last day of the annual spring meeting in May, with representatives of all ten members in attendance, the commissioner likened the gathering to a kind of wedding celebration. He suggested "keeping with the traditions of this type of event."

Whereupon Iamarino reached under the table, brought out a bottle of champagne, popped the cork, and invited everyone to join in a 9:45 A.M. toast to the success of the new Southern Conference.

"It was a rough stretch," he reflected, looking back on all the upheaval. "But we came out all right on the other side."

## BEAUMONT MILL, HEADQUARTERS OF THE SOUTHERN CONFERENCE

**WHEN COMMISSIONER DANNY MORRISON** and the Southern Conference reviewed offers from four cities to become the league's headquarters, one stood out in particular.

The league visited sites in Charlotte, North Carolina; Spartanburg, South Carolina; and Greenville, South Carolina, as well as Asheville, North Carolina, which was headquarters at the time.

"Charlotte had space for us in the Coliseum where the Hornets played, and Greenville had a nice downtown location to show us," recalled Morrison. "Both were very aggressive in wanting us. But Spartanburg was the most aggressive."

*The Southern Conference offices were relocated to the former Beaumont Mill complex in Spartanburg, South Carolina, in the summer of 2005. (Paul Lollis, Southern Conference)*

Mayor Bill Barnet and the city's Chamber of Commerce convinced the conference to move to Beaumont Mill, located just outside the city's downtown. Built in 1890, the mill had a storied history in an industry—textile manufacturing—once so critical to the economic growth of the Southeast, particularly South Carolina. At its peak, Beaumont was equipped with more than 12,000 spindles and hundreds of automatic looms. It once employed more than 1,800 workers and was surrounded by approximately 150 homes in what became the neighboring Beaumont Village.

Originally a one-story edifice, the mill was expanded to three levels stretching across more than 186,000 square feet. It was conveniently adjacent to the Richmond & Danville Railroad, which later was called the Southern Railroad. At the turn of the twentieth century, the mill's primary output included carpet, seamless bags for corn and grain, and wrapping twine for domestic products. Like most mills from that era, it was constructed with a red brick exterior and featured a tall brick smokestack.

During World War II, Beaumont Mill was one of the few in the United States designated exclusively for the war effort. Production shifted to heavy cotton fabric required for uniforms, blankets, and other materials for the armed services. The plant won a number of awards from the army and navy for its scale of wartime production.

In the decades following the war, labor conditions increasingly made production of textiles more attractive overseas to parent companies. One by one, Southern mills began closing down. That fate struck Beaumont in 1999. After sitting vacant for a couple years, the complex was purchased by Spartanburg businessman Jimmy Gibbs, who sold the equipment and began the search for new tenants.

Plans also called for a NASCAR racing museum and a South Carolina sports hall of fame. Charlotte eventually landed the NASCAR museum and the hall of fame wound up in Columbia. "As I recall, the NASCAR plan was very appealing to us," said Morrison. "But even when that fell through, I thought the building would give us wonderful space."

The SoCon moved from its temporary offices in Spartanburg on East Main Street to the mill in January of 2005, setting up shop in a 6,000-square-foot set of offices on two levels located at 702 North Pine Street. A spacious boardroom, named in honor of SoCon alumnus Arnold Palmer, featured a drop-down projection screen for both satellite TV and computer presentation viewing. There were showers for both men and women, a large upstairs storage area, and an open lobby area with a flat-screen TV.

The offices retained much of the look of a textile mill. The upfitting paid for by the conference left exposed brick on the walls and kept the support poles and the large windows

*His full name resembled an optometrist's eyechart. UNDRAKHBAYAR KHISHIGNYAM. His Citadel wrestling teammates and fans were encouraged to call him by a simpler handle—"Ugi." The native of Ulaanbaatar, capital of Mongolia, did not compete his freshman year at the Citadel due to NCAA eligibility restrictions placed on international students who do not attend high school. The next year, competing in the 141-pound weight class, Ugi flourished. He won the 2013 Southern Conference championship at 141 pounds, thereby qualifying for the NCAA nationals. Seeded sixth in his weight class, he reached the tournament's semifinal round. He was voted Freshman of the Year in the conference and the Student-Athlete of the Year at the Citadel.*

*Cleared for an additional season of competition by the NCAA, Ugi continued his success in 2013–14, once again winning in the 141-pound group in the SoCon championship and qualifying for another NCAA national appearance. He did not wrestle in his final academic year at the Citadel, instead serving as a student assistant coach prior to his graduation in May of 2015. He wound up his Citadel career with an overall record of 64-11, an .853 winning percentage. He went on to coach high school wrestling in Ohio and work as a manager for a transportation company in the Chicago area.*

that stretched nearly from floor to ceiling. Embedded in much of the hardwood floor on the second level were hundreds of ring travelers, the small circular metal pieces that guide the yarn to be spun or twisted on a spindle.

In 2015, Spartanburg Regional Health Services purchased the mill to house most of their administrative personnel, thereby freeing up space for an expansion of the nearby Spartanburg Regional Medical Center. The following summer, after nearly twelve months of renovation and construction, some 600 employees were relocated to the facility. The Southern Conference lease was transferred to the hospital.

"We have better security and more visibility with our logo displayed next to theirs on a sign off a busy road like Pine Street," said Morrison's successor, John Iamarino. "We're much more connected to the building now that we're not the only ones here. It's been a very positive change."

## THE OLDEST CONTINUOUS CONFERENCE TOURNAMENT

**WHEN THE IVY LEAGUE ANNOUNCED** in 2017 that it would begin conducting a postseason tournament to determine its automatic qualifier to the NCAA men's basketball tournament, it meant that all thirty-two Division I conferences sponsored championship tournaments. ESPN annually proclaims this stretch as Championship Week.

The Southern Conference has the distinction of owning the longest continuous conference basketball tournament in NCAA history. Technically, conference members have been competing in such a tournament since 1921, although it might be more accurate to pinpoint 1924 as the first true Southern Conference basketball championship.

The murky timeline owes to the fact that basketball teams in the South once belonged to a loose regulatory organization known as the Southern Intercollegiate Athletic Association (SIAA). Formed in 1894, the SIAA had no mandatory regular-season scheduling. A set of regulations addressed amateurism and athletic eligibility, but organization meetings eventually focused on ways to bring programs together at one site for a championship. This was first done in track and field. By the beginning of the 1920s, talk centered on a similar event for basketball.

University of Georgia basketball coach Herman J. Stegeman had long advocated for a Southern championship. Stegeman was a spectator at an Amateur Athletic Union (AAU) tournament in Atlanta that featured teams from the East, Midwest, and West. He saw how the fans were fascinated by a faster style of play than was generally played in the South.

"The fact that a brand of basket ball [*sic*] much faster than was ever seen in the south before can be played with a minimum of bodily contact was an eye-opener to all spectators and many Southern players," said Stegeman in an article on the AAU for the 1920–21 *Spalding Official Basket Ball Guide*. "And this lesson should last a long time. The fast dribbling game of the northern teams proved to be immensely popular."

It's worth noting that at the time, the sport of basketball was less than thirty years old and very much in a developmental stage. It was 1891 when Dr. James Naismith wrote a set of thirteen rules and nailed two peach baskets to the balcony of an indoor track at a YMCA in Springfield, Massachusetts. Differences in style of play from region to region still existed. The sport was evolving.

When the SIAA held its annual meeting in 1920, it authorized a tournament among members to be held at the downtown Atlanta City Auditorium in February of 1921. Participation would be by invitation only—not all SIAA members were invited. Programs had to apply to participate and were asked to submit rosters and season results to validate their worthiness. A committee was appointed to invite and seed the teams.

Ironically, the opening day of the first SIAA Tournament—Friday, February 25—was the same day that faculty representatives met in Atlanta and agreed to launch what ultimately became the Southern Conference.

Fifteen teams participated in the inaugural SIAA Tournament. Only three of the fifteen—Birmingham Southern, Millsaps, and Newberry—would never hold membership in the Southern Conference. Seven games were played on the first day. Alabama, the highest seed, drew a bye to the quarterfinals. Ultimately, the championship was won by Kentucky, 20–19, over Stegeman's Georgia Bulldogs. The game's ending illustrates how differently the sport was administered in its formative years.

With time winding down and the score tied 19–19, Kentucky's Paul Adkins was fouled taking a shot under the basket. Rules allowed the coach in such circumstances to select the player to take the free throw. William King of the Wildcats was chosen to attempt the try. Just as King steadied himself, the timer fired his pistol signifying the end of regulation time. King later admitted being rattled by the sudden noise, but still managed to sink the winning foul shot.

"Billy King had established himself as the man of the hour," wrote Guy Butler in the next day's *Atlanta Georgian.* "He was lifted upon the shoulders of his Kentucky teammates and borne about the court."

The tournament would remain an SIAA-run entity for two more years. Interestingly enough, the two teams beaten in each of those championship games would eventually become present-day SoCon members—Mercer in 1922 and Chattanooga in 1923. Commenting on the '22 tournament, the minutes of the conference's basketball committee reported that "the 1922 Tournament was, in the opinion of the committee, the finest crowd of college men ever gathered together for an athletic event, with the possible exception of a few large college track meets."

At the annual league meetings at the Raleigh Hotel in Washington, DC, in December of 1923, conference legislators finally made a clean break from the SIAA, adopting an amendment declaring that "no teams except those members of this Conference shall take part in the annual track meet or basketball tournament of the Southern Conference without the consent of the Conference or its Executive Committee."

*When Western Carolina's J. T. POSTON sank a birdie putt on the first hole of a sudden-death playoff at the 2015 Southern Conference men's golf championship, he became the first player in nearly forty years to win consecutive SoCon titles. Poston's birdie at Pinehurst's No. 9 course gave the Catamounts their fourth individual champion in the past ten tournaments. Poston had won the previous year at Pinehurst by shooting a 206 over the fifty-four holes, the lowest total for a SoCon champion in more than a decade.*

*Once the subject of a* Sports Illustrated *"Faces in the Crowd" piece for shooting a 63 while at Hickory (North Carolina) High School, Poston went on to earn his PGA Tour card. He became the first tour winner in forty-five years to shoot bogey-free golf when he captured the 2019 Windham Championship.*

In just two seasons of competition, Mercer's KYLE LEWIS (pictured) became one of the most honored players in Southern Conference baseball history. A two-time SoCon Player of the Year, Lewis won the 2016 Golden Spikes Award as USA Baseball's premier amateur player, was named Player of the Year by Baseball America, and was a first-team All-America selection. The Snellville, Georgia, native led the SoCon in seven different offensive categories during his career at Mercer.

Lewis was voted Most Valuable Player of the 2015 Southern Conference Baseball Tournament, leading the champion Bears to a subsequent NCAA tournament appearance. One year later, the Seattle Mariners made him the eleventh player chosen in the first round of the major league draft. No other Southern Conference baseball player has ever been drafted higher. Called up by the Mariners in September of 2019, he displayed above-average power, hitting six home runs in only eighteen games. (Todd Drexler, SoCon Photos)

Thus, the first SoCon members-only tournament occurred in 1924 in Atlanta. Jack Cobb of the Tar Heels scored fifteen of his team's twenty-six points as North Carolina defeated Alabama, 26–18. The tournament remained in Atlanta through the 1932 championship. When the thirteen Southeastern Conference-bound programs left the Southern, the league's executive committee moved the event to the newly rebuilt Raleigh Memorial Auditorium, which had a basketball seating capacity of 5,000. Organized and run by the Raleigh Junior Chamber of Commerce, the championship would enjoy a fourteen-year run in the North Carolina state capital.

Surviving through the Depression and World War II eras, the league basketball tournament became an ever-increasing source of revenue for Southern Conference operations. By 1951, the tournament revenue of $42,774.75 represented 60 percent of the conference's total revenues of $70,981.18. The larger members grew increasingly frustrated by the lack of traveling fans and poor crowds attending tournament games of the smaller institutions. This became just another factor to be stacked on the pile of concerns that led to the withdrawal of the soon-to-be members of the Atlantic Coast Conference in 1953.

With neither Raleigh nor Durham a viable site any longer, the conference basketball championship moved north. A 1954 trial in Morgantown, West Virginia, did not go so well when the host West Virginia Mountaineers lost in the semifinals. The now-defunct Richmond Arena became the tournament venue from 1955 through 1963. The league then moved into the larger 11,666-seat Charlotte Coliseum on Independence Blvd. for an eight-year run that coincided nicely with the emergence of the nearby Davidson College program coached by Lefty Driesell.

Facing greater competition for spectators and media coverage from the wildly popular ACC tournament, the SoCon began experimenting with formats and locations in the mid-seventies. From 1975 through 1982, first-round games were played on campus sites, with the semifinals and championship games played a week later at one site. The membership eventually yearned again for a single-site championship with a community that would help market and promote the event.

Led by Commissioner Ken Germann, the league entered negotiations with the City of Asheville, North Carolina, to host the tournament. The city was seeking to burnish its reputation as a desirable tourist destination in the mountains of western North Carolina. It boasted a downtown arena, the Asheville Civic Center, built in 1974, that had a suitable capacity of approximately 6,500 seats. Bolstered by local ticket sales marketed by the Junior League, Asheville became the host of an increasingly popular Southern Conference championship for a twelve-year period. Capacity crowds for games involving East Tennessee State and Marshall, in particular, became quite common.

At the coordination of Athletic Director Dave Braine, Marshall fans would come to Asheville armed with a large supply of $2 bills to spend in a coordinated effort to show the impact the Thundering Herd community had on the local economy. One year's estimate had Huntington, West Virginia, banks distributing an estimated 16,000 $2 bills to Marshall supporters.

When civic leaders were slow to address needed renovations to the civic center, the conference tournament left Asheville in 1996 and entered an era where the championship seemed to rotate among cities beginning with the letters GR or CH. Tournament sites included Greensboro (1996–99); Greenville, South Carolina (2000–01); Charleston (2002–04; 2006–08); Chattanooga (2005, 09, 11) and Charlotte (2010).

Finally, with a pledge to renovate and modernize the newly renamed U.S. Cellular Center, Asheville was awarded a three-year contract to host the men's and women's tournaments starting in 2012. Two subsequent renewals pushed the conference's commitment to Asheville through 2021. In May of 2019, it was announced that Harrah's Resort in Cherokee, North Carolina, had won future naming rights to the arena. Beginning in January of 2020, the facility would be known as Harrah's Cherokee Center Asheville. Part of the agreement called for the installation of state-of-the-art video boards.

Regardless of whether one considers the 1921 SIAA Tournament the first in the string, or if it's the 1924 SoCon members-only championship, no other Division I conference has conducted a championship basketball tournament longer than the Southern Conference. The tournament remains one of the signature pieces in the league's history.

# TODAY'S SOUTHERN CONFERENCE

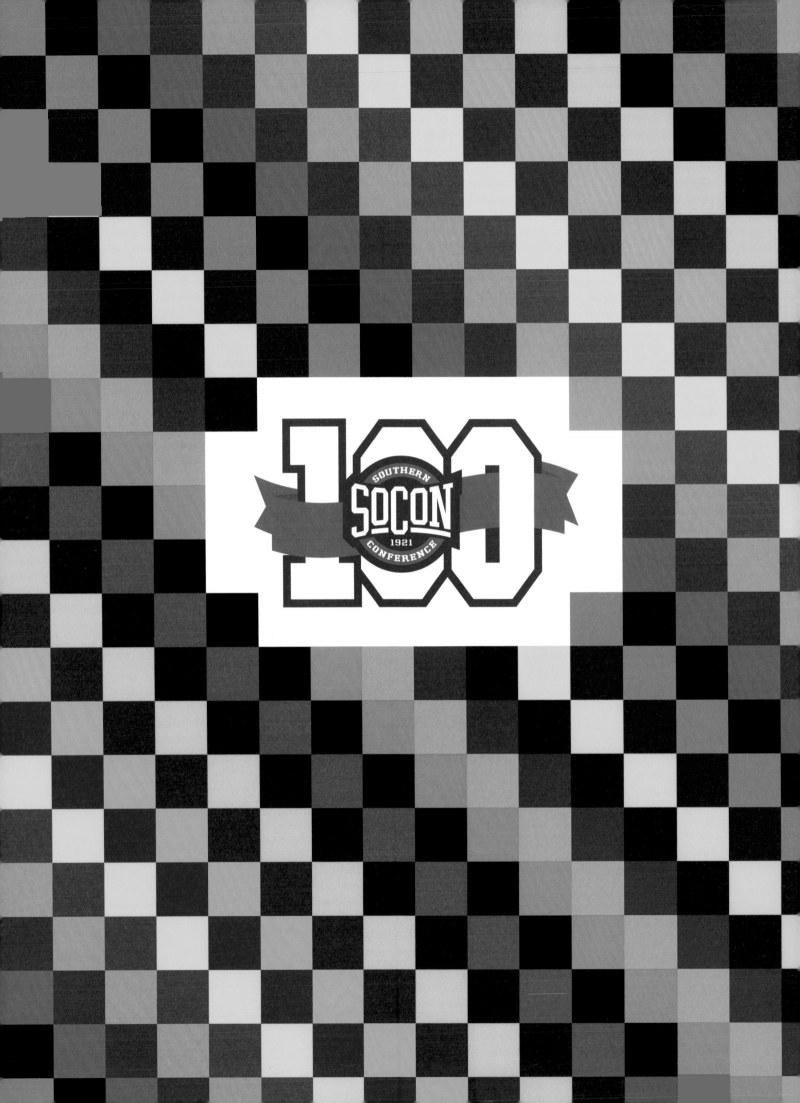

# THE CITADEL

*"The competitive nature that each team brings to the table on a daily basis adds to the level of play and excitement in this conference. Everyone plays to win, so the SoCon is extremely competitive through and through. I've made lots of friends over the past two years just by competing against them and having fun with it."*

## BROOKS O'BRIEN
### THE CITADEL BASEBALL

Named "Best Public College in the South" by *U.S. News & World Report* for eight consecutive years, the Citadel offers a classic military college education for young men and women who strive to become leaders through a rigorous combination of academic, military, and physical training. The Citadel's primary undergraduate population is comprised of the South Carolina Corps of Cadets, about 2,300 students. One in four cadets is a Pell Grant recipient. Cadets are not required to serve in the military, but about one-third graduate to become officers in all branches of United States service.

The Citadel's core values are honor, duty, respect. Through these values, the Citadel is dedicated to fostering a culture of diversity and inclusion to best support its mission of educating and developing principled leaders. Incoming cadet applicants are assessed for character, maturity, motivation, academic readiness for college, amenability to a regimented lifestyle, emotional stability, and potential to contribute to cadet life. Cadet applicants must also meet physical standards similar to those required by the US military.

The Citadel Athletics Department has sixteen varsity sport teams. The Citadel is affiliated with NCAA Division I athletics, and in football with the NCAA Football Championship Subdivision. The average cadet-athlete GPA has typically been slightly higher than the average of non-athlete cadets.

### FAST FACTS

Location
**Charleston, SC**

Founded
**1842**

Joined SoCon
**1936**

Enrollment
**2,300**

Colors
**Citadel Blue & White**

Athletic Nickname
**Bulldogs**

*Above, The Citadel, the Military College of South Carolina, was established in 1842. (Louis Brems, The Citadel); Center left, Dress uniform parades are a regular part of the Citadel's academic schedule. ( Louis Brems, the Citadel); Below left, The Citadel president, Gen. Glenn M. Walters and cadet Brooks O'Brien; Below right; Morning physical training (PT) at the Citadel (The Citadel).*

Excelling as a member of the South Carolina Corps of Cadets requires hard work, organization, and commitment, but through the leadership development model all cadet and cadet-athletes are propelled toward success and meaningful employment.

The iconic Citadel campus, situated along the Ashley River in Charleston, South Carolina, is a part of what has led Charleston to be named the No. 1 city in the United States by the readers of *Condé Nast Traveler* magazine for eight consecutive years.

## FROM THE PRESIDENT'S OFFICE

**"THE SOUTHERN CONFERENCE IS PERFECT** for the Citadel. We are an institution that values tradition, so it's incredible to be a part a conference with a 100-year legacy. There's tremendous diversity among the institutions in our conference—public and private institutions and military colleges, each with its own unique ethos and traditions. The proximity of our colleges means that cadet-athletes and student-athletes can easily travel between campuses to compete. The conference provides our athletes a rich experience and a special bond that all of us can be proud of.**"**

*General Glenn M. Walters*
*President, The Citadel*

# EAST TENNESSEE STATE UNIVERSITY

*"Every team plays like it's their last game in the SoCon. They always give you their best effort. When teams are giving you their all every single game, it makes for a fun atmosphere."*

## QUAY HOLMES
### ETSU FOOTBALL

East Tennessee State University was founded in 1911 for a singular purpose—to improve the quality of life for the people of the region. ETSU is committed to collaboration, civic engagement, and academic excellence, and the footprints being left by its students, faculty, staff, and alumni are the greatest examples of the institution's focus on its mission.

Through eleven colleges and schools, ETSU awards degrees in more than 100 programs of study, with offerings at the undergraduate, graduate, and professional levels. In addition to on-ground degree programs, it offers many programs online and at sites beyond the 350-acre main campus in Johnson City.

ETSU is home to the only major Academic Health Sciences Center between Knoxville, Tennessee, and Roanoke, Virginia. It is comprised of five colleges: the Quillen College of Medicine, Gatton College of Pharmacy, College of Nursing, College of Public Health, and

*Above, an aerial view of the campus, with the ETSU Foundation Carillon and Alumni Plaza at the center. (East Tennessee State University archives); Center left, William B. Greene Jr. Stadium was completed in time for the start of the 2017 football season. (Charlie Warden, ETSU); Below left, ETSU president, Dr. Brian Noland and student-athlete Quay Holmes; Below right, an ETSU class studies the lunar surface. (Charlie Warden, ETSU)*

College of Clinical and Rehabilitative Health Sciences. The university recently opened its Interprofessional Education and Research Center for all students in the health sciences.

Unique offerings at ETSU include a graduate program in storytelling, which is the only one of its type. ETSU became the first university in America to offer a four-year degree in bluegrass, old-time, and country music. The Center of Excellence in Paleontology and its five-acre Gray Fossil Site is one of the richest sources of information in the nation about the early Pliocene Epoch. The university is also home to a US Olympic Training Site where elite athletes from around the world train every year.

In 2017, ETSU opened the William B. Greene Jr. Stadium as the home of Buccaneer football and subsequently opened the doors of the James C. and Mary B. Martin Center for the Arts.

## FROM THE PRESIDENT'S OFFICE

**"ETSU'S MEMBERSHIP IN THE SOUTHERN CONFERENCE** is one of the defining aspects of our institution and has provided an experience we would not have realized in another conference. As a university steeped in history and defined by tradition, ETSU is grateful for this opportunity to engage with our peers at well-known and highly respected colleges and universities throughout the region. It is there where friendships are made, and rivalries are built. **"**

*Dr. Brian Noland*
*President, East Tennessee State University*

### FAST FACTS

Location
**Johnson City, TN**

Founded
**1911**

Joined SoCon
**1978; 2014**

Enrollment
**14,500**

Colors
**Navy Blue & Old Gold**

Athletic Nickname
**Buccaneers**

# FURMAN UNIVERSITY

*"I love that because the conference is smaller, we are able to treat each other as friends rather than exclusively as competitors. The sportsmanship at the Southern Conference seems to be stronger than what I see at other high-level meets."*

## EMMA KUNTZ
### FURMAN CROSS COUNTRY, TRACK AND FIELD

Founded in 1826, Furman University is a premier liberal arts and sciences university that offers students rigorous academics, broad research opportunities, a robust visual and performing arts program, and NCAA Division I athletics. Located in Greenville, South Carolina, the campus is just minutes from downtown Greenville, one of America's emerging destinations.

At the heart of the university's academic experience is the Furman Advantage, which guarantees every student an unparalleled education combining classroom learning with real-world experiences and self-discovery. This integrated four-year pathway, guided by a diverse community of mentors, prepares students for lives of purpose and accelerated career and community impact—demonstrating in concrete terms the value of a Furman education. Students live and learn on a campus that is internationally recognized for its traditional beauty and modern facilities, a short drive from the Blue Ridge Mountains, the Carolina beaches, and major metropolitan centers.

Furman provides students the opportunity to explore and solve community issues through its centers and institutes. The Riley Institute leads programs in public policy, education, and diversity in South Carolina and

## FAST FACTS

Location
**Greenville, SC**

Founded
**1826**

Joined SoCon
**1936**

Enrollment
**2,800**

Colors
**Purple & White**

Athletic Nickname
**Paladins**

*Above, the bell tower and lake contribute to the beauty of the Furman campus. (Elizabeth Lichtenberg, Furman University); Center left, a Furman chemistry department classroom. (Elizabeth Lichtenberg, Furman University); Below left, Furman president, Dr. Elizabeth Davis and student-athlete Emma Kuntz; Below right, the Furman Rose Garden. (Elizabeth Lichtenberg, Furman University)*

beyond. The Shi Center for Sustainability connects students, educators, and community leaders on issues related to human and environmental well-being. And the Institute for the Advancement of Community Health connects campus and the community to advance education and research devoted to supporting and improving health.

As the Prisma Health's primary undergraduate partner, Furman works with the community hospital system to develop internships, observation programs, and research activities that engage students and faculty in all aspects of health care.

## FROM THE PRESIDENT'S OFFICE

**WITH A UNIQUE MIX** of private and public colleges and military institutions, and a footprint that covers a swath of the Southeast, the Southern Conference fosters great and historic rivalries, provides fertile recruiting opportunities, and, unlike most other conferences, embraces a philosophy that gives every student-athlete an opportunity to compete in league championships. All of which Furman is proud to be part of as a member since 1936.

*Dr. Elizabeth Davis*
*President, Furman University*

# MERCER UNIVERSITY

*"I think the best part of being a student athlete in the SoCon is being able to compete against friends and fellow athletes you might've played against outside of college ball. The SoCon feels like a tight-knit community of athletes that love to compete against each other."*

## KAREVE RICHARDS
### MERCER MEN'S SOCCER

Mercer University is one of America's oldest and most distinctive institutions of higher learning, offering rigorous programs that span the undergraduate liberal arts to doctoral-level degrees. Founded by early-nineteenth-century Baptists, Mercer—while no longer formally denominationally affiliated—remains committed to an educational environment that embraces the historic Baptist principles of intellectual and religious freedom.

With more than 8,700 students enrolled in twelve schools and colleges on major campuses in Macon and Atlanta and medical school sites in Macon, Savannah, and Columbus, Mercer is classified as a Doctoral University with High Research Activity by the Carnegie Classification of Institutes of Higher Education and ranked among the top tier of national research universities by *U.S. News & World Report*. Mercer's nearly 80,000 alumni are making important contributions to their professions and communities throughout Georgia, the Southeast, and the world.

The Mercer Health Sciences Center includes the university's School of Medicine and Colleges of Nursing, Health Professions, and Pharmacy. Mercer is affiliated with five teaching hospitals. The university also has

**FAST FACTS**

Location
**Macon, GA**

Founded
**1833**

Joined SoCon
**2014**

Enrollment
**8,700**

Colors
**Orange & Black**

Athletic Nickname
**Bears**

*Above, a pedestrian bridge spans Mercer University Drive. (Chris Ian Smith, Mercer University); Center left, a student conducts research using an electron microscope. (John Carrington, Mercer University); Below left, Mercer president, William Underwood and student-athlete Kareve Richards; Below right, Mercer held a watch party for students to view the 2017 solar eclipse. (Chris Ian Smith, Mercer University)*

an educational partnership with the Warner Robins Air Logistics Complex. It operates an academic press and a performing arts center in Macon and an engineering research center in Warner Robins.

Mercer is one of only 286 institutions nationwide to shelter a chapter of the Phi Beta Kappa Society, the nation's most prestigious academic honor society, one of eight institutions to hold membership in the Georgia Research Alliance, and the only private university in Georgia to field an NCAA Division I athletic program. Mercer's uniqueness is found in the way the university integrates five defining components of its mission: liberal learning, professional knowledge, discovery, service to humankind, and community.

## FROM THE PRESIDENT'S OFFICE

**THE SOUTHERN CONFERENCE IS AMONG THE MOST PRESTIGIOUS** intercollegiate athletics associations, with a proud heritage of fostering competition among true student-athletes. The exceptional quality of Southern Conference institutions that share our commitment to high academic standards and competing with honor makes the Southern Conference an especially attractive home to Mercer University. Our student-athletes benefit from competing against other student-athletes who are first and foremost committed to academic achievement. **"**

*Mr. William D. Underwood*
*President, Mercer University*

# SAMFORD UNIVERSITY

*"Being an athlete in the Southern Conference definitely has its perks, but my favorite part is the support the student-athletes receive. Since most of the schools are relatively small in comparison to other major D-1 schools, the athletes in our conference can better know our peers around campus. This helps create a sense of community across the campuses."*

## SIERRA RAYZOR
### SAMFORD WOMEN'S SOCCER

Samford University is a premier nationally ranked Christian university located in Birmingham, Alabama. Founded in 1841, Samford is the eighty-seventh-oldest institution of higher learning in the United States. It enrolls more than 5,600 students from forty-four states and thirty countries.

The university's history is one of academic excellence and leadership. Samford is the top-ranked university in Alabama in rankings by *The Wall Street Journal* and national publications. Additionally, *The Wall Street Journal* ranks Samford twelfth in the country for student engagement. *Kiplinger's Personal Finance* ranks Samford fiftieth among private universities in the US for value and affordability.

Samford offers numerous undergraduate and graduate/professional degrees through ten academic schools: Arts, Arts and Sciences, Business, Divinity, Education, Health Professions, Law, Nursing, Pharmacy, and Public Health. The faculty-to-student ratio is 1:13. Central to its Christian mission, Samford provides students with numerous opportunities to integrate faith, learning, leadership, and service through experiential learning, service

## FAST FACTS

Location
**Birmingham, AL**

Founded
**1841**

Joined SoCon
**2008**

Enrollment
**5,600**

Colors
**Red & Dark Blue**

Athletic Nickname
**Bulldogs**

*Above, the Centennial Walk is a prime feature of the Samford campus. (Samford University); Center left, a student in the McWhorter School of Pharmacy. (Samford University); Below left, Samford president, Dr. Andrew Westmoreland and student-athlete Sierra Rayzor; Below right, an outdoor class takes place in front of the A. H. Reid Chapel. (Caroline Summers, Samford University)*

immersion, and volunteer opportunities. Each year, Samford students spend more than 927,000 hours serving and learning in communities at home and abroad.

Among Samford's 51,926 alumni are more than sixty members of the US Congress, eight state governors, two US Supreme Court justices, one secretary of state, four Rhodes Scholars, multiple Emmy and Grammy award-winning artists, two national championship football coaches, and recipients of the Pulitzer and Nobel Peace prizes.

The university fields seventeen varsity sports—eight men's and nine women's—that participate at the NCAA Division I level in the Southern Conference. Samford's athletics teams are ranked number one in Alabama for Graduation Success Rate (GSR) by the NCAA with an average score of 97 percent.

## FROM THE PRESIDENT'S OFFICE

**"FINDING THE RIGHT BALANCE** of academics and athletics is a priority for Samford University that is shared with the Southern Conference member institutions. Samford's long history is one of academic excellence and leadership. As a private, Christian institution, we also have a very public purpose directly tied to the economic and social development of our region and beyond. We are delighted with the athletic competition and the academic collaboration we enjoy within the Southern Conference. **"**

*Dr. Andrew Westmoreland*
*President, Samford University*

# UNC GREENSBORO

*"It has been an honor to play in the SoCon. We play against some incredible league competition and get to travel to awesome cities. The league produces live streams as well, which has been awesome for friends and families back home. It provides fantastic opportunities, and pushes us, as we are often overlooked by the bigger Power 5 schools."*

## AIYANAH TYLER-COOPER
### UNCG WOMEN'S SOCCER

UNC Greensboro was founded as a college for women in 1891. In 1932, it became one of the "original three" institutions to form the UNC System. Men were enrolled beginning in 1964. Today, UNCG is a growing research university with more than 20,000 students representing ninety nationalities and about 3,000 faculty and staff. UNCG offers 125-plus undergraduate areas of study and 100-plus master's and doctoral programs. It fields seventeen Division I athletic teams. UNCG offers nationally recognized, highly ranked programs in a wide range of disciplines, from nursing and education to business and the performing arts.

UNC Greensboro takes pride in the vast array of students who find their way here. It is among the most diverse universities in North Carolina. UNCG's student body includes nearly 40 percent first-generation students. About half of its students are people of color and nearly a third of faculty hired since 2016 are racial minorities. UNCG is in the top three in the UNC System for Hispanic/Latino enrollment. It has been honored multiple times as a military-friendly institution.

**FAST FACTS**

Location
**Greensboro, NC**

Founded
**1897**

Joined SoCon
**1997**

Enrollment
**20,000**

Colors
**Navy Blue, Gold & White**

Athletic Nickname
**Spartans**

*Abover, overhead view of the UNCG campus, looking down College Avenue. (UNC Greensboro); Center left, Students comparing notes in organic chemistry. (UNC Greensboro); Below left, UNCG chancellor, Dr. Franklin Gilliam Jr. and student-athlete Aiyanah Tyler-Cooper; Below right, new UNCG students participate in SOAR— Spartan Orientation, Advising & Registration. (UNC Greensboro)*

Nationally recognized for combining academic excellence and value, UNCG is one of only fifty doctoral institutions distinguished by the Carnegie Foundation for both higher research activity and community engagement. Annually, the university generates a $1 billion economic impact on the region and more than a million hours of community service.

UNCG is not just a top institution in the UNC System, but a true national model for how a university can blend opportunity, excellence, and impact to transform the lives of its students and make a major positive impact on the prosperity of its community and its state.

## FROM THE CHANCELLOR'S OFFICE

**THE SOUTHERN CONFERENCE REPRESENTS TWO VALUES** that are also at the core of who we are at UNCG—Opportunity and Excellence. Our student-athletes get the opportunity to compete for championships on a regional and national stage. They get to develop their work ethic, sharpen their skills, and reach their potential by going up against strong competition every time they take the field or hit the court. Our student-athletes realize that competing in the Southern Conference not only helps them become better athletes, but it helps them raise their game academically, socially, and culturally so they are better prepared to face the world and succeed when they graduate. **"**

*Dr. Franklin D. Gilliam Jr.*
*Chancellor, University of North Carolina at Greensboro*

# UNIVERSITY OF TENNESSEE AT CHATTANOOGA

*"Every year the competition gets better and better and it makes teams work harder to succeed. I have never entered a Southern Conference game and thought that we weren't going to have to compete and play hard until the last out is made. I am very fortunate to be able to play against the best of the best."*

## ALLISON SWINFORD
### CHATTANOOGA SOFTBALL

As a national model for metropolitan universities, the University of Tennessee at Chattanooga offers a rich, experiential learning environment that incorporates the city as its laboratory. Students have countless opportunities to apply classroom knowledge to real-world problems of regional entities in partnering to find solutions.

Founded as private Chattanooga University in 1886, UTC affiliated with the UT system in 1969 and today is the second-largest university in that statewide system. Over its 133-year history, UTC has developed a reputation for excellence—built on an unusual blend of the private and public traditions of American higher education—and continually raising the achievement bar.

UTC offers 109 undergraduate, sixty-one master's, nine doctoral programs with twenty-four graduate-certificate programs, and three specialist-degree programs. The student body of more than 11,000 undergraduate and graduate students are enrolled in five academic colleges:

*Above, a drone offers an aerial view of the center of the UTC campus. (University of Tennessee at Chattanooga); Center left, the UTC Library opened in January of 2015. (University of Tennessee at Chattanooga); Below left, UTC chancellor, Dr. Steven Angle and student-athlete Allison Swinford; Below right, Chattanooga's spirit squads are among the most enthusiastic in the Southern Conference. (D. Rutemeyer, University of Tennessee at Chattanooga)*

Arts and Sciences; Business; Engineering and Computer Science; Health, Education, and Professional Studies; and the Honors College.

Just blocks from downtown, UTC puts students in the heart of Chattanooga, a boomtown between the banks of the Tennessee River and the base of the mountains. Chattanooga is a city with an uninhibited, energetic, forward-looking attitude, populated by a diverse mix of those who love good food, live music, and seek to exceed expectations and shatter stereotypes.

UTC is committed to embracing diversity, inspiring positive change, and enriching the community. The university's goal is to make a difference in Chattanooga and the region surrounding it as well as in the lives of its students.

## FROM THE CHANCELLOR'S OFFICE

**“ THE SOUTHERN CONFERENCE PROVIDES A WONDERFUL** experience for our student-athletes and the entire university community. The level of competition, both in the sport and in the classroom, is extremely high. The mix of public, private, and military institutions affords each university added depth to the student-athlete experience. The academic partnerships of the conference provide additional depth and meaning to members of this incredible conference. **”**

*Dr. Steven R. Angle*
*Chancellor, The University of Tennessee at Chattanooga*

### FAST FACTS

Location
**Chattanooga, TN**

Founded
**1886**

Joined SoCon
**1976**

Enrollment
**11,600**

Colors
**Navy Blue, Old Gold & Silver**

Athletic Nickname
**Mocs**

# VIRGINIA MILITARY INSTITUTE

*"If I had to choose one word to use to describe my experience as a student-athlete in the Southern Conference it is 'grateful.' I am treated with the utmost respect by the people that work in this conference, and they all want the best for all student-athletes. The Southern Conference takes pride in what they do for athletics and allows us the best opportunity to achieve the goals we set for ourselves."*

## CLIFTON CONWAY
### VMI WRESTLING

Founded in 1839, Virginia Military Institute is the nation's oldest state-supported military college. VMI offers a rigorous education that includes a broad undergraduate program with fourteen majors spread among engineering, the sciences, liberal arts, and social sciences. Leadership and character development are woven into the curriculum with the goal of producing citizen-soldiers capable of meeting national and international challenges. The Institute is consistently ranked among the nation's top five public colleges by *U.S. News & World Report.*

Just over half of each year's graduating class accepts a commission into the armed services. All cadets, whether they plan to commission or not, are required to participate in four years of ROTC training. The Institute offers Army, Naval, and Air Force ROTC, and offers a pathway for commissioning into the Coast Guard.

VMI's cadet-run regimental system offers a wealth of leadership opportunities. Freshmen, known as "rats," are led by a cadre of upper-class cadets whose goal is to inculcate discipline

*Above, a drone view of the VMI post in Lexington, VA. (John Robertson IV); Center left, cadets march in the annual New Market Ceremony, honoring those VMI cadets killed in the Civil War battle of New Market in May of 1864. (John Robertson IV, Virginia Military Institute); Below left, VMI superintendent, Gen. J. H. Binford Peay III and cadet Clifton Conway; Below right, the Corps Physical Training Facility at VMI features a hydraulic track for championship meets. (John Robertson IV, Virginia Military Institute)*

and duty. With each passing year, cadets have the chance to take on leadership roles of increasing responsibility. VMI's single-sanction honor system is girded by the Institute's Honor Code—"A cadet will not lie, cheat, steal, or tolerate those who do"—and administered entirely by cadets elected by their peers to the Honor Court.

Athletics have long been a part of the Institute's tradition, and VMI has been a member of the Southern Conference for almost the entirety of the conference's existence. All of VMI's NCAA athletic teams compete in the Southern Conference with the exception of water polo and swimming and diving.

VMI's 1,700 cadets all live in the barracks, a National Historic Landmark designed by renowned nineteenth-century architect Alexander Jackson Davis. Women make up approximately 10 percent of the Corps of Cadets, and 61 percent of all cadets are from Virginia.

## FROM THE SUPERINTENDENT'S OFFICE

**❝ VMI WAS ONE OF THE EARLY** founding members of the Southern Conference, dating back to 1923. The Institute departed in 2003 and joined the Big South Conference for a decade before returning to its Southern Conference roots in 2014. That 'brief' move highlighted for us the convergence of institutional values with a shared vision of student-athletes and academics that we find appealing among the member colleges. VMI believes that athletics and leadership are intertwined and enjoys competing in seventeen sports in a Conference with such a rich history and an admired national reputation. ❞

*General J. H. Binford Peay III*
*Superintendent, Virginia Military Institute*

# WESTERN CAROLINA UNIVERSITY

*"Over the last few years especially, SoCon women's tennis is becoming less predictable and more competitive. I think what will continue to set us apart is the way that we encourage each other on the court, fight for every single point, and maintain a drive to do better."*

## JORDYN KING
### WESTERN CAROLINA WOMEN'S TENNIS

As the westernmost institution in the University of North Carolina system, Western Carolina University provides comprehensive educational opportunities to residents in the state's western region and attracts students from around the globe to explore the region's vast natural diversity.

Founded in 1889 as a teaching college, Western Carolina now provides a quality education to more than 10,000 students with 120-plus undergraduate and more than forty graduate programs. There is a student/faculty ratio of 17 to 1. The university focuses its undergraduate, master's and doctoral programs, educational outreach, research, and creative and cultural activities to sustain and improve individual lives and enhance economic and community development in western North Carolina and beyond.

The Carnegie Foundation for the Advancement of Teaching recognized Western Carolina's emphasis on community engagement and its link to

## FAST FACTS

Location
**Cullowhee, NC**

Founded
**1889**

Joined SoCon
**1976**

Enrollment
**11,600**

Colors
**Purple & Gold**

Athletic Nickname
**Catamounts**

*Above, an aerial view of the WCU campus in the hills of western North Carolina. (Western Carolina University); Center left, a student on-campus festival takes place underneath the clock on Alumni Tower. (Western Carolina University); Below left, WCU chancellor, Dr. Kelli Brown and student-athlete Jordyn King; Below right, the university campus following a fresh snowfall. (Western Carolina University)*

engaged teaching, research, and service by selecting the university to receive its 2015 Community Engagement Classification.

Western Carolina's unique mountain location helps fuel a vibrant campus community with more than 170 student clubs and organizations, a busy performing arts center, and the campus's own adventure guide service.

In addition, Western Carolina is home to sixteen Southern Conference athletic teams featuring more than 375 student-athlete competitors. Since 2008, WCU programs have captured conference championships in men's and women's track and field (both indoor and outdoor), women's basketball, baseball, and women's soccer.

## FROM THE CHANCELLOR'S OFFICE

**I BELIEVE THAT A STRONG INTERCOLLEGIATE** athletics program is a vital component in the fabric of campus life. In addition to providing a communal rallying point for students, faculty, staff and alumni, a successful athletics program serves as the institution's front porch for many members of the external community. Perhaps the most important aspect is what an athletics program means for those most closely associated with it—the student-athletes. They will gain essential life skills in the areas of hard work, time management, self-discipline, and teamwork, which will help them succeed in life long after their playing days have concluded.

*Dr. Kelli R. Brown*
*Chancellor, Western Carolina University*

# WOFFORD COLLEGE

*"In the SoCon, there is no compromise between the athletic side and the student side. The SoCon works to push their student-athletes in the classroom just as much as they push on the court or on the field. It's great because it helps the student-athletes realize there is no athletics without academics."*

## STORM MURPHY
### WOFFORD MEN'S BASKETBALL

Wofford College, established in 1854, is a four-year, independent, residential liberal arts college located in Spartanburg, South Carolina. It offers a distinctive program with twenty-six major fields of study to a student body of 1,650 undergraduates.

Nationally known for its strong academic program, outstanding faculty, study-abroad participation, and successful graduates, Wofford ranks well in published ratings from *U.S. News & World Report, Princeton Review, The Fiske Guide to College,* and *Kiplinger's Personal Finance.* The college also is recognized consistently as a "best value college" and is among the *New York Times's* "Top Colleges Doing the Most for the American Dream," a ranking based on accessibility for low- and middle-income students.

A leader in offering high-impact learning opportunities to students, Wofford encourages students to take advantage of all that Wofford, and through it the world, has to offer. These opportunities include internships with scientific, corporate, and nonprofit organizations across the globe; undergraduate research opportunities; service-learning in the local commu-

Above, Wofford's administration building is commonly referred to as "Old Main." (Mark S. Olencki, Wofford College); Center left Wofford students support their Terriers in a game vs. North Carolina. (Mark S. Olencki, Wofford College); Below left, Wofford president, Dr. Nayef Samhat and student-athlete Storm Murphy; Below right, patrons enjoy the newly constructed Rosalind Sallenger Richardson Center for the Arts on the Wofford campus. (Mark S. Olencki, Wofford College)

nity; international study-abroad programming; and a thriving host of cocurricular opportunities on campus.

Student and residence life on campus include exciting Division I NCAA athletics, opportunities to participate in one of the college's Greek-letter fraternities or sororities, competitive intramurals, a diverse selection of clubs, student publications, and a housing plan that helps students progress from first year through fourth in a close-knit community that builds independence.

The college recently completed three major construction projects on campus. The Rosalind Sallenger Richardson Center for the Arts, the Jerry Richardson Indoor Stadium, and the Stewart H. Johnson Greek Village all bring new, exciting, and diverse opportunities for academic and social enrichment.

## FROM THE PRESIDENT'S OFFICE

**"I THINK OUR STUDENTS DERIVE BENEFITS** from the regional intimacy of the conference membership and the commitment—and this is so very important it cannot be emphasized enough—to allow access to conference championships for all. Beyond the athletic realm, the focus on shared academic experiences broadens the conference's relevance and appeal beyond student-athletes. In my mind, this makes the Southern Conference a model for Division I athletics *and* academics. **"**

*Dr. Nayef H. Samhat*
*President, Wofford College*

A PROUD ATHLETIC HISTORY

# HALL
# OF FAME

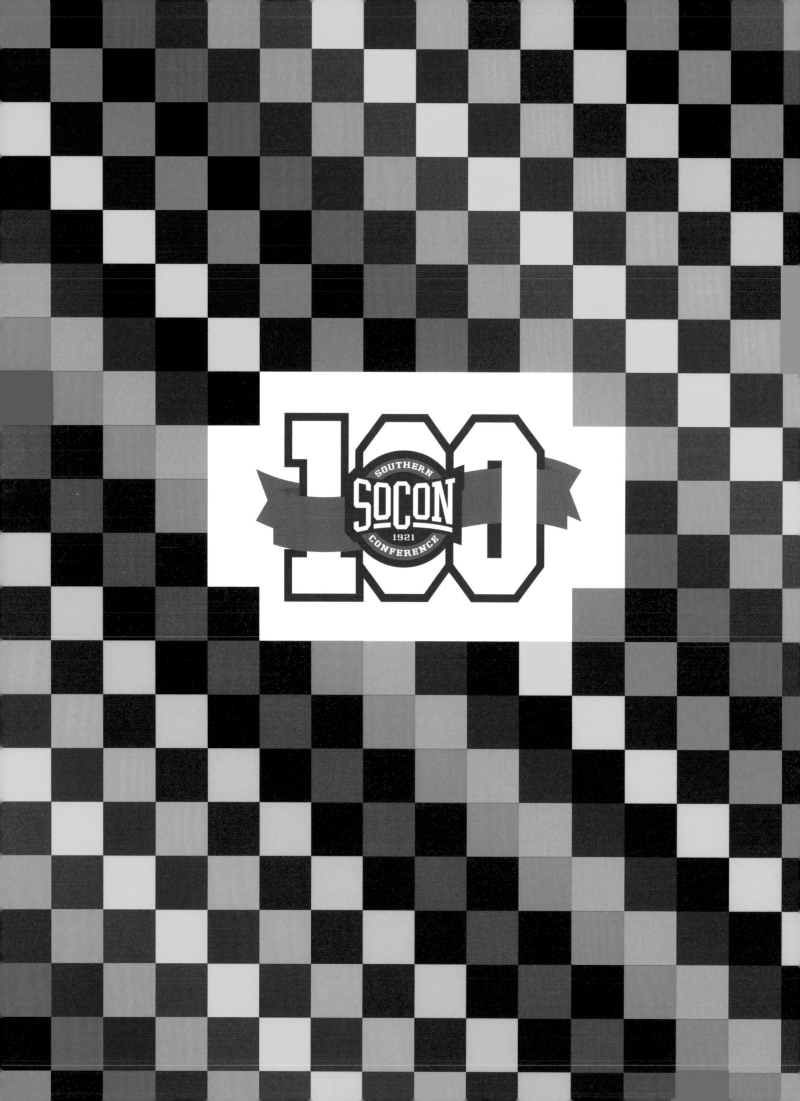

# THE SOUTHERN CONFERENCE HALL OF FAME

Within six months of being named commissioner, John Iamarino told his council of presidents that he wanted their approval to go forward with the creation of a Southern Conference Hall of Fame. He made it clear that he did not want to create any committees or get entangled in bureaucratic red tape.

"I wanted them to trust us to handle this the right way," he remembered. "To their credit, they gave us the autonomy and resources to do what we thought was necessary."

Personnel from each of the twelve members, combined with media representatives and some administrators from former members, comprised a twenty-person voting panel in the fall of 2008. A ballot of forty names was culled from more than 200 nominations from all former and current conference members. Voting guidelines ensured that there would be diversity among former and current members as well as male and female candidates.

It was decided to conduct the first induction ceremony at the Chapman Cultural Center in the league's headquarters city of Spartanburg, South Carolina. The date selected was May 4, 2009.

Laura Hayes, assistant to the commissioner, organized the logistics, which included air and ground transportation and lodging for the ten inductees, a pre-event dinner, gift bags, an open-bar pre-ceremony reception for attending guests, and a post-induction reception for the inductees and their families. Introductions of the inductees were made via videos produced by Mandi Copeland, director of multimedia services.

The charter class of the Hall of Fame truly spoke to the history of the Southern Conference. Inductees included Jerry West, Arnold Palmer, Sam Huff, Dick Groat, Charlie Justice, Frank Selvy, Adrian Peterson, Valorie Whiteside, Megan Dunigan, and Melissa Morrison-Howard.

Iamarino welcomed the guests to "a night 88 years in the making." West acknowledged the presence in the audience of West Virginia athletic director Ed Pastilong, football coach Bill Stewart, and basketball coach Bob Huggins. "That's what happens when you donate money to your alma mater," he joked. "They have to come to things like this."

Huff, a fellow Mountaineer, recalled earning extra money parking cars outside the basketball arena on game nights. Selvy pulled some notes out of his jacket and read off scores of famous Furman basketball victories he played a part in. Palmer, the only living inductee unable to attend, was in Wales opening a new golf course he had designed. He sent along a video reminiscing about his days at Wake Forest. The evening was a huge success for the SoCon.

The conference subsequently decided to conduct inductions in alternating years. By 2018, forty-four former student-athletes, coaches, administrators, and officials were part of the Hall. Their plaques, which Iamarino designed to replicate those enshrined at the Baseball Hall of Fame in Cooperstown, New York, are displayed on a wall inside the league office.

## MEGAN DUNIGAN

### Furman University
### 1999–2002, Tennis

- Four-time SoCon Player of Year.
- Freshman of Year, 1999.
- MVP of SoCon Tournament, 2000 and 2001.
- Earned Female Athlete of Year Award, 2002.
- Finished career at Furman with overall 79-19 singles record.

*(Furman University Athletics)*

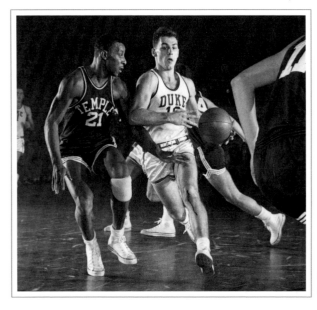

## DICK GROAT

### Duke University
### 1949–52, Basketball/Baseball

- SoCon basketball Player of Year and first-team All-America, 1951 and 1952.
- Helms Foundation national Player of Year, 1951.
- Led NCAA in scoring and assists, 1952.
- Elected to College Basketball Hall of Fame, 2007.
- Voted 1960 National League MVP as starting shortstop for Pittsburgh Pirates.

*Dick Groat, shown here against Temple, was a basketball and baseball star at Duke. (Duke University Athletics)*

(Appalachian State University Athletics)

## MELISSA MORRISON-HOWARD

*Appalachian State University*
*1989–93, Track and Field*

- Captured seventeen individual SoCon championships in six different events during four-year career.
- All-America in 55-meter and 100-meter hurdles, 1993.
- Voted Most Valuable Performer at both indoor and outdoor conference meets, 1992 and 1993.
- Earned bronze medals in 100-meter hurdles, 2000 and 2004 Olympic Games.
- Four-time US indoor 60-meter hurdles champion.

Two of the greatest athletes in West Virginia University history, Sam Huff (left) and Jerry West, display their SoCon Hall of Fame plaques. (Todd Drexler, SoCon Photos)

## SAM HUFF

*West Virginia University*
*1952–55, Football*

- First-team All-America lineman, 1955.
- Played both offense and defense, leading Mountaineers to 31-7 record over four years.
- Drafted by New York Giants in third round of 1956 NFL draft.
- Elected to College Football Hall of Fame, 1980.
- Elected to Pro Football Hall of Fame, 1982.

## CHARLIE (CHOO CHOO) JUSTICE

*University of North Carolina*
*1946–49, Football*

- Four-time All-SoCon back following four years of service in the navy during World War II.
- Conference Player of Year, 1948 and 1949.
- Heisman Trophy runner-up, 1948 and 1949.
- Ran or threw for sixty-four career touchdowns, compiling 4,883 total yards.
- Elected to College Football Hall of Fame, 1961.

Charlie Justice. (University of North Carolina Athletics)

## ARNOLD PALMER
### *Wake Forest University*
### *1948–50, 1954, Golf*
- NCAA Tournament medalist, 1949 and 1950.
- Captured SoCon individual championship, 1948 and '49.
- Led Wake Forest to SoCon team title, 1950.
- Captured sixty-two PGA events and seven major tournaments, including four Masters.
- PGA Player of Year, 1960 and 1962.

*Arnold Palmer led Wake Forest to the 1950 Southern Conference golf championship. (Wake Forest University Athletics)*

## ADRIAN PETERSON
### *Georgia Southern University*
### *1998–2001, Football*
- Walter Payton Award winner in 1999 as top Division I-AA offensive player in nation.
- Graduated as NCAA Division I all-time leading rusher with 6,559 yards.
- Four-time All-America selection.
- Voted SoCon Player of Year, 1998 and 2001.
- Drafted in sixth round by Chicago Bears, played in Super Bowl XLI.

*Adrian Peterson (No. 3) carries the ball for Georgia Southern against Montana. (Georgia Southern University Athletics)*

## FRANK SELVY
### *Furman University*
### *1951–54, Basketball*
- Led NCAA in scoring as a junior (29.5) and senior (41.7).
- First player in NCAA history to score 1,000 points in a season and average more than forty points per game.
- Scored NCAA all-time record 100 points in a single game, February 13, 1954.
- Voted UPI national Player of Year, 1954.
- Three-time All-America, twice voted SoCon Player of Year.

*Frank Selvy, the "Corbin Comet." (Furman University Athletics)*

## JERRY WEST

*West Virginia University*
*1957–60, Basketball*

• SoCon Player of Year, 1959 and 1960.
• Three-time MVP of SoCon Tournament.
• Scored 2,309 points at West Virginia, averaging 24.8 per game.
• Started for gold medal-winning USA team in 1960 Olympics.
• Named NBA All-Star in all fourteen seasons with Los Angeles Lakers.

*The NBA logo is a silhouette of Jerry West, pictured here as a West Virginia Mountaineer. (West Virginia University Athletics)*

## VALORIE WHITESIDE

*Appalachian State University*
*1984–88, Basketball*

• All-time leading scorer (men's or women's basketball) in SoCon history.
• Finished career with 2,944 points and 1,369 rebounds.
• MVP of SoCon Tournament, 1987 and 1988.
• Led conference in scoring three times.
• Led Appalachian State to consecutive SoCon championships, 1987 and 1988.

*(Appalachian State University Athletics)*

## EVERETT CASE

*North Carolina State University*
*1946–64, Basketball*

• Pioneering basketball coach who led Wolfpack to six consecutive Southern Conference championships from 1947–52.
• Guided NC State teams to 87-11 league record in seven years in SoCon.
• Finished with four more championships in ACC and was three-time ACC Coach of Year.
• Innovator widely credited with inaugurating tradition of cutting down the nets to celebrate a championship.

*Everett Case, named to the Basketball Hall of Fame in 1982, coached North Carolina State to six straight Southern Conference titles. (North Carolina State University Athletics)*

CLASS OF 2010

## MARY JAYNE HARRELSON

*Appalachian State University*
*1996–2001, Track and Field, Cross Country*
• Two-time Female Athlete of Year in SoCon (1999, 2001).
• Voted NCAA Woman of Year from North Carolina, 2001.
• Captured twenty-three SoCon championships in cross country, indoor and outdoor track.
• Two-time winner of 1,500 meters at NCAA outdoor track championships.
• Won silver medal in same event at 2003 PanAm Games.

*Appalachian State's Mary Jayne Harrelson established herself as one of the greatest distance runners in conference history. (Appalachian State University Athletics)*

## FRED HETZEL

*Davidson College*
*1962–65, Basketball*
• Three-time SoCon Player of Year (1963, '64,'65) and three-time consensus All-America.
• Twice named Most Outstanding Player of conference tournament.
• Finished career with 2,032 points and 1,094 rebounds.
• Led Wildcats to 29-5 conference record and two SoCon titles.
• First overall pick of 1965 NBA draft by San Francisco Warriors, played six seasons in league.

*(Davidson College Athletics)*

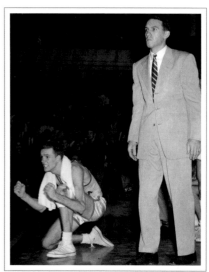

## ROD HUNDLEY

*West Virginia University*
*1954–57, Basketball*
• Conference Player of Year, 1956–57.
• Two-time All-America selection and three-time All-Conference choice.
• SoCon's leading scorer in 1956–57 (23.1), finished career with 2,180 points.
• Led Mountaineers to three straight league championships.
• No. 1 overall pick of 1957 NBA draft by Minneapolis Lakers.

*Rod Hundley, here with head coach Fred Schaus, was an emotional and talented basketball performer at West Virginia. (West Virginia University Athletics)*

## BANKS McFADDEN

*Clemson University*
*1936–40, Football, Basketball, Track and Field*

- Only Clemson athlete to have jersey retired in both football and basketball.
- Voted greatest athlete in Clemson history in 1999 media poll.
- Led Tigers to 1939 SoCon Basketball Tournament Championship.
- Named to basketball and football All-America teams, and also starred for Tigers' track team.
- Inducted into College Football Hall of Fame, 1959.

*Clemson retired jerseys in football and basketball to honor the career of Banks McFadden. (Clemson University Athletics)*

## J. DALLAS SHIRLEY

*Southern Conference*
*1967–88, Basketball Administration*

- One of preeminent authorities on basketball officiating for more than four decades.
- Began officiating in SoCon in 1930s.
- Had a lengthy career in the ACC and officiated in the 1960 Olympic games in Rome.
- Served conference for more than forty years as assistant to the commissioner and coordinator of all game officials.
- Elected to Basketball Hall of Fame, 1980.

*J. Dallas Shirley worked for the Southern Conference in a variety of capacities for more than forty years. (Southern Conference)*

## WALLACE WADE

*University of Alabama, 1923–30*
*Duke University, 1931–50, Football*

- Won three national championships (1925, 1926, 1930) and two Rose Bowls as head coach at Alabama.
- Led Crimson Tide to four SoCon titles.
- Began coaching career at Duke in 1931 and earned six conference titles.
- Finished career with 171-49-10 overall record and SoCon mark of 113-28-5 (.801 winning percentage).
- Inducted into College Football Hall of Fame, 1955.

*Wallace Wade made five appearances in the Rose Bowl coaching then-SoCon members Alabama and Duke. (Duke University Athletics)*

## DEXTER COAKLEY

*Appalachian State University*
*1993–96, Football*

- Two-time Buck Buchanan Award recipient as Division I-AA national defensive player of year (1995, '96).
- Three-time SoCon Defensive Player of Year.
- SoCon Freshman of Year, 1993.
- Played 155 games in ten-year NFL career for Dallas Cowboys and St. Louis Rams.
- Selected to three Pro Bowls (1999, 2001, 2003).

*(Appalachian State University Athletics)*

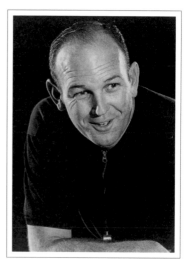

## CHARLES (LEFTY) DRIESELL

*Davidson College*
*1960–69, Basketball*

- Coached Wildcats to five first-place finishes and three SoCon tournament championships.
- Reached NCAA Elite Eight in 1968 and '69.
- Four-time SoCon Coach of Year.
- During his tenure, Davidson won 73 percent of league games.
- Elected to Basketball Hall of Fame, 2018.

*Under Lefty Driesell, the Davidson basketball program became nationally known in the 1960s. (Davidson College Athletics)*

## REGINA KIRK

*University of Tennessee at Chattanooga*
*1984–88, Basketball*

- Four-time All-Conference selection.
- SoCon Player of Year, 1987–88.
- Led Chattanooga to conference championships in 1985, '86.
- MVP of 1986 SoCon Tournament.
- Finished career with 2,376 points and 1,086 rebounds, both UTC records.

*(University of Tennessee at Chattanooga Athletics)*

## ROBERT NEYLAND

### University of Tennessee
### 1926–32, Football

- Directed Vols to 61-2-5 overall record in seven years in SoCon.
- Served three stints as head coach at UT in between military service.
- 1939 Vols were last team to complete regular season unbeaten and unscored upon.
- Elected to College Football Hall of Fame, 1956.
- Neyland Stadium on UT campus dedicated in his honor, 1962.

*A brigadier general in the US Army, Robert Neyland coached the Tennessee Volunteers' football program for twenty-one years. (University of Tennessee Athletics)*

*(University of North Carolina Athletics)*

## VIC SEIXAS

### University of North Carolina
### 1947–49, Tennis

- Captured SoCon championships in singles (1948) and doubles (1949).
- Earned All-America honors in 1948, reaching NCAA singles championship final.
- Won sixty-three of sixty-six singles matches for Tar Heels.
- Earned two Grand Slam singles events, winning 1953 Wimbledon and '54 US Open.
- Elected to International Tennis Hall of Fame, 1971.

## SHANNON WOMMACK

### University of Tennessee at Chattanooga
### 2001–06, Track and Field, Cross Country

- Captured twenty SoCon championships in track and field and cross country.
- Twice voted national Academic All-America.
- Named SoCon Female Athlete of Year, 2006.
- Earned five All-America honors in track and cross country.
- Set conference indoor and outdoor records in mile run.

*(University of Tennessee at Chattanooga Athletics)*     *Hall of Fame*    

### ANGIE BARKER

*East Tennessee State University*
*1987–89, Track and Field*

- Three-time SoCon shot put champion, twice indoors (1988, '89), once outdoors (1989).
- Captured NCAA indoor shot put title, 1988.
- Named indoor track All-America in consecutive years, 1988 and '89.
- Remains conference record-holder in indoor shot put with mark of 54'6".
- Inducted into ETSU Hall of Fame, 1998.

*(East Tennessee State University Athletics)*

### PERCY BEARD

*Auburn University*
*1926–29, Track and Field*

- Two-time champion hurdler in SoCon and earned All-America honors at Auburn in 1928.
- Set world record (14.2 seconds) in 120-yard high hurdles in 1931 and tied mark three years later.
- Earned silver medal in 110-meter high hurdles at 1932 Olympics in Los Angeles.
- Seven-time national AAU high hurdles champion.
- Named to US Track and Field Hall of Fame, 1981.

*Auburn's Percy Beard was among the first Olympic medal winners from the Southern Conference. (Auburn University Athletics)*

*Jim Burch is honored during the 2011 men's basketball championship game, with conference staffers Sue Arakas and Geoff Cabe making the presentations. (Todd Drexler, SoCon Photos)*

### JIM BURCH

*Southern Conference*
*1967–2011, Basketball Administration*

- Served forty-four years as both basketball official and coordinator of conference officials.
- Spent twenty-three years in latter capacity, training hundreds of young collegiate officials, many of whom would ultimately work postseason NCAA events.
- Joined SoCon in 1967 as first African-American basketball official in conference history.
- Worked fifteen SoCon tournaments and four NCAA regionals.
- Elected to Fayetteville (NC) State University Hall of Fame, 1990.

*(University of Maryland Athletics)*

## DICK MODZELEWSKI

*University of Maryland*
*1950–52, Football*

- Two-time All-America selection at Maryland.
- Earned 1952 Outland Trophy as nation's outstanding lineman.
- Helped SoCon-champion Terrapins to unbeaten season in 1951, climaxed by Sugar Bowl victory over Tennessee.
- Drafted by Washington Redskins in 1953 and played fourteen years as a defensive tackle, winning championships in 1956 (New York Giants) and 1964 (Cleveland Browns).
- Elected to College Football Hall of Fame, 1993.

*(Furman University Athletics)*

## PAUL SCARPA

*Furman University*
*1967–2011, Tennis*

- Retired as winningest tennis coach in NCAA Division I history with 853 dual-match victories.
- Spent forty-five seasons at Furman, earning 817 wins and guiding Paladins to seventeen SoCon championships.
- Voted Coach of Year SoCon-record nine times.
- Crafted the "Scarpa System" of dual-match scoring (doubles matches using eight-game pro set, followed by singles), which was adopted by NCAA in 1993.
- Elected to Furman Hall of Fame, 1994.

## RUSHIA BROWN

*Furman University*
*1989–94, Basketball*

- First-team All-Southern Conference selection in all four years.
- Ranks among SoCon's top ten in career points (2,169), rebounds (1,023), field goals (908), and steals (338).
- Selected Player of Year, 1991–92.
- Led Paladins to three conference championships.
- Competed professionally in Europe and for seven seasons with Cleveland and Charlotte of WNBA.

*Rushia Brown, taking a short jump shot vs. ETSU, was the 1991–92 SoCon Player of the Year. (Furman University Athletics)*

*Hall of Fame*

(Duke University Athletics)

## EDDIE CAMERON

*Duke University*
*1929–45, Basketball, Football*

- Highly successful coach for more than forty years.
- Named head basketball coach in 1929; led Blue Devils to two SoCon championships and three tournament crowns.
- Compiled overall mark of 226-99 (.695) in fourteen seasons.
- Guided Duke to 25-11-1 record in four wartime football seasons, capped by 29–26 Sugar Bowl victory over Alabama (1945).
- Later spent twenty-one years as Duke's AD and played key role in formation of ACC in 1953.

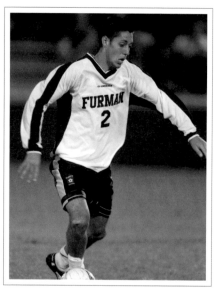
(Furman University Athletics)

## CLINT DEMPSEY

*Furman University*
*2001–03, Soccer*

- Three-time All-Southern Conference midfielder.
- Voted Freshman of Year, 2001.
- Finished career with fifty-three points in sixty-two games and led Paladins to two league championships.
- Entered ranks of professional and international soccer in 2004, becoming captain of US national team.
- Scored fifty-seven goals playing for the American national team, tied with Landon Donovan for the most in US history.

(Appalachian State University Athletics)

## JERRY MOORE

*Appalachian State University*
*1989–2012, Football*

- Winningest coach in SoCon football history.
- Led ASU to 215-87 mark over twenty-four seasons, earning ten conference titles, including six straight (2005–10).
- Eight-time league Coach of Year.
- Led Mountaineers to three consecutive Division I national championships (2005, '06, '07).
- Guided ASU to 34–32 victory at Michigan in 2007, considered among greatest upsets in college football history.

(Wake Forest University Athletics)

## CHARLIE TEAGUE

*Wake Forest University*
*1947–50, Baseball*

- Selected ABCA first-team All-America three times (1947, '49, '50).
- A second baseman, he finished with a lifetime batting average of .335.
- Led Demon Deacons to 31-4 record in 1949 and championship game of College World Series, hitting .353 for season.
- First Wake Forest player inducted into College Baseball Hall of Fame (2010).
- Named to SoCon's 75th Anniversary baseball team in 1995.

Steph Curry, flanked by Jason Richards (left) and head coach Bob McKillop, was nicknamed the "Baby-Faced Assassin" after his success at Davidson. (Tim Cowie, Tim Cowie Photography)

## STEPHEN CURRY

*Davidson College*
*2006–09, Basketball*

- All-time leading scorer in Southern Conference men's basketball history with 2,635 points.
- Two-time Player of Year and twice selected Most Outstanding Player of conference tournament.
- Led Davidson to Elite Eight in 2008 NCAA Tournament, averaging thirty-two points in four games.
- Set then-league record for most career three-point field goals with 414.
- Drafted in first round by Golden State Warriors, was named MVP in leading Warriors to 2014–15 NBA title. Unanimously voted MVP again in succeeding season.

## ARMANTI EDWARDS

*Appalachian State University*
*2006–09, Football*

- Led Mountaineers to two national championships (2006, 2007) and overall 11-2 record in FCS playoffs.
- Two-time Walter Payton Award winner as top offensive performer in FCS.
- Became first Division I quarterback to exceed 10,000 yards passing and 4,000 yards rushing.
- SoCon Male Athlete of the Year, 2010.
- Later played professionally in the NFL and CFL.

Armanti Edwards, pictured on a media guide cover. (Appalachian State University Athletics)

Brad Faxon was voted the premier collegiate golfer in 1983 while competing for Furman. (Furman University Athletics)

## BRAD FAXON

*Furman University*
*1979–83, Golf*

- Two-time All-America selection, he earned the Haskins Award as the leading collegiate golfer in US in 1983.
- Medalist at '83 Southern Conference Championship, winning by eleven strokes.
- Three-time All-Conference selection at Furman.
- Joined PGA Tour and won eight events, earning reputation as one of the best putters on the tour.
- Led the PGA in lowest putting average three times, establishing single-season record in 2000.

(East Tennessee State University Athletics)

## KEITH (MISTER) JENNINGS

*East Tennessee State University*
*1987–91, Basketball*

- Winner of 1991 Frances Pomeroy Naismith Award as nation's best player under six feet tall.
- Named first team All-Conference twice and was two-time Most Outstanding Player of Southern Conference Tournament (1990, '91).
- All-time conference leader with 983 assists.
- Led NCAA in three-point FG percentage (.592) as a senior.
- Guided Bucs to three consecutive NCAA tournaments.

## KAREN PELPHREY

*Marshall University*
*1982–86, Basketball*

- Finished varsity career with 2,746 points and 891 rebounds.
- Scored 2,163 points in three years of SoCon play.
- Shares league record for most points in a single game, 48.
- Three-time All-Conference selection and voted Player of Year as a senior (1985–86).
- Led Thundering Herd to pair of regular-season conference championships.

(Marshall University Athletics)

*Wofford's Mike Ayers ranks third all-time among head football coaches in Southern Conference victories. (Wofford College Athletics)*

### MIKE AYERS

*East Tennessee State University, 1985–87*
*Wofford College, 1988–2017, Football*
- Won 218 games over course of thirty-three seasons at ETSU and Wofford.
- Coached Terriers to Division II playoffs twice before guiding program into SoCon in 1997.
- Led Wofford to five league championships, including undefeated season in 2003.
- Competed in FCS playoffs eight times, reaching semifinals in 2003.
- Won at least nine or more games on ten different occasions.

### RON CARTER

*Virginia Military Institute*
*1974–78, Basketball*
- Finished with 2,228 career points, third all-time at VMI.
- Two-time SoCon Player of Year, three-time selection as first team All-Conference.
- Led Keydets to back-to-back NCAA tournament appearances, including trip to Elite Eight in 1976.
- Most Outstanding Player in 1976 SoCon Tournament.
- VMI posted .707 overall winning percentage in his four years and captured two SoCon championships.

*Ron Carter of VMI played a key role in the Keydets' march to the NCAA Tournament's Elite Eight in 1976. (Virginia Military Institute Athletics)*

### SUSAN GARDNER

*Western Carolina University*
*1989–93, Track and Field, Cross Country*
- Captured numerous honors in both track and field and cross country.
- Earned eighteen All-SoCon awards in indoor track and twelve outdoors.
- Won 800-meter run in both indoor and outdoor SoCon meets (1992) as well as outdoor high jump in '91 and indoor mile in '92.
- All-SoCon in cross country, 1991.
- Named North Carolina's NCAA Woman of Year, 1993.

*Susan Gardner Mayhorn was an exceptional performer in cross country and indoor and outdoor track and field for the Catamounts of Western Carolina. (Western Carolina University Athletics)*

Chal Port coached the Citadel's baseball program for twenty-seven years. (The Citadel archives)

## CHAL PORT

*The Citadel*
*1965–91, Baseball*

- Compiled 641-386-2 record as coach of Citadel baseball program for twenty-seven seasons.
- Led Bulldogs to 1990 College World Series and five NCAA regional appearances.
- Named SoCon Coach of Year unprecedented six times.
- Named *Sporting News* National Coach of Year, 1990.
- Voted into both ABCA Hall of Fame and Citadel Hall of Fame in 1996.

Les Robinson both coached and served as athletic director at three institutions: ETSU, North Carolina State, and the Citadel. (The Citadel Athletics)

## LES ROBINSON

*The Citadel, 1974–85; 2000–08*
*East Tennessee State University, 1985–90,*
*Basketball*

- Forged successful career as both a basketball coach and administrator at two SoCon institutions.
- Spent eleven years as head coach at the Citadel, earning two Coach of Year honors and winning twenty games in 1978–79.
- At ETSU, led Bucs to pair of NCAA tournament appearances while also serving as AD.
- Later moved to NC State as coach, then AD, before concluding career as AD at the Citadel (2000–08).
- Served as member of both Division I Basketball Committee and NIT Selection Committee.

Debbie Southern coached Furman's women's tennis team to 19 Southern Conference regular-season titles and 16 tournament championships. (Furman University Athletics)

## DEBBIE SOUTHERN

*Furman University*
*1985–2015, Tennis*

- Coached women's tennis at Furman for thirty-one seasons, winning 461 matches.
- Led Paladins to nineteen regular-season conference titles and sixteen tournament championships.
- Finished with an overall SoCon record of 213-22, a .906 winning percentage.
- Guided Furman to 100 consecutive SoCon victories (1998–2010), longest such streak in conference history in any sport.
- Voted Coach of Year in SoCon fourteen times, including seven straight years from 2003–09.

# SOUTHERN CONFERENCE COMMISSIONERS

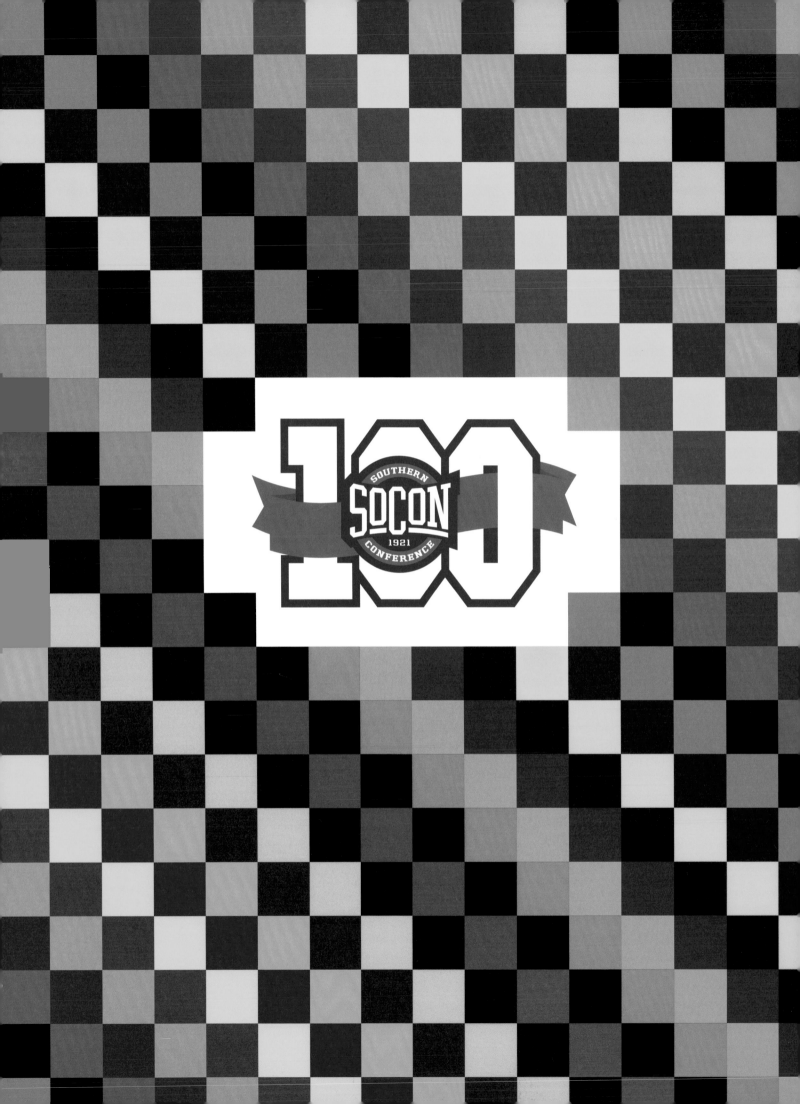

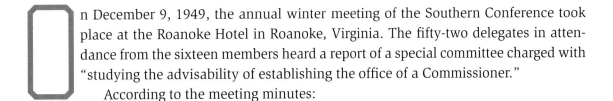

# WALLACE WADE

## 1951–1960

O n December 9, 1949, the annual winter meeting of the Southern Conference took place at the Roanoke Hotel in Roanoke, Virginia. The fifty-two delegates in attendance from the sixteen members heard a report of a special committee charged with "studying the advisability of establishing the office of a Commissioner."

According to the meeting minutes:

> Beginning July 1, 1950, or earlier if possible, the Southern Conference shall engage the services of a person who shall be called Commissioner. He shall be charged with the responsibility of endorcing [sic] the rules and regulations of the Conference.
>
> He shall be paid an annual salary not to exceed twelve thousand ($12,000) dollars. There shall be provided, for the necessary expenses in the operation of his office, an annual sum not to exceed ten thousand ($10,000) dollars, and an additional amount of eight thousand ($8,000) dollars for the maintenance of booking officials.

The committee's recommendation was seconded and adopted. Another special committee was assigned the task of identifying the right person for the job. After sifting through applications and resumes for much of 1950, the committee felt it became obvious that the right person was Wallace Wade.

Perhaps no individual associated with the Southern Conference had achieved such fame and success over such a long period of time as Wade. He had just completed his sixteenth season as head football coach at Duke. Before that, Wade had built a powerhouse program at Alabama beginning in 1923, winning two Rose Bowls and three mythical national championships.

For three decades the SoCon had been a viable, well-respected organization. But the increasing pressures to succeed in college athletics, particularly with the emergence of television, made presidents, chancellors, and athletic directors realize the need for an executive director who could view issues through a neutral, nonpartisan lens. Wade's assignment was to monitor national trends, establish and enforce regulations, and promote a sprawling league that stretched from Washington, DC, to Charleston, South Carolina.

It wasn't long before he was staring at his first crisis. Seven large, high-profile members formally announced their departure to form a new league called the Atlantic Coast Confer-

*Commissioner-elect Wallace Wade presents the Most Outstanding Player Award to North Carolina State's Sammy Ranzino at the 1950 Southern Conference Basketball Tournament. (Duke University Athletics)*

ence. The ACC defections left the remaining Southern Conference members reeling.

"Wallace Wade was our inspiration," the Citadel faculty representative D. S. McAlister would later tell a Columbia, South Carolina, reporter. "He had come to Duke from Alabama to coach football and told everybody in the Southern that our football could match that of the SEC with hard work. He did the same thing after the conference split in 1953. He told us we had to get to work.

"We did, and we earned respectability."

Wade was so highly thought of that the departing ACC programs contacted him to serve as commissioner of the fledgling league while keeping his SoCon duties. He accepted, telling members of both conferences that although it might not be the advisable thing to do, and could lead to problems and confusion, he would "serve as ably as he could." The joint commissionership lasted for almost a year before Wake Forest AD Jim Weaver was named ACC commissioner on May 7, 1954.

"I was told unofficially that the ACC would like me to join them, but I felt loyal to the Southern," Wade recalled years later.

The formation of the ACC marked the end of the Southern Conference being recognized as one of the top two or three conferences in the United States. But it wasn't a death knell, either.

"Of course, we had some other difficulties, mostly minor," remembered Wade. "But the new Southern had better relations among the members. There wasn't quite the tendency to go all out and there was more conforming to the rules."

The conference did not add any new members during Wade's nine years in office. Toward the latter part of his term, Wade convinced the members to create and use the first Southern Conference logo. Rifle was added as a league sport in 1956, mostly at the urging of Virginia Tech and the latest addition to the league, West Virginia.

Success in at least one sport proved more elusive under Wade. The 1951 conference baseball tournament showed net gate receipts of $12.84 in Greensboro. It was moved to Raleigh for two years and fared better, but once the ACC teams left, it was decided to eliminate the baseball tournament. It would not be revived until 1984.

One of Wade's proudest moments as commissioner was attending the championship game of the 1959 NCAA Basketball Tournament in Louisville's Freedom Hall where his West Virginia Mountaineers competed in the national championship game, falling to California in the final seconds by a single point.

Nine months later, the 67-year-old Wade stepped down as commissioner and settled on his 120-acre farm in an unincorporated community near Durham, where he and his wife, Virginia, raised prize Hereford cattle. He enjoyed a long retirement, living to see Duke rename its football stadium in his honor in 1967. He died on October 7, 1986, at the age of 94.

# LLOYD JORDAN

## 1960–1973

The longest-serving commissioner in Southern Conference history, Lloyd Jordan was a three-sport athlete at the University of Pittsburgh. He entered the coaching ranks in both basketball and football, eventually concentrating his efforts on the latter. After a stint as an assistant at Colgate, Jordan became the head football coach at Amherst College, spending fifteen seasons interrupted by military service in World War II. His teams won six conference championships and nearly 70 percent of their contests. His success earned him the head-coaching job at Harvard, where he spent seven unremarkable seasons before being released in January of 1957.

Jordan's appointment as commissioner was announced in late August of 1959, with speculation that his annual salary would be $10,000. "I have always had the greatest respect for Wallace Wade as a coach and as a person," said Jordan of his predecessor. "I am delighted to have the privilege of following in his footsteps."

Jordan took over on the first day of a new decade, January 1, 1960. He immediately moved the league offices to the prestigious Virginia Building at 1 N. Fifth Street in the heart of downtown Richmond. Built in 1905, the building was for many years the tallest in the central district of the city. Today it is listed on the National Register of Historic Places.

Shortly after setting up his new office, Jordan sat down with a local TV sportscaster and was asked what his initial impressions were of the Southern Conference. "I think they're doing one of the finest jobs with less to work with than any group I know of," he said. "If they all work to make progress, nothing can hold them back."

Mindful of the history and tradition of the organization he was heading up, Jordan took steps to preserve the official record of the Southern Conference. In 1967, he hired J. Dallas Shirley, a long-time basketball official and clinician, as assistant to the commissioner. The Washington, DC, native had been working as a high school principal. Shirley collected and organized all

*Lloyd Jordan remains the longest tenured commissioner in Southern Conference history, having served fourteen years. (Southern Conference)*

the league minutes dating back to 1921 and became the recording secretary at meetings and special events until his retirement in 1988.

In basketball, Jordan put an end to the dubious practice of allowing a two-thirds majority vote of head coaches to blackball an official from working SoCon games. "It is gratifying to report that Commissioner Lloyd Jordan will end this privilege," said *Sports Illustrated* in September of 1964.

In 1966, Jordan oversaw the introduction of the first new sport (soccer) in the conference in ten years. He initiated the Commissioner's Cup, emblematic of broad sports excellence among member programs. He also worked to strengthen ties between the SoCon and the Orlando-based Tangerine Bowl, resulting in six Southern Conference teams participating from 1964–71.

Initially, the institutional lineup Jordan inherited remained the same. East Carolina was added in 1964, but a year later Virginia Tech departed, followed soon thereafter by West Virginia and George Washington. The once twenty-three-member SoCon was reduced to seven members by 1970. A year later, the conference added Appalachian State, a Division I independent, and again stabilized.

The membership appreciated his efforts. "In the face of many difficulties and numerous problems," read a resolution from the athletic directors to Jordan at the annual meeting in 1971, "Lloyd Jordan has performed his duties as commissioner with great competence, absolute integrity, complete fairness and profound wisdom."

Upon leaving the position in December of 1973, Jordan remained in the Richmond area, where he still kept up with the Southern Conference. "My real interest was then, and is now, the welfare of the student-athlete," he said in 1979. "Some positive steps have been taken in that direction and I'm glad of it."

His coaching accomplishments earned him induction into the College Football Hall of Fame in December of 1978. He died on February 24, 1990, at the age of 89.

# KEN GERMANN

## 1974–1986

At first glance, Kenneth Germann was an unlikely candidate to become the third commissioner of the Southern Conference. His roots were all in the Northeast. He was born in New York, attended high school and college there, and coached football in the metropolitan New York area. But he also presented an impressive sports background as both an athlete and a coach. Moreover, he displayed the leadership qualities gleaned by service in the Marines Corps and as athletic director at Columbia University, his alma mater.

Germann (pronounced GUR-man), was a talented enough running back to be invited to training camp with the original Buffalo Bills of the All-America Football Conference. He eventually taught in high school and coached football before stints as an assistant coach at Columbia and Rutgers. He also worked in the winter as a college basketball official.

When he became commissioner in 1974, Germann decided to find a more southern location for the league office and moved the operations from Richmond to 5 Woodlawn Green in Charlotte. His primary assistant, J. Dallas Shirley, continued to worked out of his home in Reston, Virginia. In time, the office added John Geis as director of the service bureau.

Germann presided over seismic changes within the Southern Conference. There were members on the way out (Richmond, William & Mary, East Carolina) and those on the way in (Chattanooga, Marshall, Western Carolina, ETSU). The historic Title IX ruling of 1972 paved the way for the NCAA to supplant the Association of Intercollegiate Athletics for Women (AIAW) and sanction women's championship sports in 1981. Two years later, at the conference's June meeting in Myrtle Beach, Germann received approval from the membership to hold women's championships in volleyball and basketball.

Germann was an active commissioner. He served a term as president of the Collegiate Commissioners Association (CCA). He wrote feature articles for the Charlotte newspapers. He approached Bob James of the ACC about a postseason football bowl game between the SoCon champion and the ACC's runner-up team. (James respectfully declined.)

He continually looked for ways to improve the competitive quality of the league. "We certainly haven't reached the level we want," he told a West Virginia writer in 1981. "We're striving to do better and better and better."

Germann was the first SoCon commissioner to push the concept of television coverage and providing local TV stations in conference cities with packaged highlights they could use. He started the league office's first service bureau to maintain accurate statistics and records.

Ken Germann awards the Most Outstanding Player trophy to VMI's Dave Montgomery at the 1977 conference basketball tournament. (Southern Conference)

In May of 1985 he announced his plans to serve one more year before retiring, thereby providing for "an orderly transition process." In advance of the 1986–87 academic year, the conference created an all-sports trophy to recognize overall program excellence in women's athletics. The award was named the Germann Cup after the outgoing commissioner, who had led the way in bringing women's athletics under the Southern Conference umbrella.

Germann and his wife, Ruth, retired to a home in suburban Richmond. He passed away in August of 2005 at the age of 84.

# DAVE HART SR.

## 1986–1991

The legacy of Dave Hart Sr. with the Southern Conference is inextricably linked to the city he made his home and headquarters for the conference office—Asheville, North Carolina. Hart's efforts to promote the SoCon basketball tournament in Asheville, his involvement there in the local community, and his tireless efforts to promote and market the league helped elevate the conference in numerous ways.

The basketball tournament had been in Asheville since 1984, but it truly gathered momentum as a hot ticket after Hart became commissioner in July of '86. He worked to enhance the tournament on several fronts. He sold a title sponsorship to First Commercial Bank, and a significant corporate package to Coca-Cola. He negotiated coverage of the championship game in prime time on ESPN. He worked with city and county officials, most notably the Junior League of Asheville, to sell tickets and raise awareness. Soon, the SoCon was routinely averaging more than 5,000 fans per session in an Asheville Civic Center that held right around 6,500.

Hart arranged to bring baseball and tennis championships to Asheville as well. "The Southern Conference/Asheville marriage is a good one for both parties," he told a feature writer in 1987. "I want to bring as many Southern Conference events to Asheville as possible."

A native of Connellsville, Pennsylvania, Hart earned his undergraduate degree as a football student-athlete at St. Vincent College in Latrobe, Pennsylvania, hometown of Arnold Palmer. He went on to coach high school football before moving on to the collegiate ranks. From 1966 to '68, Hart was the head coach at the University of Pittsburgh. After a brief stint as a scout for the Dallas Cowboys, he was appointed athletic director at the University of Louisville, and five years later, in 1978, at the University of Missouri.

"He kept the program clean," wrote Don Kausler in the *Columbia* (MO) *Tribune* when Hart announced he was leaving Mizzou for the SoCon in March of 1986. "You never could question his integrity. And he recognized the value in maintaining a good relationship with the media."

Looking for a new challenge, Hart found it at the Southern Conference, but he didn't back away. "We're not trying to be something we aren't—that's why I wanted this job," he told the *Huntington* (WV) *Herald-Dispatch* in October of '87. "We have good academic institutions and good people."

Hart was the first Southern Conference commissioner to truly emphasize the league's TV and corporate marketing efforts. He hired a TV consultant and eventually signed agreements with the Liberty Sports Network and the cable channel SCORE.

"I know a lot about television and know how to increase the chances of a lesser-known program getting on television," he once said. "We've got to knock down doors. We've got to be aggressive and go all out and sell ourselves."

He also operated the first truly modern conference office with more personnel than had ever been employed before. In 1988 Hart hired Wright Waters from Tulane to become assistant commissioner for rules compliance. Jimmy Wilder was hired that same year to succeed John Geis as director of the service bureau, a position Geis had held for ten years.

Also in '88, Hart hired the office's first intern, Geoff Cabe, a UNC Asheville graduate. Cabe would go on to serve the SoCon for more than thirty years, skillfully handling such varied areas as media relations, scheduling, championships, and marketing. The internship program Hart started has been in place continuously to the present day.

*Dave Hart relocated the SoCon offices to Asheville, NC, in 1987 and was instrumental in the basketball tournament's success there. (Southern Conference)*

His football roots convinced Hart that the SoCon should strengthen its pedigree on the gridiron. Toward that end, he led discussions that resulted in the addition of Georgia Southern as a full league member in 1991. The Eagles' program had already captured four national Division I-AA championships as an independent.

Hart also laid the groundwork for the first postgraduate scholarships awarded by the Southern Conference in the spring of 1991.

At the 1990 June spring meeting in Myrtle Beach, Hart announced he would retire after one more year. "I feel I need to spend more time with my family," he told reporters. "The job has been very time consuming in the last year. I'm a workaholic. I work too much."

Hart was the first of three generations of successful athletic administrators. His son, Dave Hart Jr., served as athletic director at four large state institutions—East Carolina, Florida State, Alabama, and Tennessee. His grandson, Rick Hart, spent six years in the Southern Conference as the athletic director at Chattanooga before becoming AD at Southern Methodist University in July of 2012.

Dave Hart and his wife, Earlyn, remained in Asheville after he left the SoCon. He continued to follow the athletic programs headed by his son and, later, his grandson. He stayed active in the community and helped sponsor a fundraising golf tournament for UNC Asheville. In 2006, he attended his final Southern Conference football media day. At the event's golf outing, he played in a threesome with grandson Rick and new commissioner John Iamarino.

Dave Hart Sr. passed away on March 14, 2009, at the age of 83.

# WRIGHT WATERS

## 1991–1998

Wright Waters was hired in June of 1988 to become the first compliance officer for the Southern Conference. Ostensibly, his duties were to make sure member institutions followed the rules and regulations of the conference and the NCAA, but his responsibilities quickly expanded and he became an obvious choice to replace Dave Hart Sr. in July of 1991.

Waters attended the University of Alabama before earning his undergraduate and graduate degrees from Livingston University. He began a career in collegiate athletics administration that included stops at Southern Mississippi, Florida, Southwestern Louisiana, and Tulane before joining the SoCon. He gained extensive experience in all aspects of running an athletic department—compliance, scheduling, radio and TV negotiations, ticketing, promotions.

An innovative thinker, Waters focused his efforts as commissioner on boosting revenues, improving the student-athlete experience, and making the basketball championship an event that would be regarded as first class. Like many of predecessors, he also had to deal with questions of expansion.

Under his guidance, conference finances were brought entirely in-house for the first time. Waters hired local Asheville businessperson Sue Arakas in 1994 to handle the league's daily financial matters. Previously, a secretary/treasurer was appointed among one of the conference's administrators. Arakas would eventually be promoted to associate commissioner and remain on staff for more than twenty-five years.

To impart leadership skills in Southern Conference student-athletes, Waters established the Student-Athlete Leadership Institute (SALI), a weekend summer retreat in the mountains of western North Carolina for team captains and other athletes exhibiting leadership qualities. Under Arakas's direction, the retreat ran annually for more than two decades. Waters also initiated awards designed to recognize success in academic performance and graduation rates among league members.

When the Asheville Civic Center, site of the league's basketball tournament, began showing signs of age, Waters negotiated an agreement with the Greensboro Coliseum to move the tournament there in 1996 for a four-year run that added significant revenue to the league's budget.

The SoCon added new championships for women in soccer, softball, and golf. "I am proud that we have expanded not only the support and quality of our championships, but we have expanded the championship offerings," he wrote in a summation letter prior to his departure.

*Commissioner Wright Waters presents Mrs. Wallace Wade with an award in memory of her late husband from the Collegiate Commissioners Association. (Duke University Athletics)*

Looking to increase membership to twelve, Waters steered the Southern Conference through two expansions. When Marshall University left in 1997, Wofford College and the University of North Carolina at Greensboro were added, bringing the league total to eleven members. A year later, the College of Charleston entered the fold.

"We have twice expanded the league without compromising our standards," wrote Waters. "The new members have all enhanced the conference."

The Montgomery, Alabama, native was always interested in new horizons. So it was not a complete surprise when he announced that he would not sign an extension of his contract. "I personally need a new challenge," he wrote the Citadel's Gerald Runey, president of the conference. "I have toyed with this issue for over a year. It is not made as a snap judgment."

At 49, he was certainly not thinking retirement. After a year working in marketing for Crimson Tide Properties at his beloved University of Alabama, Waters spent fourteen years in New Orleans as commissioner of the Sun Belt Conference, adding football as a league sport, lining up bowl affiliations, and eventually bringing that conference its present FBS divisional status.

In 2012, he left the Sun Belt to become the executive director of the Football Bowl Association, a position he held through 2020. A statement by the association upon his hire said, "Wright has extensive experience in athletics administration and is capable of communicating with stakeholders throughout collegiate athletics as we navigate adjustments to college football's postseason."

# ALFRED WHITE

## 1998–2001

When he was named the new commissioner of the Southern Conference, Alfred White became the first African-American in that role at a Division I league not consisting of historically black colleges and universities. He addressed it straight on during his introductory press conference on April 6, 1998, at Asheville's Grove Park Inn.

"I respect the fact that I'm the first African-American to be a Commissioner, but I don't plan on dwelling on it a whole bunch," he said. "I do think it's kind of an honor."

White joined the Southern Conference after a distinguished fifteen-year career at the NCAA, working his way up from a communications assistant to director of promotions to director of corporate marketing. He began his career in intercollegiate athletics working in media relations at his alma mater, Texas Tech University.

White quickly laid out his primary goals—enhancing the SoCon's position among Division I-AA conferences, building a corporate partner structure, and improving the league's internal governance.

"I thought getting the ball rolling on a marketing initiative that was more encompassing than just at the championships was a step in the right direction," White recalled. "But basically, getting the governance groups talking and respecting each other was my proudest accomplishment. I sensed that I inherited a culture of communicating 'to' rather than 'with.'"

White became an outspoken advocate for making I-AA football viable and attractive for institutions and conferences that realized they could not compete with the greater-resourced I-A (now FBS) members. He saw that an unstructured landscape for I-AA meant more programs trying to reclassify, as former SoCon member Marshall did in leaving for the Mid-American Conference in 1997.

"Anyone who's considering a jump needs to get their arms around what I-A is doing," he told Bob Gillespie of the *Columbia* (SC) *State*. "That division is going more to the super conferences. They need to do some soul searching about why they think they need to move up."

White toured all twelve campuses in short order, including that of the newest member, the College of Charleston. He met with presidents, chancellors, faculty, coaches, and administrators, listening to their concerns. He laid out a meticulous three-page plan for his first 100 days in office. "I thought unifying the members around a strategic plan was monumental because it was a conversation that the presidents, ADs, SWAs, and faculty reps had never had before," recalled White.

*Alfred White is interviewed by Keith Jarrett of the Asheville Citizen-Times. (Southern Conference)*

After the conference's agreement expired with the Greensboro Coliseum for its basketball tournament, White negotiated a deal with the Bi-Lo Center in Greenville, South Carolina, and brought the event there for two years. Additionally, White's office worked with the arena to secure the first and second rounds of the 2002 NCAA Tournament, a major coup for Greenville and the Southern Conference.

By the time the event came, however, White was no longer part of the conference. In July of 2001 he announced he was stepping down as commissioner to accept a position as president of the Asheville Altitude of the NBA's development league (now known as the G League). The move would allow White, his wife, Judy, and their daughter, Cassidy, to remain in their home in Asheville.

"This has been an extremely difficult decision for my family and me," White said in a statement. "I will forever be indebted to the Southern Conference for giving me the opportunity. The SoCon will always have a special place in my heart."

After three years with the Altitude, White returned to Division I conference work as the senior associate commissioner of Conference USA. In 2016, he left to join the College Football Playoff as senior director of marketing and strategic partnerships, utilizing his many years of marketing expertise to sell special VIP ticket packages, hospitality suites, and other incentives for college football's championship game.

"I've thoroughly enjoyed working on both of the premier sporting events in college athletics during my career—the Final Four and the College Football Playoff national championship," White said.

# DANNY MORRISON

## 2001–2005

Danny Morrison came to the Southern Conference with as varied a background as any of his predecessors. He had experience as a student-athlete, math teacher, basketball coach, director of athletics, and college senior vice president. The latter position came at Wofford College, his alma mater, and included duties in business operations and enrollment management.

Prior to that, Morrison had been the AD at Wofford and paved the way for the college to go from a bare-bones NAIA athletic program to the ranks of Division I and an invitation to join the Southern Conference in 1997.

When thinking about the commissioner position, the native of Burlington, North Carolina, wondered how he would react to no longer being on a campus. Before making up his mind, he spoke with John Swofford, commissioner of the ACC and a former North Carolina athletic director.

"He said he loved working for more than one school," Morrison told writer Rick Nelson of the *Charleston* (SC) *Post and Courier*. "I thought it was great to hear he loved his role."

Hired in November of 2001, Morrison built upon the work of Alfred White in increasing the conference's corporate marketing efforts. He hired Pete Moore, a former Duke football player, to head up corporate relations. He began a program to recognize and honor boosters and benefactors contributing to Southern Conference institutions. Additional postgraduate scholarships were awarded each year.

"Having been on a campus, I wanted to look for ways to help our programs with development," Morrison recalled. "The distinguished service award concept was part of an effort to bring some harmony to the group. We consciously built social events into meeting schedules. We tried to upgrade our annual spring meeting by moving it to Hilton Head and that seemed to work well."

Morrison and his staff successfully hosted the 2002 NCAA Basketball Tournament first and second rounds at Greenville's Bi-Lo Center. It was the first time the tournament had been played in the state of South Carolina in thirty-two years.

When the lease in Asheville was due for renewal, he decided to look at other possible sites for the conference office. Ultimately, the league accepted an offer from Spartanburg, South Carolina, to settle in a renovated textile mill. The conference office moved to Spartanburg in the summer of 2002.

Morrison created a fall retreat at the Biltmore Estate in Asheville to conduct meetings and bring in high-level professionals from intercollegiate athletics to talk with the presidents and chancellors. He worked to obtain TV coverage with a number of regional sports networks.

In the spring of 2005, Morrison announced that he was leaving to become the director of athletics at Texas Christian University. He remained at TCU until accepting the position as president of the NFL's Carolina Panthers in 2009. He was with the franchise when it played in the Super Bowl following the 2015 season.

Morrison left the Panthers two years after that and taught a sports management course at the University of South Carolina before being named executive director of the Charlotte Sports Foundation in early 2019. He always spoke highly of his time at the SoCon.

"I see the conference office as a place where you take ideas from all the institutions, pick the very best ones, and find a way to collectively move forward."

*Danny Morrison delivers the 2003 SoCon Football Championship trophy to head coach Mike Ayers of the Wofford Terriers. (Wofford College Athletics)*

# JOHN IAMARINO

## 2006–2019

In the summer of 2001, John Iamarino applied for the vacant commissioner position at the Southern Conference. He was among the many applicants not invited for an interview. Four years later, when Danny Morrison left the position, Iamarino applied again. This time he was interviewed and offered the position shortly before Christmas.

The native of Monsey, New York, came to Spartanburg with extensive experience at the conference level. He was in his ninth year as commissioner of the Northeast Conference. Prior to that, he spent eleven years with the Sun Belt Conference, starting in media relations and gradually rising to the level of associate commissioner.

Iamarino's professional career began as a sports writer in the suburban New York area, but a college friend's suggestion to pursue a vacant sports information position at Georgetown University led him into college athletics.

Taking over at the eleven-member Southern Conference in January of 2006, Iamarino realized expansion would be a high priority. He became convinced that Samford University was the right fit and made logical sense geographically. He built consensus to add the Birmingham-based university in 2008.

"Samford's transition to the SoCon was probably far more tranquil than is often the case in such matters," said Samford president Dr. Andrew Westmoreland. "There appeared to be no disruption within the existing SoCon membership regarding Samford's entrance, so we were welcomed from the very beginning."

From the time he started, Iamarino had pushed for creation of a Southern Conference Hall of Fame. In 2008, the Council of Presidents approved the concept, and on May 4, 2009, the first ten inductees were honored at a reception and ceremony at the Chapman Cultural Center in Spartanburg.

"I distinctly remember sitting there on the stage looking across at Jerry West, Sam Huff, Dick Groat, Frank Selvy, and the others and thinking how awesome it was that we pulled all this together," Iamarino recalled. "It was just a tremendous night for the Conference and for the city of Spartanburg."

Within a couple years, membership issues became just as problematic for Iamarino as they had for so many previous Southern Conference leaders. "The discussions at league meetings seemed to focus more on the diversity of our institutions, and how that was a negative instead of a positive," he recalled. "It had not been that way my first few years."

*John Iamarino stands with Davidson's Stephen Curry after awarding him All-Conference and Player of the Year plaques for the 2008–09 season. (Todd Drexler, SoCon Photos)*

In a nine-month period, five Southern Conference members announced plans to leave the league. Iamarino spent countless hours on the phone, researching and visiting campuses of potential new members, and networking with other commissioners. Eventually, offers were sent to, and accepted by, Mercer University and two former members seeking to return—East Tennessee State and Virginia Military Institute.

"Losing members and having to call other Commissioners and tell them you're going to contact their schools, those are difficult things to deal with," Iamarino said. "You just try to be professional about it and set your emotions to the side. I think we managed to get through it without sacrificing our reputation as a conference."

With a new group of ten members looking to stabilize, Iamarino addressed some league-wide needs. Using exit fees from departing members, the conference office purchased video equipment for each member to launch the SoCon Digital Network in 2014. Shortly thereafter, video coordinators began producing live content for ESPN platforms. By 2017–18, Southern Conference institutions were producing more than 800 live events for video-streaming outlets.

In 2014, the Southern Conference Academic Exchange was formed, a collaborative effort directed by the chief academic officers. The group created conference awards honoring faculty and staff members, launched an annual student research forum, and began a program designed to instill leadership and development skills in faculty members.

In March of 2019, Iamarino announced he would retire at the end of June, saying, "It's been a privilege to serve the SoCon, but I feel this is the right time for me to step aside."

# JIM SCHAUS

## 2019–PRESENT

The son of one of the most successful head basketball coaches in league history, Jim Schaus was named the ninth commissioner of the Southern Conference on June 4, 2019. He was introduced at a press conference two days later.

"I look forward to working with the staff and conference membership," he said, "to build upon past successes in the quest to become the premier mid-major conference in the country."

Schaus joined the SoCon after an impressive career that included lengthy stops as director of athletics at Wichita State and Ohio University. His programs at OU were successful both athletically and academically. The football team participated in ten bowl games during his eleven years there. The men's basketball team advanced to an NCAA tournament Sweet Sixteen. And in 2017, twelve of the Bobcats' sixteen varsity sports recorded perfect scores of 1,000 in the NCAA's Academic Progress Rate (APR).

A graduate of Purdue University, Schaus grew up with a fuller knowledge of college athletics than most people. His father was Fred Schaus, who steered West Virginia to five Southern Conference regular-season championships from 1954–60, winning four Coach of the Year awards. Fred Schaus later coached the Los Angeles Lakers, then rejoined the college ranks at Purdue.

"I've always followed the Southern Conference from afar," Jim Schaus told the *Spartanburg Herald Journal*. "But to have an opportunity to be the Commissioner, well, if my dad was alive today he'd be really proud of that."

Schaus's career included a variety of jobs at both the collegiate and professional levels. He was an intern for the New England Patriots, served as a publicity assistant with the LPGA, spent three years in the marketing department of the Washington Redskins, and worked for a television production company. But he eventually focused on a career in college athletics administration. His resume included positions at West Virginia, Oregon, Northern Illinois, and Cincinnati before he became the AD at Wichita State and Ohio.

"Jim is among the most well-respected athletic directors in the nation, and he brings a vision and a wealth of experience that will be highly valuable to the league," said ETSU president Brian Noland, who chaired the conference's internal search committee.

Schaus immediately identified a number of goals for the SoCon. Among them were securing a television/digital-streaming contract to maximize exposure and rights fees, steering the league toward the top of the FCS in football, and succeeding despite the ever- widening gap between the so-called Power Five conferences and the rest of Division I.

He also planned to spend time with basketball coaches and ADs to encourage non-conference scheduling that would place the league's better teams in a more advantageous position to obtain higher NCAA tournament seeds and an elusive at-large berth in the tournament field. This would be another area in which the new commissioner would be speaking from experience, having served on the prestigious NCAA Basketball Committee from 2015–18.

*Jim Schaus speaks during a press conference introducing him as the ninth commissioner in SoCon history. (Haley Shotwell, Southern Conference)*

## A PROUD ATHLETIC HISTORY

# CHAMPIONSHIP SPORTS

# INTRODUCTION OF CHAMPIONSHIP SPORTS

| MEN | YEAR | | WOMEN | YEAR |
|---|---|---|---|---|
| Basketball | 1921 | | Volleyball | 1983 |
| Football | 1922 | | Basketball | 1983 |
| Outdoor Track and Field | 1923 | | Tennis | 1984 |
| Baseball | 1923 | | Cross Country | 1985 |
| Cross Country | 1926 | | Outdoor Track and Field | 1987 |
| Boxing<br>*(discontinued after 1939)* | 1927 | | Indoor Track and Field | 1988 |
| Wrestling | 1927 | | Softball | 1994 |
| Tennis | 1928 | | Golf | 1994 |
| Golf | 1930 | | Soccer | 1994 |
| Indoor Track and Field | 1930 | | Lacrosse | 2018 |
| Swimming & Diving<br>*(discontinued after 1982)* | 1930 | | | |
| Soccer | 1966 | | | |
| Lacrosse | 2015 | | | |

| COED | YEAR |
|---|---|
| Rifle<br>*(discontinued after 1985; restored in 2016)* | 1956 |

*Asher Wojciechowski was the winning pitcher twice in the Citadel's march to the 2010 SoCon Championship. (Todd Drexler, SoCon Photos)*

## BASEBALL

*Championship tournament not held until 1950; discontinued 1954–83; restored in 1984.*

| YEAR | REGULAR SEASON CHAMPION | TOURNAMENT CHAMPION | TOURNAMENT MOST OUTSTANDING PLAYER | TOURNAMENT HOST / SITE |
|------|-------------------------|---------------------|-------------------------------------|-------------------------|
| 1923 | Georgia Tech | — | — | — |
| 1924 | North Carolina State | — | — | — |
| 1925 | Alabama | — | — | — |
| 1926 | Georgia Tech | — | — | — |
| 1927 | Auburn | — | — | — |
| 1928 | Georgia | — | — | — |
| 1929 | Duke | — | — | — |
| 1930 | Alabama | — | — | — |
| 1931 | Duke | — | — | — |
| 1932 | Alabama | — | — | — |
| 1933 | South Carolina | — | — | — |

| YEAR | REGULAR SEASON CHAMPION | TOURNAMENT CHAMPION | TOURNAMENT MOST OUTSTANDING PLAYER | TOURNAMENT HOST / SITE |
|---|---|---|---|---|
| 1934 | North Carolina | — | — | — |
| 1935 | Duke | — | — | — |
| 1936 | Maryland | — | — | — |
| 1937 | Duke | — | — | — |
| 1938 | Duke | — | — | — |
| 1939 | Duke | — | — | — |
| 1940 | Clemson | — | — | — |
| 1941 | North Carolina | — | — | — |
| 1942–45 | *Limited participation due to war.* | | | |
| 1946 | North Carolina State | — | — | — |
| 1947 | Clemson | — | — | — |
| 1948 | North Carolina | — | — | — |
| 1949 | Wake Forest | — | — | — |
| 1950 | Virginia Tech (North) *Wake Forest (South)* | Wake Forest | — | Greensboro, NC |
| 1951 | Maryland (North) *Clemson (South)* | Duke | — | Greensboro, NC |
| 1952 | Richmond (North) *Duke (South)* | Duke | — | Raleigh, NC |
| 1953 | Maryland (North) *North Carolina (South)* | Duke | — | Raleigh, NC |
| 1954 | Virginia Tech | — | — | — |
| 1955 | West Virginia | — | — | — |
| 1956 | George Washington | — | — | — |
| 1957 | George Washington | — | — | — |
| 1958 | George Washington & Richmond (tie) | — | — | — |
| 1959 | George Washington | — | — | — |
| 1960 | The Citadel & Richmond (tie) | — | — | — |
| 1961 | West Virginia | — | — | — |
| 1962 | West Virginia | — | — | — |
| 1963 | West Virginia | — | — | — |
| 1964 | West Virginia | — | — | — |
| 1965 | Furman | — | — | — |
| 1966 | East Carolina | — | — | — |

*A Proud Athletic History: 100 Years of the Southern Conference*

| YEAR | REGULAR SEASON CHAMPION | TOURNAMENT CHAMPION | TOURNAMENT MOST OUTSTANDING PLAYER | TOURNAMENT HOST / SITE |
|---|---|---|---|---|
| 1967 | West Virginia | — | — | — |
| 1968 | East Carolina | — | — | — |
| 1969 | William & Mary (North) *Furman (South)* | — | — | — |
| 1970 | William & Mary (North) *East Carolina (South)* | — | — | — |
| 1971 | The Citadel & Furman (tie) | — | — | — |
| 1972 | Richmond | — | — | — |
| 1973 | Appalachian State | — | — | — |
| 1974 | East Carolina | — | — | — |
| 1975 | The Citadel | — | — | — |
| 1976 | Furman | — | — | — |
| 1977 | East Carolina | — | — | — |
| 1978 | Marshall | — | — | — |
| 1979 | The Citadel | — | — | — |
| 1980 | ETSU | — | — | — |
| 1981 | ETSU, Marshall & Western Carolina (tie) | — | — | — |
| 1982 | The Citadel | — | — | — |
| 1983 | The Citadel | | | |
| 1984 | Appalachian State (North) *Western Carolina (South)* | Appalachian State | Rusty Weaver, App St. | Western Carolina |
| 1985 | Appalachian State (North) *Davidson (South)* | Western Carolina | Mike Carson, WCU | Appalachian State |
| 1986 | Appalachian State (North) *Western Carolina (South)* | Western Carolina | David Hyatt, WCU | Western Carolina |
| 1987 | Appalachian State (North) *Western Carolina (South)* | Western Carolina | Clint Fairey, WCU | Asheville, NC |
| 1988 | VMI (North) *Western Carolina (South)* | Western Carolina | Keith LeClair, WCU | Asheville, NC |
| 1989 | Western Carolina | Western Carolina | Paul Menhart, WCU | Asheville, NC |
| 1990 | The Citadel | The Citadel | Billy Baker, The Citadel | Charleston, SC |
| 1991 | The Citadel | Furman | Brent Williams, Furman | Charleston, SC |
| 1992 | Western Carolina | Western Carolina | Joey Cox, WCU | Charleston, SC |
| 1993 | Georgia Southern | Western Carolina | Phillip Grundy, WCU | Charleston, SC |
| 1994 | Western Carolina | The Citadel | Jermaine Shuler, The Citadel | Charleston, SC |
| 1995 | The Citadel | The Citadel | Donald Morillo, The Citadel | Charleston, SC |

| YEAR | REGULAR SEASON CHAMPION | TOURNAMENT CHAMPION | TOURNAMENT MOST OUTSTANDING PLAYER | TOURNAMENT HOST / SITE |
|------|------------------------|---------------------|-----------------------------------|------------------------|
| 1996 | Georgia Southern | Georgia Southern | Mark Hamlin, GSU | Charleston, SC |
| 1997 | Georgia Southern & Western Carolina (tie) | Western Carolina | J. P. Burwell, WCU | Charleston, SC |
| 1998 | UNCG | The Citadel | Brian Rogers, The Citadel | Charleston, SC |
| 1999 | The Citadel | The Citadel | Rodney Hancock, The Citadel | Charleston, SC |
| 2000 | The Citadel & Georgia Southern (tie) | Georgia Southern | Matt Easterday, GSU | Charleston, SC |
| 2001 | Georgia Southern | The Citadel | Randy Corn, The Citadel | Charleston, SC |
| 2002 | The Citadel | Georgia Southern | Brett Lewis, GSU | Charleston, SC |
| 2003 | Western Carolina | Western Carolina | Brian Sigmon, WCU | Charleston, SC |
| 2004 | College of Charleston | The Citadel | Jonathan Ellis, The Citadel | Charleston, SC |
| 2005 | College of Charleston | Furman | Nick Hollstegge, Furman | Charleston, SC |
| 2006 | Elon | College of Charleston | Nick Chiggers, C of C & Jess Easterling, C of C (tie) | Charleston, SC |
| 2007 | College of Charleston & Western Carolina (tie) | Wofford | Brandon Waring, Wofford | Charleston, SC |
| 2008 | Elon | Elon | Cory Harrilchak, Elon | Charleston, SC |
| 2009 | Elon | Georgia Southern | Kyle Blackburn, GSU | Greenville, SC |
| 2010 | The Citadel | The Citadel | Justin Mackert, The Citadel | Charleston, SC |
| 2011 | Elon | Georgia Southern | Chris Beck, GSU | Charleston, SC |
| 2012 | Appalachian State & College of Charleston (tie) | Samford* | Josh Martin, Samford | Greenville, SC |
| 2013 | Western Carolina | Elon | Joe Jackson, The Citadel | Greenville, SC |
| 2014 | Western Carolina | Georgia Southern | Jason Richman, GSU | Charleston, SC |
| 2015 | Mercer | Mercer | Eric Nyquist, Mercer | Charleston, SC |
| 2016 | Mercer | Western Carolina | Matt Smith, WCU | Greenville, SC |
| 2017 | Mercer | UNCG | Tripp Shelton, UNCG | Greenville, SC |
| 2018 | UNCG | Samford | Brooks Carlson, Samford | Greenville, SC |
| 2019 | Samford | Mercer | Trevor Austin, Mercer | Greenville, SC |

*Championship subsequently vacated due to NCAA violations.

*A Proud Athletic History: 100 Years of the Southern Conference*

*Fletcher Magee of Wofford led the Terriers to the 2019 conference tournament championship and a first-round victory in the NCAA tournament. (Todd Drexler, SoCon Photos)*

# MEN'S BASKETBALL

The 1921, 1922, and 1923 championship tournaments were sponsored by the Southern Intercollegiate Athletic Association (SIAA). All Southern Conference members were eligible to qualify. In 1924, the event became a Southern Conference members-only tournament.

*No tournament Most Outstanding Player selection until 1948.*

| YEAR | REGULAR SEASON CHAMPION | TOURNAMENT CHAMPION | TOURNAMENT MOST OUTSTANDING PLAYER | TOURNAMENT HOST / SITE |
|------|-------------------------|---------------------|-----------------------------------|------------------------|
| 1920–21 | No conference play | Kentucky | — | Atlanta |
| 1921–22 | Virginia | North Carolina | — | Atlanta |
| 1922–23 | North Carolina | Mississippi State | — | Atlanta |
| 1923–24 | Tulane | North Carolina | — | Atlanta |
| 1924–25 | North Carolina | North Carolina | — | Atlanta |
| 1925–26 | Kentucky | North Carolina | — | Atlanta |

| YEAR | REGULAR SEASON CHAMPION | TOURNAMENT CHAMPION | TOURNAMENT MOST OUTSTANDING PLAYER | TOURNAMENT HOST / SITE |
|---|---|---|---|---|
| 1926–27 | South Carolina | Vanderbilt | — | Atlanta |
| 1927–28 | Auburn | Mississippi | — | Atlanta |
| 1928–29 | Washington & Lee | North Carolina State | — | Atlanta |
| 1929–30 | Alabama | Alabama | — | Atlanta |
| 1930–31 | Georgia | Maryland | — | Atlanta |
| 1931–32 | Kentucky & Maryland (tie) | Georgia | — | Atlanta |
| 1932–33 | South Carolina | South Carolina | — | Raleigh, NC |
| 1933–34 | South Carolina | Washington & Lee | — | Raleigh, NC |
| 1934–35 | North Carolina | North Carolina | — | Raleigh, NC |
| 1935–36 | Washington & Lee | North Carolina | — | Raleigh, NC |
| 1936–37 | Washington & Lee | Washington & Lee | — | Raleigh, NC |
| 1937–38 | North Carolina | Duke | — | Raleigh, NC |
| 1938–39 | Wake Forest | Clemson | — | Raleigh, NC |
| 1939–40 | Duke | North Carolina | — | Raleigh, NC |
| 1940–41 | North Carolina | Duke | — | Raleigh, NC |
| 1941–42 | Duke | Duke | — | Raleigh, NC |
| 1942–43 | Duke | George Washington | — | Raleigh, NC |
| 1943–44 | North Carolina | Duke | — | Raleigh, NC |
| 1944–45 | South Carolina | North Carolina | — | Raleigh, NC |
| 1945–46 | North Carolina | Duke | — | Raleigh, NC |
| 1946–47 | North Carolina State | North Carolina State | — | Duke |
| 1947–48 | North Carolina State | North Carolina State | Jere Bunting, W&M | Duke |
| 1948–49 | North Carolina State | North Carolina State | Chet Giermak, W&M | Duke |
| 1949–50 | North Carolina State | North Carolina State | Sammy Ranzino, NC State | Duke |
| 1950–51 | North Carolina State | North Carolina State | Dick Groat, Duke | Raleigh, NC |
| 1951–52 | West Virginia | North Carolina State | Dick Groat, Duke | Raleigh, NC |
| 1952–53 | North Carolina State | Wake Forest | Gene Shue, Maryland | Raleigh, NC |
| 1953–54 | George Washington | George Washington | Joe Holup, GWU | West Virginia |
| 1954–55 | West Virginia | West Virginia | Rod Hundley, WVU | Richmond, VA |
| 1955–56 | George Washington & West Virginia (tie) | West Virginia | Rod Hundley, WVU | Richmond, VA |
| 1956–57 | West Virginia | West Virginia | Lloyd Sharrar, WVU | Richmond, VA |
| 1957–58 | West Virginia | West Virginia | Jerry West, WVU | Richmond, VA |
| 1958–59 | West Virginia | West Virginia | Jerry West, WVU | Richmond, VA |

*A Proud Athletic History: 100 Years of the Southern Conference*

| YEAR | REGULAR SEASON CHAMPION | TOURNAMENT CHAMPION | TOURNAMENT MOST OUTSTANDING PLAYER | TOURNAMENT HOST / SITE |
|---|---|---|---|---|
| 1959–60 | Virginia Tech | West Virginia | Jerry West, WVU | Richmond, VA |
| 1960–61 | West Virginia | George Washington | Jon Feldman, GWU | Richmond, VA |
| 1961–62 | West Virginia | West Virginia | Rod Thorn, WVU | Richmond, VA |
| 1962–63 | West Virginia | West Virginia | Rod Thorn, WVU | Richmond, VA |
| 1963–64 | Davidson | VMI | Fred Hetzel, Davidson | Charlotte, NC |
| 1964–65 | Davidson | West Virginia | Fred Hetzel, Davidson | Charlotte, NC |
| 1965–66 | Davidson | Davidson | Dick Snyder, Davidson | Charlotte, NC |
| 1966–67 | West Virginia | West Virginia | Johnny Moates, Richmond | Charlotte, NC |
| 1967–68 | Davidson | Davidson | Mike Maloy, Davidson | Charlotte, NC |
| 1968–69 | Davidson | Davidson | Doug Cook, Davidson | Charlotte, NC |
| 1969–70 | Davidson | Davidson | Doug Cook, Davidson | Charlotte, NC |
| 1970–71 | Davidson | Furman | Jerry Martin, Furman | Charlotte, NC |
| 1971–72 | Davidson | East Carolina | Roy Simpson, Furman | Greenville, SC |
| 1972–73 | Davidson | Furman | Clyde Mayes, Furman | Richmond, VA |
| 1973–74 | Furman | Furman | Aron Stewart, Richmond | Richmond, VA |
| 1974–75 | Furman | Furman | Clyde Mayes, Furman | Greenville, SC |
| 1975–76 | VMI | VMI | Ron Carter, VMI | Greenville, SC |
| 1976–77 | Furman & VMI (tie) | VMI | Dave Montgomery, VMI | Roanoke, VA |
| 1977–78 | Appalachian State | Furman | Jonathan Moore, Furman | Roanoke, VA |
| 1978–79 | Appalachian State | Appalachian State | Darryl Robinson, App State | Roanoke, VA |
| 1979–80 | Furman | Furman | Jonathan Moore, Furman | Roanoke, VA |
| 1980–81 | Appalachian State, Chattanooga & Davidson (tie) | Chattanooga | Nick Morken, UTC | Roanoke, VA |
| 1981–82 | Chattanooga | Chattanooga | Russ Schoene, UTC | Charleston, WV |
| 1982–83 | Chattanooga | Chattanooga | Willie White, UTC | Charleston, WV |
| 1983–84 | Marshall | Marshall | LaVerne Evans, Marshall | Asheville, NC |
| 1984–85 | Chattanooga | Marshall | Gay Elmore, VMI | Asheville, NC |
| 1985–86 | Chattanooga | Davidson | Gerry Born, Davidson | Asheville, NC |
| 1986–87 | Marshall | Marshall | Derek Rucker, Davidson | Asheville, NC |
| 1987–88 | Marshall | Chattanooga | Benny Green, UTC | Asheville, NC |
| 1988–89 | Chattanooga | ETSU | John Taft, Marshall | Asheville, NC |
| 1989–90 | ETSU | ETSU | Keith Jennings, ETSU | Asheville, NC |
| 1990–91 | Chattanooga, ETSU & Furman (tie) | ETSU | Keith Jennings, ETSU | Asheville, NC |
| 1991–92 | Chattanooga & ETSU (tie) | ETSU | Greg Dennis, ETSU | Asheville, NC |

| YEAR | REGULAR SEASON CHAMPION | TOURNAMENT CHAMPION | TOURNAMENT MOST OUTSTANDING PLAYER | TOURNAMENT HOST / SITE |
|---|---|---|---|---|
| 1992–93 | Chattanooga | Chattanooga | Tim Brooks, UTC | Asheville, NC |
| 1993–94 | Chattanooga | Chattanooga | Chad Copeland, UTC | Asheville, NC |
| 1994–95 | Marshall (North) *Chattanooga (South)* | Chattanooga | Frankie King, WCU | Asheville, NC |
| 1995–96 | Davidson (North) *Western Carolina (South)* | Western Carolina | Anquell McCollum, WCU | Greensboro, NC |
| 1996–97 | Davidson & Marshall (tie North) *Chattanooga (South)* | Chattanooga | John Brannen, Marshall | Greensboro, NC |
| 1997–98 | App. State& Davidson (tie North) *Chattanooga (South)* | Davidson | Ben Ebong, Davidson | Greensboro, NC |
| 1998–99 | App. State (North) *Coll. of Charleston (South)* | Coll. of Charleston | Marshall Phillips, App State | Greensboro, NC |
| 1999–2000 | App. State (North) *Coll. of Charleston (South)* | Appalachian State | Tyson Patterson, App State | Greenville, SC |
| 2000–01 | ETSU (North) *Coll. of Charleston (South)* | UNCG | Toot Young, UTC | Greenville, SC |
| 2001–02 | Davidson, ETSU & UNCG (tie North) *Chattanooga, Coll. of Charleston & Georgia Southern (tie South)* | Davidson | Peter Anderer, Davidson | N. Charleston, SC |
| 2002–03 | Appalachian State, Davidson & ETSU (tie North) *Coll. of Charleston (South)* | ETSU | Tim Smith, ETSU | N. Charleston, SC |
| 2003–04 | ETSU (North) *Coll. of Charleston, Davidson & Georgia Southern (tie South)* | ETSU | Tim Smith, ETSU | N. Charleston, SC |
| 2004–05 | Chattanooga (North) *Davidson (South)* | Chattanooga | Mindaugas Katelynas, UTC | Chattanooga, TN |
| 2005–06 | Elon (North) *Georgia Southern (South)* | Davidson | Brendan Winters, Davidson | N. Charleston, SC |
| 2006–07 | App. State (North) *Davidson (South)* | Davidson | Stephen Curry, Davidson | N. Charleston, SC |
| 2007–08 | Appalachian State & Chattanooga (tie North) *Davidson (South)* | Davidson | Stephen Curry, Davidson | N. Charleston, SC |
| 2008–09 | Chattanooga & Western Carolina (tie North) *Davidson (South)* | Chattanooga | Stephen McDowell, UTC | Chattanooga, TN |
| 2009–10 | App. State (North) *Wofford (South)* | Wofford | Noah Dahlman, Wofford | Charlotte, NC |

| YEAR | REGULAR SEASON CHAMPION | TOURNAMENT CHAMPION | TOURNAMENT MOST OUTSTANDING PLAYER | TOURNAMENT HOST / SITE |
|---|---|---|---|---|
| 2010–11 | Chattanooga & Western Carolina (tie North) *Coll. of Charleston & Wofford (tie South)* | Wofford | Noah Dahlman, Wofford | Chattanooga, TN |
| 2011–12 | UNCG (North) *Davidson (South)* | Davidson | De'Mon Brooks, Davidson | Asheville, NC |
| 2012–13 | Elon (North) *Davidson (South)* | Davidson | De'Mon Brooks, Davidson | Asheville, NC |
| 2013–14 | Davidson | Wofford | Karl Cochran, Wofford | Asheville, NC |
| 2014–15 | Wofford | Wofford | Lee Skinner, Wofford | Asheville, NC |
| 2015–16 | Chattanooga | Chattanooga | Greg Pryor, UTC | Asheville, NC |
| 2016–17 | ETSU, Furman & UNCG (tie) | ETSU | T.J. Cromer, ETSU | Asheville, NC |
| 2017–18 | UNCG | UNCG | Francis Alonso, UNCG | Asheville, NC |
| 2018–19 | Wofford | Wofford | Fletcher Magee, Wofford | Asheville, NC |

## WOMEN'S BASKETBALL

| YEAR | REGULAR SEASON CHAMPION | TOURNAMENT CHAMPION | TOURNAMENT MOST OUTSTANDING PLAYER | TOURNAMENT HOST / SITE |
|---|---|---|---|---|
| 1983–84 | Chattanooga | Chattanooga | Tina Chairs, UTC | Chattanooga |
| 1984–85 | Chattanooga & Marshall (tie) | Chattanooga | Chris McClure, UTC | ETSU |
| 1985–86 | Chattanooga & Marshall (tie) | Chattanooga | Regina Kirk, UTC | Appalachian State |
| 1986–87 | Appalachian State & Marshall (tie) | Appalachian State | Valorie Whiteside, App State | Western Carolina |
| 1987–88 | Appalachian State & Marshall (tie) | Appalachian State | Valorie Whiteside, App State | Marshall |
| 1988–89 | Appalachian State & Marshall (tie) | Chattanooga | Janice Rhynehardt, Furman & Nancy Smith, UTC (tie) | ETSU |
| 1989–90 | Furman | Appalachian State | Shannon Thomas, App State | ETSU |
| 1990–91 | Chattanooga | Appalachian State | Nicole Hopson, ETSU | ETSU |
| 1991–92 | Chattanooga & Furman (tie) | Chattanooga | Kim Brown, UTC | ETSU |
| 1992–93 | Furman | Georgia Southern | Janice Johnson, GSU | ETSU |

*Chattanooga's Alex Anderson, pictured in a 2008 NCAA Tournament game, was the first Southern Conference player chosen in the WNBA draft. (University of Tennessee at Chattanooga Athletics)*

| YEAR | REGULAR SEASON CHAMPION | TOURNAMENT CHAMPION | TOURNAMENT MOST OUTSTANDING PLAYER | TOURNAMENT HOST / SITE |
|---|---|---|---|---|
| 1993–94 | Georgia Southern | Georgia Southern | Rushia Brown, Furman | Furman |
| 1994–95 | ETSU | Furman | DeShawne Blocker, ETSU | Asheville, NC |
| 1995–96 | Appalachian State | Appalachian State | Stephanie Wine, Marshall | Greensboro, NC |
| 1996–97 | Furman | Marshall | Keri Simmons, Marshall | Greensboro, NC |
| 1997–98 | Georgia Southern | UNCG | Telly Hall, GSU | Greensboro, NC |
| 1998–99 | UNCG | Appalachian State | Beth Schoolfield, App State | Greensboro, NC |
| 1999–2000 | Chattanooga | Furman | Brianne Dodgen, UNCG | Greenville, SC |
| 2000–01 | Chattanooga & Georgia Southern (tie) | Chattanooga | ChoRhonda Gwaltney, UNCG | Greenville, SC |
| 2001–02 | Chattanooga & UNCG (tie) | Chattanooga | Miranda Warfield, UTC | Charleston, SC |
| 2002–03 | Chattanooga | Chattanooga | Miranda Warfield, UTC | Charleston, SC |

*A Proud Athletic History: 100 Years of the Southern Conference*

| YEAR | REGULAR SEASON CHAMPION | TOURNAMENT CHAMPION | TOURNAMENT MOST OUTSTANDING PLAYER | TOURNAMENT HOST / SITE |
| --- | --- | --- | --- | --- |
| 2003–04 | Chattanooga | Chattanooga | Katasha Brown, UTC | Charleston, SC |
| 2004–05 | Chattanooga | Western Carolina | Jennifer Gardner, WCU | Chattanooga |
| 2005–06 | Chattanooga | Chattanooga | Tiffani Roberson, UTC | N. Charleston, SC |
| 2006–07 | Chattanooga & Western Carolina (tie) | Chattanooga | Alex Anderson, UTC | N. Charleston, SC |
| 2007–08 | Chattanooga | Chattanooga | Alex Anderson, UTC | N. Charleston, SC |
| 2008–09 | Chattanooga | Western Carolina | Brooke Johnson, WCU | Chattanooga |
| 2009–10 | Chattanooga | Chattanooga | Shanara Hollinquest, UTC | Charlotte, NC |
| 2010–11 | Appalachian State | Samford | Savannah Hill, Samford | Chattanooga |
| 2011–12 | Appalachian State & Davidson (tie) | Samford | Shelby Campbell, Samford | Asheville, NC |
| 2012–13 | Chattanooga | Chattanooga | Ashlen Dewart, UTC | Asheville, NC |
| 2013–14 | Chattanooga | Chattanooga | Taylor Hall, UTC | Asheville, NC |
| 2014–15 | Chattanooga | Chattanooga | Jasmine Joyner, UTC | Asheville, NC |
| 2015–16 | Chattanooga & Mercer (tie) | Chattanooga | Alicia Payne, UTC | Asheville, NC |
| 2016–17 | Chattanooga & Mercer (tie) | Chattanooga | Jasmine Joyner, UTC | Asheville, NC |
| 2017–18 | Mercer | Mercer | Kahlia Lawrence, Mercer | Asheville, NC |
| 2018–19 | Mercer | Mercer | KeKe Calloway, Mercer | Asheville, NC |

# BOXING

| YEAR | REGULAR SEASON CHAMPION | TOURNAMENT CHAMPION | TOURNAMENT MOST OUTSTANDING PLAYER | TOURNAMENT HOST / SITE |
|------|------|------|------|------|
| 1927 | — | Virginia | — | Virginia |
| 1928 | — | North Carolina | — | Virginia |
| 1929 | — | North Carolina | — | Virginia |
| 1930 | — | Florida | — | Virginia |
| 1931 | — | Virginia | — | Virginia |
| 1932 | — | Virginia | — | Virginia |
| 1933 | — | Virginia | — | Virginia |
| 1934 | — | Virginia | — | Virginia |
| 1935 | — | Virginia | — | Virginia |
| 1936 | — | Virginia | — | Virginia |
| 1937 | — | Maryland | — | Maryland |
| 1938 | — | Clemson | — | Maryland |
| 1939 | — | Maryland | — | South Carolina |

*Memorial Gym on the University of Virginia campus hosted the first ten Southern Conference boxing tournaments, including this one, circa 1928. (Albert and Shirley Small Special Collections Library, University of Virginia)*

*Aaron Templeton (52) and Ryan Adams (48) lead a Furman contingent in the 2018 cross country championship won by the Paladins. (Todd Drexler, SoCon Photos)*

## MEN'S CROSS COUNTRY

| YEAR | MEET CHAMPION | MEET INDIVIDUAL CHAMPION | TOURNAMENT HOST / SITE |
|------|---------------|--------------------------|------------------------|
| 1926 | North Carolina | Galen Elliott, UNC | Georgia |
| 1927 | North Carolina | Galen Elliott, UNC | North Carolina |
| 1928 | North Carolina | Bob Young, Georgia | Georgia Tech |
| 1929 | North Carolina | Bob Young, Georgia | North Carolina |
| 1930 | VMI | Ham Smith & H. A. Wise, VMI (tie) | North Carolina |
| 1931 | North Carolina | Clarence Jensen, UNC | North Carolina |
| 1932 | Duke | Bob Bird & Jerry Bray, Duke (tie) | North Carolina |
| 1933 | Duke | Meceslaus Dunaj, W & L | North Carolina |
| 1934 | North Carolina | Ed McRae, UNC | North Carolina |
| 1935 | Duke | Bill Morse, Duke | North Carolina |
| 1936 | North Carolina | Bill Morse, Duke | North Carolina |

| YEAR | MEET CHAMPION | MEET INDIVIDUAL CHAMPION | TOURNAMENT HOST / SITE |
|------|---------------|--------------------------|------------------------|
| 1937 | North Carolina | Bill Hendrix, UNC | North Carolina |
| 1938 | North Carolina | Bill Hendrix, UNC | North Carolina |
| 1939 | North Carolina | Fred Hardy, UNC | North Carolina |
| 1940 | North Carolina | Tommy Fields, Maryland | Maryland |
| 1941 | North Carolina | Wendell Lockwood, Duke | Maryland |
| 1942–45 *No championship conducted due to war.* | | | |
| 1946 | North Carolina | Jimmy Miller, UNC | North Carolina |
| 1947 | Maryland | Bob Palmer, Maryland | Maryland |
| 1948 | Maryland | Bob Palmer, Maryland | Maryland |
| 1949 | Maryland | Bob Palmer, Maryland | Maryland |
| 1950 | Maryland | Clyde Garrison, NCSU | North Carolina State |
| 1951 | North Carolina State | Clyde Garrison, NCSU | Duke |
| 1952 | North Carolina State | Buzz Sawyer, NCSU | Richmond |
| 1953 | West Virginia | Russell Thoburn, WVU | West Virginia |
| 1954 | VMI | Ben Angle, VMI | William & Mary |
| 1955 | William & Mary | Dave Pitkethly, VMI | Davidson |
| 1956 | William & Mary | Dave Pitkethly, VMI | Lexington, VA |
| 1957 | William & Mary | Bob DeTombe, W&M | West Virginia |
| 1958 | VMI | Bob DeTombe, W&M | Furman |
| 1959 | VMI | Louis Castagnola, Va. Tech | Richmond |
| 1960 | VMI | Louis Castagnola, Va. Tech | William & Mary |
| 1961 | Furman | Coppley Vickers, Furman | VMI |
| 1962 | West Virginia | Dennis Patterson, Furman | The Citadel |
| 1963 | William & Mary | Jim Johnson, W&M | Virginia Tech |
| 1964 | William & Mary | Jim Johnson, W&M | Davidson |
| 1965 | Furman | Jim Johnson, W&M | Davidson |
| 1966 | William & Mary | Terry Donnelly, W&M | Furman |
| 1967 | William & Mary | Terry Donnelly, W&M | Richmond |
| 1968 | William & Mary | George Davis, W&M | East Carolina |
| 1969 | William & Mary | Howell Michael, W&M | William & Mary |
| 1970 | William & Mary | Ron Martin, W&M | VMI |
| 1971 | William & Mary | Ron Martin, W&M | Charleston, SC |
| 1972 | William & Mary | Bill Louv, W&M | Davidson |
| 1973 | William & Mary | Ron Martin, W&M | Furman |

| YEAR | MEET CHAMPION | MEET INDIVIDUAL CHAMPION | TOURNAMENT HOST / SITE |
|------|---------------|--------------------------|------------------------|
| 1974 | William & Mary | Reggie Clark, W&M | William & Mary |
| 1975 | William & Mary | Mac Collins & Chris Tulou, W&M (tie) | East Carolina |
| 1976 | Furman | Mike Ellington, W&M | Blowing Rock, NC |
| 1977 | Marshall | Rex Wiggins, VMI | VMI |
| 1978 | ETSU | Adrian Leek, ETSU | Charleston, SC |
| 1979 | ETSU | Louis Kenny, ETSU | Davidson |
| 1980 | ETSU | Adrian Leek, ETSU | Furman |
| 1981 | ETSU | Dennis Stark, ETSU | Marshall |
| 1982 | ETSU | Dennis Stark, ETSU | Western Carolina |
| 1983 | ETSU | Dennis Stark, ETSU | Appalachian State |
| 1984 | ETSU | Brian Dunne, ETSU | VMI |
| 1985 | ETSU | Brian Dunne, ETSU | Charleston, SC |
| 1986 | Marshall | David Tabor, Marshall | Chattanooga |
| 1987 | Appalachian State | Shamus Hynes, ETSU | Davidson |
| 1988 | ETSU | Thomas O'Gara, ETSU | Furman |
| 1989 | Appalachian State & ETSU (tie) | James Hynes, ETSU | Marshall |
| 1990 | ETSU | Seamus Power, ETSU | Western Carolina |
| 1991 | ETSU | Seamus Power, ETSU | Blowing Rock, NC |
| 1992 | ETSU | Seamus Power, ETSU | VMI |
| 1993 | Appalachian State | Seamus Power, ETSU | Furman |
| 1994 | Appalachian State | Tommy Holland, App State | Chattanooga |
| 1995 | ETSU | Derek Murphy, ETSU | Furman |
| 1996 | ETSU | Nic Crider, UTC | Western Carolina |
| 1997 | Appalachian State | Nic Crider, UTC | Georgia Southern |
| 1998 | Chattanooga | Nic Crider, UTC | Davidson |
| 1999 | Chattanooga | Brent Ferrell, Davidson | VMI |
| 2000 | Appalachian State | Ryan Kendall, UTC | Appalachian State |
| 2001 | Appalachian State | Ryan Kendall, UTC | Charleston, SC |
| 2002 | Appalachian State | Gediminas Banevicius, UTC | Charleston, SC |
| 2003 | Chattanooga | Steven Kocsis, UTC | Davidson |
| 2004 | Chattanooga | Steven Kocsis, UTC | Furman |
| 2005 | Appalachian State | Ian Mayne, UTC | Georgia Southern |
| 2006 | Appalachian State | Phil Mitchell, App State | Chattanooga |
| 2007 | Appalachian State | Brian Deal, App State | Western Carolina |

| YEAR | MEET CHAMPION | MEET INDIVIDUAL CHAMPION | TOURNAMENT HOST / SITE |
|---|---|---|---|
| 2008 | Appalachian State | Emmanuel Kirwa, UTC | Spartanburg, SC |
| 2009 | Appalachian State | Emmanuel Kirwa, UTC | Elon |
| 2010 | Appalachian State | Emmanuel Kirwa, UTC | Appalachian State |
| 2011 | UNCG* | Paul Chelimo, UNCG | Charleston, SC |
| 2012 | Appalachian State | Paul Chelimo, UNCG | Charleston, SC |
| 2013 | Furman | Paul Chelimo, UNCG | Samford |
| 2014 | Furman | Tripp Hurt, Furman | Kernersville, NC |
| 2015 | Furman | Arsene Guillorel, Samford | Furman |
| 2016 | Furman | Frank Lara, Furman | Chattanooga |
| 2017 | Furman | Aaron Templeton, Furman | Spartanburg, SC |
| 2018 | Furman | Aaron Templeton, Furman | Western Carolina |

*Championship subsequently vacated due to NCAA violations.*

## WOMEN'S CROSS COUNTRY

| | | | |
|---|---|---|---|
| 1985 | ETSU | Beth Ruggles, App State | Charleston, SC |
| 1986 | Appalachian State | Michelle Crow, App State | Chattanooga |
| 1987 | Appalachian State | Beth Ruggles, App State | Davidson |
| 1988 | Appalachian State | Whitney Ball, App State | Furman |
| 1989 | Appalachian State | Whitney Ball, App State | Marshall |
| 1990 | Appalachian State | Cate Pichon, Furman | Western Carolina |
| 1991 | Appalachian State | Cate Pichon, Furman | Blowing Rock, NC |
| 1992 | Appalachian State | Carrie Hogg, App State | VMI |
| 1993 | Furman | Heather VandeBrake, Furman | Charleston, SC |
| 1994 | Furman | Heather VandeBrake, Furman | Chattanooga |
| 1995 | Furman | Heather VandeBrake, Furman | Furman |
| 1996 | Appalachian State | Lynn Kepper-Hudson, Furman | Western Carolina |
| 1997 | Chattanooga | Catherine Berry, ETSU | Georgia Southern |
| 1998 | Chattanooga | Mary Jayne Harrelson, App State | Davidson |
| 1999 | ETSU | Mary Jayne Harrelson, App State | VMI |
| 2000 | Furman | Mary Jayne Harrelson, App State | Appalachian State |
| 2001 | Chattanooga | Gina Recher, UTC | Charleston, SC |

*Participants leave the starting line in the 2016 women's cross country championship at Chattanooga. (Jimmy Burgess, SoCon Photos)*

| YEAR | MEET CHAMPION | MEET INDIVIDUAL CHAMPION | TOURNAMENT HOST / SITE |
|------|---------------|--------------------------|------------------------|
| 2002 | Appalachian State | Shannon Wommack, UTC | Charleston, SC |
| 2003 | Davidson | Katie Sujkowski, App State | Davidson |
| 2004 | Chattanooga | Shannon Wommack, UTC | Furman |
| 2005 | Davidson | Shannon Wommack, UTC | Georgia Southern |
| 2006 | Chattanooga | Lanni Marchant, UTC | Chattanooga |
| 2007 | Chattanooga | Kathleen Turchin, UTC | Western Carolina |
| 2008 | Chattanooga | Megan Lordi, Furman | Spartanburg, SC |
| 2009 | Samford | Brittney Caudle, App State | Elon |
| 2010 | Samford | Ashley Schnell, UNCG | Appalachian State |
| 2011 | UNCG | Ashley Schnell, UNCG | Charleston, SC |
| 2012 | Appalachian State | Lauren D'Alessio, Samford | Mt. Pleasant, SC |
| 2013 | Furman | Teghan Henderson, UTC | Samford |
| 2014 | Furman | Allie Buchalski, Furman | Kernersville, NC |
| 2015 | Furman | Allie Buchalski, Furman | Furman |
| 2016 | Furman | Karisa Nelson, Samford | Chattanooga |
| 2017 | Furman | Allie Buchalski, Furman | Spartanburg, SC |
| 2018 | Furman | Hannah Steelman, Wofford | Western Carolina |

*Devlin Hodges, passing against the Georgia Bulldogs, set numerous school and conference records in his four years at Samford. (Samford University Athletics)*

## FOOTBALL

| YEAR | REGULAR SEASON CHAMPION | YEAR | REGULAR SEASON CHAMPION |
|------|-------------------------|------|-------------------------|
| 1922 | North Carolina | 1939 | Duke |
| 1923 | Washington & Lee | 1940 | Clemson |
| 1924 | Alabama | 1941 | Duke |
| 1925 | Alabama | 1942 | William & Mary |
| 1926 | Alabama | 1943 | Duke |
| 1927 | Georgia Tech | 1944 | Duke |
| 1928 | Georgia Tech | 1945 | Duke |
| 1929 | Tulane | 1946 | North Carolina |
| 1930 | Alabama | 1947 | William & Mary |
| 1931 | Tulane | 1948 | Clemson |
| 1932 | Tennessee | 1949 | North Carolina |
| 1933 | Duke | 1950 | Washington & Lee |
| 1934 | Washington & Lee | 1951 | Maryland & VMI (tie) |
| 1935 | Duke | 1952 | Duke |
| 1936 | Duke | 1953 | West Virginia |
| 1937 | Maryland | 1954 | West Virginia |
| 1938 | Duke | 1955 | West Virginia |

| YEAR | REGULAR SEASON CHAMPION | YEAR | REGULAR SEASON CHAMPION |
|---|---|---|---|
| 1956 | West Virginia | 1989 | Furman |
| 1957 | VMI | 1990 | Furman |
| 1958 | West Virginia | 1991 | Appalachian State |
| 1959 | VMI | 1992 | The Citadel |
| 1960 | VMI | 1993 | Georgia Southern |
| 1961 | The Citadel | 1994 | Marshall |
| 1962 | VMI | 1995 | Appalachian State |
| 1963 | Virginia Tech | 1996 | Marshall |
| 1964 | West Virginia | 1997 | Georgia Southern |
| 1965 | West Virginia | 1998 | Georgia Southern |
| 1966 | East Carolina & William & Mary (tie) | 1999 | Appalachian State, Furman & Georgia Southern (tie) |
| 1967 | West Virginia | 2000 | Georgia Southern |
| 1968 | Richmond | 2001 | Furman & Georgia Southern (tie) |
| 1969 | Davidson & Richmond (tie) | 2002 | Georgia Southern |
| 1970 | William & Mary | 2003 | Wofford |
| 1971 | Richmond | 2004 | Furman & Georgia Southern (tie) |
| 1972 | East Carolina | 2005 | Appalachian State |
| 1973 | East Carolina | 2006 | Appalachian State |
| 1974 | VMI | 2007 | Appalachian State & Wofford (tie) |
| 1975 | Richmond | 2008 | Appalachian State |
| 1976 | East Carolina | 2009 | Appalachian State |
| 1977 | Chattanooga & VMI (tie) | 2010 | Appalachian State & Wofford (tie) |
| 1978 | Chattanooga & Furman (tie) | 2011 | Georgia Southern |
| 1979 | Chattanooga | 2012 | Appalachian State, Georgia Southern & Wofford (tie) |
| 1980 | Furman | 2013 | Chattanooga, Furman & Samford* (tie) |
| 1981 | Furman | 2014 | Chattanooga |
| 1982 | Furman | 2015 | Chattanooga & The Citadel (tie) |
| 1983 | Furman | 2016 | The Citadel |
| 1984 | Chattanooga | 2017 | Wofford |
| 1985 | Furman | 2018 | ETSU, Furman & Wofford (tie) |
| 1986 | Appalachian State | | |
| 1987 | Appalachian State | | |
| 1988 | Furman & Marshall (tie) | | |

*Championship subsequently vacated due to NCAA violations.*

# MEN'S GOLF

| YEAR | TOURNAMENT CHAMPION | TOURNAMENT MEDALIST | TOURNAMENT HOST / SITE |
|------|---------------------|---------------------|------------------------|
| 1930 | Alabama | Sam Perry, Alabama | CC of Birmingham, Birmingham, AL |
| 1931 | Tulane | Albert Wheeler, Vanderbilt | Athens CC, Athens, GA |
| 1932 | North Carolina | Jesse Rainwater, Tulane | Athens CC, Athens, GA |
| 1933 | Duke | Roger Peacock, Duke | Sedgefield CC, Greensboro, NC |
| 1934 | Washington & Lee | Cliff Perry, Duke | Cascades CC, Hot Springs, VA |
| 1935 | Duke | Erwin Laxton, North Carolina | Sedgefield CC, Greensboro, NC |
| 1936 | Duke | Cliff Perry, Duke | Cascades CC, Hot Springs, VA |
| 1937 | Duke | Johnny Morris, Duke | Pinehurst No. 2, Pinehurst, NC |
| 1938 | Duke | Skip Alexander, Duke | Cascades CC, Hot Springs, VA |
| 1939 | Duke | Skip Alexander, Duke | Pinehurst No. 2, Pinehurst, NC |
| 1940 | Duke | Henry Russell, Duke | Sedgefield CC, Greensboro, NC |
| 1941 | Duke | Grover Poole, Duke | Cascades CC, Hot Springs, VA |
| 1942 | Duke | Grover Poole, Duke | Old Town Club, Winston-Salem, NC |
| 1943–46 | *No tournament held due to war.* | | |
| 1947 | North Carolina | Jimmy McNair, Duke & Dick Doeschler, North Carolina (tie) | Old Town Club, Winston-Salem, NC |
| 1948 | Duke | Arnold Palmer, Wake Forest | Pinehurst No. 2, Pinehurst, NC |
| 1949 | Duke | Arnold Palmer, Wake Forest | Old Town Club, Winston-Salem, NC |
| 1950 | Wake Forest | Harvie Ward, North Carolina | Old Town Club, Winston-Salem, NC |
| 1951 | Duke | Lou McLennan, Duke | Cascades CC, Hot Springs, VA |
| 1952 | North Carolina | Tommy Langley, North Carolina | Old Town Club, Winston-Salem, NC |
| 1953 | North Carolina | Jim Ferree, North Carolina | Old Town Club, Winston-Salem, NC |
| 1954 | Davidson | Bill Wood, VMI | James River GC, Lexington, VA |
| 1955 | Washington & Lee | Teddy Kerr, Washington & Lee | Danville CC, Danville, VA |
| 1956 | Virginia Tech | Harry Devine, The Citadel & Maurice Tanner, Virginia Tech (tie) | Danville CC, Danville, VA |
| 1957 | George Washington | Jay Randolph, George Washington | Danville CC, Danville, VA |
| 1958 | Davidson & George Washington (tie) | Bill Dennis, Davidson | Danville CC, Danville, VA |
| 1959 | George Washington | Heyward Sullivan, Furman | Woodmont CC, Bethesda, MD |
| 1960 | Davidson | Verner Stanley, Davidson | Mid Pines CC, Southern Pines, NC |
| 1961 | Virginia Tech | Dick Horne, The Citadel & Bob Haney, George Washington (tie) | Richmond CC, Richmond, VA |

*Adrian Meronk of ETSU won the 2016 SoCon Men's Golf Championship at Pinehurst No. 9. (Todd Drexler, SoCon Photos)*

| YEAR | TOURNAMENT CHAMPION | TOURNAMENT MEDALIST | TOURNAMENT HOST / SITE |
|---|---|---|---|
| 1962 | Virginia Tech | Walter Smith, Furman | Dunes GC, Myrtle Beach, SC |
| 1963 | Virginia Tech | Bill Etheridge, The Citadel | Dunes GC, Myrtle Beach, SC |
| 1964 | The Citadel | Bill Etheridge, The Citadel & Charles Collett, George Washington (tie) | Dunes GC, Myrtle Beach, SC |
| 1965 | Virginia Tech | Neff McClary, Virginia Tech | Cascades CC, Hot Springs, VA |
| 1966 | Davidson | Doug McKeever, Davidson | CC of NC, Southern Pines, NC |
| 1967 | Davidson | Mike Spann, Davidson | Dunes GC, Myrtle Beach, SC |
| 1968 | Davidson | David Joesbury, The Citadel | Dunes GC, Myrtle Beach, SC |
| 1969 | East Carolina | David Strawn, Furman | Pinehurst No. 2, Pinehurst, NC |
| 1970 | Furman | David Strawn, Furman | CC of NC, Southern Pines, NC |
| 1971 | East Carolina | Lynwood Edwards, The Citadel | Quail Ridge GC, Sanford, NC |
| 1972 | East Carolina | Eddie Pinnix, East Carolina | Quail Ridge GC, Sanford, NC |
| 1973 | Furman | Rusty Boyd, Davidson | CC of SC, Florence, SC |

| YEAR | TOURNAMENT CHAMPION | TOURNAMENT MEDALIST | TOURNAMENT HOST / SITE |
|---|---|---|---|
| 1974 | Appalachian State | Dean Sigmon, App State | CC of SC, Florence, SC |
| 1975 | Furman | Ken Ezell, Furman | CC of SC, Florence, SC |
| 1976 | Furman | Ken Ezell, Furman | CC of SC, Florence, SC |
| 1977 | Furman | Ken Ezell, Furman | CC of SC, Florence, SC |
| 1978 | Appalachian State | Donnie Green, Chattanooga | CC of SC, Florence, SC |
| 1979 | ETSU | Terry May, ETSU | Pinehurst No. 2, Pinehurst, NC |
| 1980 | ETSU | Mike Hulbert, ETSU | Pinehurst No. 2, Pinehurst, NC |
| 1981 | ETSU | Eric Lawhon, ETSU | Raintree CC, Charlotte, NC |
| 1982 | ETSU | Steve Munson, ETSU | Raintree CC, Charlotte, NC |
| 1983 | ETSU | Brad Faxon, Furman | Raintree CC, Charlotte, NC |
| 1984 | Furman | Eddie Kirby, Furman | Raintree CC, Charlotte, NC |
| 1985 | Furman | Gary Rusnak, Marshall | Raintree CC, Charlotte, NC |
| 1986 | Furman | Tom Kies, Marshall | Raintree CC, Charlotte, NC |
| 1987 | Chattanooga | Kelly Leonhardt, Western Carolina | Raintree CC, Charlotte, NC |
| 1988 | Furman | Todd White, Furman | Raintree CC, Charlotte, NC |
| 1989 | ETSU | Bobby Gage, ETSU | Raintree CC, Charlotte, NC |
| 1990 | ETSU | Rex Kuramoto, ETSU | Raintree CC, Charlotte, NC |
| 1991 | ETSU | Eric Shaffer, Marshall | Raintree CC, Charlotte, NC |
| 1992 | ETSU | Chris Stutts, ETSU | Raintree CC, Charlotte, NC |
| 1993 | Furman | Nick Cifelli, Furman | Raintree CC, Charlotte, NC |
| 1994 | ETSU | Garrett Willis, ETSU | Council Fire GC, Chattanooga, TN |
| 1995 | ETSU | Neil Gibson, Georgia Southern | Forest Heights CC, Statesboro, GA |
| 1996 | ETSU | Garrett Willis, ETSU | Stoney Creek GC, Greensboro, NC |
| 1997 | Furman | Jordan Byrd, Furman | Stoney Creek GC, Greensboro, NC |
| 1998 | ETSU | Rion Moore, Wofford | Carolina CC, Spartanburg, SC |
| 1999 | ETSU | Chris Wisler, ETSU | CC of Sapphire Valley, Sapphire, NC |
| 2000 | ETSU | Pat Beste, ETSU | Lexington GC, Lexington, VA |
| 2001 | ETSU | William McGirt, Wofford | Chattanooga GC, Chattanooga, TN |
| 2002 | College of Charleston | Daniel Brunson, Col. of Charleston | Furman Univ. GC, Greenville, SC |
| 2003 | Georgia Southern | Bruce McDonald, Col. of Charleston | Forest Heights CC, Statesboro, GA |
| 2004 | Furman | Matt Davidson, Furman | The Ridges GC, Jonesborough, TN |
| 2005 | ETSU | Rhys Davies, ETSU | River Run CC, Davidson, NC |
| 2006 | Georgia Southern | Matt Cook, Western Carolina | Links at Stono Ferry, Hollywood, SC |
| 2007 | Chattanooga | J. D. Bass, UNCG | CC of SC, Florence, SC |

| YEAR | TOURNAMENT CHAMPION | TOURNAMENT MEDALIST | TOURNAMENT HOST / SITE |
|---|---|---|---|
| 2008 | Chattanooga | Matt Cook, Western Carolina | CC of SC, Florence, SC |
| 2009 | Chattanooga | Drew Lethem, Georgia Southern | CC of SC, Florence, SC |
| 2010 | Furman | Austin Reeves, Furman | CC of SC, Florence, SC |
| 2011 | Georgia Southern | Richard Fountain, Davidson | CC of SC, Florence, SC |
| 2012 | Chattanooga | Stephan Jaeger, Chattanooga | Daniel Isl. GC, Daniel Island, SC |
| 2013 | Chattanooga | Josh Lorenzetti, Col. of Charleston | Daniel Isl. GC, Daniel Island, SC |
| 2014 | Georgia Southern | J. T. Poston, Western Carolina | National GC, Pinehurst, NC |
| 2015 | ETSU | J. T. Poston, Western Carolina | Pinehurst No. 9, Pinehurst, NC |
| 2016 | ETSU | Adrian Meronk, ETSU | Pinehurst No. 9, Pinehurst, NC |
| 2017 | ETSU | Geuntae Kim, ETSU | Pinehurst No. 9, Pinehurst, NC |
| 2018 | UNCG | Nick Lyerly, UNCG | Pinehurst No. 9, Pinehurst, NC |
| 2019 | UNCG | Shiso Go, ETSU | Pinehurst No. 9, Pinehurst, NC |

## WOMEN'S GOLF

| YEAR | TOURNAMENT CHAMPION | TOURNAMENT MEDALIST | TOURNAMENT HOST / SITE |
|---|---|---|---|
| 1994 | Furman | Caroline Peek, Furman | Furman GC, Greenville, SC |
| 1995 | Furman | Dawn Turner, Furman | Jefferson Landing GC, West Jefferson, NC |
| 1996 | Furman | Dawn Turner, Furman | Stoney Creek GC, Greensboro, NC |
| 1997 | Furman | Diana D'Alessio, Furman | Stoney Creek GC, Greensboro, NC |
| 1998 | Furman | Jen Hanna, Furman | Furman GC, Greenville, SC |
| 1999 | Furman | Lotta Jonson, UNCG | The Ridges GC, Jonesborough, TN |
| 2000 | Furman | Jennifer Perri, Furman | Patriots Point Links, Mt. Pleasant, SC |
| 2001 | Furman | Jennifer Perri, Furman | Hound Ears CC, Blowing Rock, NC |
| 2002 | Furman | Brandi Jackson, Furman | Wescott Plantation, N. Charleston, SC |
| 2003 | Western Carolina | Brandy Andersen, WCU | Waynesville GC, Waynesville, NC |
| 2004 | Furman | Sarah Johnston, Furman | Starmount Forest CC, Greensboro, NC |
| 2005 | Furman | Jenny Suh, Furman | Furman GC, Greenville, SC |
| 2006 | College of Charleston | Angie Hill, C of C | Mill Creek GC, Mebane, NC |
| 2007 | Western Carolina | Blair Lamb, Furman | Patriots Point Links, Mt. Pleasant, SC |
| 2008 | Furman | Stefanie Kenoyer, Furman | Links at Stono Ferry, Hollywood, SC |
| 2009 | Furman | Stefanie Kenoyer, Furman | Moss Creek GC, Hilton Head, SC |
| 2010 | Chattanooga | Yue Xu, Appalachian St. | Moss Creek GC, Hilton Head, SC |
| 2011 | Chattanooga | Emma de Groot, UTC | Moss Creek GC, Hilton Head, SC |

| YEAR | TOURNAMENT CHAMPION | TOURNAMENT MEDALIST | TOURNAMENT HOST / SITE |
|---|---|---|---|
| 2012 | Chattanooga | Jordan Britt, UTC | Moss Creek GC, Hilton Head, SC |
| 2013 | Chattanooga | Agathe Sauzon, UTC | Moss Creek GC, Hilton Head, SC |
| 2014 | Chattanooga | Emily McLennan, UTC | Moss Creek GC, Hilton Head, SC |
| 2015 | Furman | Taylor Totland, Furman | Club at Savannah Quarters, Pooler, GA |
| 2016 | Furman | Megan Woods, UTC | Club at Savannah Quarters, Pooler, GA |
| 2017 | Furman | Natalie Srinivasan, Furman | CC of Lexington, Lexington, SC |
| 2018 | Furman | Reona Hirai, Furman | Moss Creek GC, Hilton Head, SC |
| 2019 | Furman | Monica San Juan, UTC | Moss Creek GC, Hilton Head, SC |

*UNCG's Louisa Tichy hits a driver at the 2017 women's golf championship at the Country Club of Lexington in Lexington, SC. (SoCon Photos)*

*Left, Andrew Tien of the Air Force is defended by Richmond's Austin Cates at the 2017 SoCon Men's Lacrosse Championship Game, won by the Falcons, 9–6. (Todd Drexler, SoCon Photos); Right, Mercer's Meghan Segreti (24) and Jo Imbriani (28) battle Detroit Mercy's Kaitlyn Wandelt (17) for a loose ball at the inaugural 2018 women's lacrosse tournament. (SoCon Photos)*

## MEN'S LACROSSE

| YEAR | REGULAR SEASON CHAMPION | TOURNAMENT CHAMPION | TOURNAMENT MOST OUTSTANDING PLAYER | TOURNAMENT HOST / SITE |
|---|---|---|---|---|
| 2015 | Richmond | High Point | Austin Geisler, High Point | Richmond |
| 2016 | Air Force | Air Force | Doug Gouchoe, Air Force | Richmond |
| 2017 | Air Force, Furman & Richmond (tie) | Air Force | Brandon Jones, Air Force | Richmond |
| 2018 | High Point & Richmond (tie) | Richmond | Teddy Hatfield, Richmond | Richmond |
| 2019 | Air Force & High Point (tie) | Richmond | Jack Rusbuldt, Richmond | High Point |

## WOMEN'S LACROSSE

| 2018 | Central Michigan & Detroit Mercy (tie) | Mercer | Kelly Hagerty, Mercer | Mercer |
|---|---|---|---|---|
| 2019 | Detroit Mercy, Furman & Mercer (tie) | Mercer | Hailey Rhatigan, Mercer | Furman |

*North Georgia's Ruthanne Conner was the small-bore rifle champion in 2017, the SoCon's first rifle championship in thirty-two years. (University of North Georgia Athletics)*

## RIFLE

*Sport discontinued by conference, 1986–2016; restored, 2017.*

| YEAR | TOURNAMENT CHAMPION | TOURNAMENT INDIVIDUAL CHAMPION | TOURNAMENT HOST / SITE |
|------|--------------------|-------------------------------|------------------------|
| 1956 | Virginia Tech | D. H. Smith, The Citadel | West Virginia |
| 1957 | Virginia Tech | Dale Hoberg, Va. Tech | West Virginia |
| 1958 | Virginia Tech | Sam Morgan, Va. Tech | West Virginia |
| 1959 | The Citadel | Robert Metsker, The Citadel | West Virginia |
| 1960 | West Virginia | Bruce Meredith, WVU | Davidson |
| 1961 | The Citadel | Charles Rowan, WVU | Virginia Tech |
| 1962 | The Citadel | F. K. Dixon, The Citadel | Fort Lee, VA |
| 1963 | The Citadel | Richard Bell, The Citadel | Fort Lee, VA |
| 1964 | VMI | Steve Cook, Va. Tech | Fort Lee, VA |
| 1965 | Virginia Tech | John Writer, WVU | Fort Lee, VA |
| 1966 | West Virginia | John Writer, WVU | Fort Lee, VA |
| 1967 | West Virginia | Jerry Luh, WVU | Fort Lee, VA |
| 1968 | The Citadel | Gregory Dalton, The Citadel | Fort Lee, VA |

| YEAR | TOURNAMENT CHAMPION | TOURNAMENT INDIVIDUAL CHAMPION | TOURNAMENT HOST / SITE |
|---|---|---|---|
| 1969 | The Citadel | Donald Johnson, The Citadel | Fort Lee, VA |
| 1970 | The Citadel | No individual champion | Fort Lee, VA |
| 1971 | VMI | No individual champion | Fort Lee, VA |
| 1972 | VMI | Calvin Brown, App State | Fort Lee, VA |
| 1973 | The Citadel | Dennis Smith, App State | Fort Lee, VA |
| 1974 | The Citadel | Dennis Smith, App State | VMI |
| 1975 | Appalachian State | Edward Scarboro, App State | VMI |
| 1976 | Appalachian State | William Piatt, App State | VMI |
| 1977 | Appalachian State | William Piatt, App State | VMI |
| 1978 | Appalachian State | Paul Timberlake, App State | VMI |
| 1979 | ETSU | John Akemon, ETSU | VMI |
| 1980 | ETSU | John Duus, ETSU | VMI |
| 1981 | ETSU | Ethel-Ann Alves, ETSU | VMI |
| 1982 | ETSU | Marie Miller, ETSU | ETSU |
| 1983 | ETSU | Joe McGuigan, ETSU | VMI |
| 1984 | ETSU | Elizabeth McKay, ETSU | The Citadel |
| 1985 | ETSU | Bill Thomas, ETSU | VMI |
| 2017 | North Georgia | Ruthanne Conner, N. Georgia (small-bore rifle) Andrew Hickey, VMI (air rifle) | The Citadel |
| 2018 | North Georgia | Dakota Spivey, N. Georgia (small-bore rifle) Allison Auten, The Citadel (air rifle) | The Citadel |
| 2019 | UAB | Tobin Sanctuary, N. Georgia (small-bore rifle) Rosemary Kramer, Ga. Southern(air rifle) | Georgia Southern |

Mercer's Will Bagrou was twice selected Male Athlete of the Year in the Southern Conference. (SoCon Photos)

## MEN'S SOCCER

*No conference tournament held until 1988.*

| YEAR | REGULAR SEASON CHAMPION | TOURNAMENT CHAMPION | TOURNAMENT MOST OUTSTANDING PLAYER | TOURNAMENT HOST / SITE |
|---|---|---|---|---|
| 1966 | West Virginia | — | — | — |
| 1967 | West Virginia | — | — | — |
| 1968 | George Washington | — | — | — |
| 1969 | George Washington | — | — | — |
| 1970 | Davidson | — | — | — |
| 1971 | Davidson | — | — | — |
| 1972 | Appalachian State | — | — | — |
| 1973 | Appalachian State | — | — | — |
| 1974 | Appalachian State | — | — | — |
| 1975 | Appalachian State | — | — | — |
| 1976 | William & Mary | — | — | — |
| 1977 | Appalachian State | — | — | — |

| YEAR | REGULAR SEASON CHAMPION | TOURNAMENT CHAMPION | TOURNAMENT MOST OUTSTANDING PLAYER | TOURNAMENT HOST / SITE |
|---|---|---|---|---|
| 1978 | Appalachian State | — | — | — |
| 1979 | Appalachian State | — | — | — |
| 1980 | Appalachian State | — | — | — |
| 1981 | Appalachian State | — | — | — |
| 1982 | Appalachian State | — | — | — |
| 1983 | Furman | — | — | — |
| 1984 | Furman | — | — | — |
| 1985 | Appalachian State | — | — | — |
| 1986 | Furman | — | — | — |
| 1987 | Furman | — | — | — |
| 1988 | Furman | Furman | Rod Underwood, Furman (Off.) Russel Rankenburg, The Citadel (Def.) | Greensboro, NC |
| 1989 | Appalachian State | Furman | Andrew Burr, Furman | Greensboro, NC |
| 1990 | Furman | Appalachian State | Andy Salandy, App State | Greensboro, NC |
| 1991 | Furman | Furman | Andrew Zorovich, Furman | Greensboro, NC |
| 1992 | Furman | Davidson | Ben Hayes, Davidson | Greensboro, NC |
| 1993 | Furman | Furman | Jay Weyer, Furman | Greensboro, NC |
| 1994 | Davidson & Furman (tie) | Furman | Brian Little, Furman | Greensboro, NC |
| 1995 | Davidson & Furman (tie) | Davidson | Alex Deegan, Davidson | Davidson |
| 1996 | Furman | Furman | Ryan Higginbotham, Furman | Furman |
| 1997 | UNCG | Furman | Ryan Higginbotham, Furman | Furman |
| 1998 | Furman & UNCG (tie) | UNCG | Nathan Kipp, UNCG | Davidson |
| 1999 | Furman | Furman | Graham Seagraves, Furman | Daniel Island, SC |
| 2000 | Furman | Furman | John Barry Nusum, Furman | Coll. of Charleston |
| 2001 | Furman | Furman | Anthony Esquivel, Furman | Coll. of Charleston |
| 2002 | Furman | — | — | Coll. of Charleston |

*(Tournament unable to be completed due to weather.)*

| YEAR | REGULAR SEASON CHAMPION | TOURNAMENT CHAMPION | TOURNAMENT MOST OUTSTANDING PLAYER | TOURNAMENT HOST / SITE |
|---|---|---|---|---|
| 2003 | Davidson | Davidson | Nick Hansell, Davidson | Coll. of Charleston |
| 2004 | UNCG | Coll. of Charleston | Ben Hollingsworth, C of C | Daniel Island, SC |
| 2005 | Davidson & UNCG (tie) | UNCG | Henning Jonasson, UNCG | Daniel Island, SC |
| 2006 | UNCG | UNCG | Henning Jonasson, UNCG | Furman |
| 2007 | Furman | Furman | Bryan Amos, Furman | UNCG |
| 2008 | Elon | UNCG* | Joe Burnett, UNCG | Davidson |
| 2009 | Wofford | Wofford | Wilson Hood, Wofford | Wofford |
| 2010 | Coll. of Charleston, Furman & UNCG* (tie) | UNCG* | Matt Strine, UNCG | Coll. of Charleston |

| YEAR | REGULAR SEASON CHAMPION | TOURNAMENT CHAMPION | TOURNAMENT MOST OUTSTANDING PLAYER | TOURNAMENT HOST / SITE |
|---|---|---|---|---|
| 2011 | UNCG* | Elon | Nick Millington, Elon | Appalachian State |
| 2012 | Elon | Elon | Gabe Latigue, Elon | Cary, NC |
| 2013 | Wofford | Elon | Jason Waterman, Elon | Furman |
| 2014 | Mercer | Furman | Clint Ritter, Furman | UNCG |
| 2015 | UNCG | Furman | Sven Lissek, Furman | ETSU |
| 2016 | ETSU | Mercer | Jeremy Booth, Mercer | UNCG |
| 2017 | ETSU | Mercer | Jeremy Booth, Mercer | Furman |
| 2018 | Mercer | Furman | Laurence Wyke, Furman | ETSU |

*Championship subsequently vacated due to NCAA violations.*

## WOMEN'S SOCCER

| YEAR | REGULAR SEASON CHAMPION | TOURNAMENT CHAMPION | TOURNAMENT MOST OUTSTANDING PLAYER | TOURNAMENT HOST / SITE |
|---|---|---|---|---|
| 1994 | Davidson | Davidson | Shannon Lowrance, Davidson | Greensboro, NC |
| 1995 | Furman | Davidson | Claudia Lombard, Davidson | Davidson |
| 1996 | Davidson | Davidson | Katherine Cornelius, Davidson | Davidson |
| 1997 | UNCG | UNCG | Kim Rosenberg, UNCG | Davidson |
| 1998 | UNCG | UNCG | Ali Lord, UNCG | Furman |
| 1999 | Furman | Furman | Kaye Brownlee, Furman | UNCG |
| 2000 | Furman | UNCG | Lynsey McLean, UNCG | Mt. Pleasant, SC |
| 2001 | Furman, UNCG & Western Carolina (tie) | UNCG | Kathryn Clewley, UNCG | Furman |
| 2002 | Furman | Furman | Andrea Morrison, Furman | UNCG |
| 2003 | Furman | UNCG | Rakel Logadottir, UNCG | UNCG |
| 2004 | UNCG | Furman | Andrea Morrison, Furman | UNCG |
| 2005 | Davidson | Western Carolina | Alesha Row, WCU | Furman |
| 2006 | UNCG | UNCG | Shannon Donovan, UNCG | Western Carolina |
| 2007 | UNCG | Furman | Rachel Fry, Furman | Davidson |
| 2008 | UNCG* | Western Carolina | Caitlin Williams, WCU | Mt. Pleasant, SC |
| 2009 | UNCG* | Davidson | Amanda Flink, Davidson | UNCG |
| 2010 | UNCG* | UNCG* | Kelsey Kearney, UNCG | Western Carolina |
| 2011 | Samford | Samford | Shanika Thomas, Samford | UNCG |
| 2012 | UNCG | Georgia Southern | Katie Merson, GSU | Samford |
| 2013 | Furman | Furman | Stephanie DeVita, Furman | Wofford |

| YEAR | REGULAR SEASON CHAMPION | TOURNAMENT CHAMPION | TOURNAMENT MOST OUTSTANDING PLAYER | TOURNAMENT HOST / SITE |
|---|---|---|---|---|
| 2014 | Samford | Mercer | Maggie Cropp, Mercer | Western Carolina |
| 2015 | Samford | Furman | Stephanie DeVita, Furman | Furman |
| 2016 | Samford | Samford | Anna Allen, Samford | ETSU |
| 2017 | Furman & Samford (tie) | UNCG | Regan Lehman, UNCG | Samford |
| 2018 | Samford | UNCG | Heida Vidarsdottir, UNCG | Mercer |

*Championship subsequently vacated due to NCAA violations.*

Quiqui Hita looks to set up a shot on goal for UNCG in the 2018 tournament, won by the Spartans. (Todd Drexler, SoCon Photos)

*Excited teammates greet Chattanooga's Amanda Beltran after her home run in the 2018 softball tournament. (Carlos Morales, SoCon Photos)*

## SOFTBALL

| YEAR | REGULAR SEASON CHAMPION | TOURNAMENT CHAMPION | TOURNAMENT MOST OUTSTANDING PLAYER | TOURNAMENT HOST / SITE |
|---|---|---|---|---|
| 1994 | Furman | Furman | Kim Currier, Furman | Furman |
| 1995 | Chattanooga & Furman (tie) | Marshall | Cristy Waring, Marshall | Furman |
| 1996 | Georgia Southern | Chattanooga | April Miller, UTC | Georgia Southern |
| 1997 | Chattanooga | Chattanooga | J. D. Staton, UTC | Marshall |
| 1998 | Chattanooga | Chattanooga | Amy Robertson, UTC | Chattanooga |
| 1999 | Chattanooga | Georgia Southern | Aimee Littlejohn, GSU | Coll. of Charleston |
| 2000 | Chattanooga | Chattanooga | Connie Ness, UTC | UNCG |
| 2001 | Chattanooga | Chattanooga | Angela Brewer, UTC | Chattanooga |
| 2002 | Chattanooga | Chattanooga | Awbrey Winckler, UTC | Chattanooga |
| 2003 | Coll. of Charleston | Chattanooga | Melissa Ramirez, UTC | Chattanooga |
| 2004 | Chattanooga | Chattanooga | Melissa Ramirez, UTC | Chattanooga |

*A Proud Athletic History: 100 Years of the Southern Conference*

| YEAR | REGULAR SEASON CHAMPION | TOURNAMENT CHAMPION | TOURNAMENT MOST OUTSTANDING PLAYER | TOURNAMENT HOST / SITE |
|---|---|---|---|---|
| 2005 | Coll. of Charleston | Coll. of Charleston | Rachael Stern, C of C | Coll. of Charleston |
| 2006 | Western Carolina | Georgia Southern | Shanita Black, GSU | Chattanooga |
| 2007 | Chattanooga | Furman | Amber Kiser, Furman | UNCG |
| 2008 | Chattanooga | Chattanooga | Brooke Loudermilk, UTC | Coll. of Charleston |
| 2009 | Chattanooga | Chattanooga | Brianna Streetmon, GSU | Chattanooga |
| 2010 | Chattanooga | Elon | Amber Harrell, UNCG | Chattanooga |
| 2011 | Chattanooga | Chattanooga | Sara Poteat, UTC | Georgia Southern |
| 2012 | Georgia Southern | Georgia Southern | Sarah Purvis, GSU | Appalachian State |
| 2013 | Appalachian State | Georgia Southern | Raeanne Hanks, UNCG | UNCG |
| 2014 | Georgia Southern | Chattanooga | Katie Henderson, UTC | UNCG |
| 2015 | Chattanooga | Chattanooga | Anyssa Robles, UTC | Chattanooga |
| 2016 | Samford | Samford | Mollie Hanson, Samford | UNCG |
| 2017 | Furman & UNCG (tie) | ETSU | Lindsey Fadnek, ETSU | Chattanooga |
| 2018 | UNCG | UNCG | Alicia Bazonski, UNCG | UNCG |
| 2019 | UNCG | Chattanooga | Stephanie Bryden, UNCG | Chattanooga |

## MEN'S SWIMMING AND DIVING

| YEAR | CHAMPION | MEET HOST / SITE | YEAR | CHAMPION | MEET HOST / SITE |
|---|---|---|---|---|---|
| 1930 | Georgia Tech | Georgia Tech | 1942 | North Carolina | North Carolina |
| 1931 | Georgia Tech | Georgia Tech | 1943 | North Carolina | Washington & Lee |
| 1932 | Georgia Tech | Georgia Tech | 1944–1946 | *No championship held due to war.* | |
| 1933 | Virginia | Virginia | 1947 | North Carolina | North Carolina |
| 1934 | Duke | Virginia | 1948 | North Carolina | North Carolina |
| 1935 | Washington & Lee | Duke | 1949 | North Carolina | North Carolina |
| 1936 | Washington & Lee | Duke | 1950 | North Carolina | North Carolina |
| 1937 | Washington & Lee | VMI | 1951 | North Carolina | North Carolina State |
| 1938 | Washington & Lee | VMI | 1952 | North Carolina | North Carolina |
| 1939 | Clemson | North Carolina State | 1953 | *No official points kept* | North Carolina State |
| 1940 | North Carolina | North Carolina | 1954 | VMI | Virginia Tech |
| 1941 | North Carolina | Virginia Tech | 1955 | VMI | Davidson |

| YEAR | CHAMPION | MEET HOST / SITE | YEAR | CHAMPION | MEET HOST / SITE |
|------|----------|-----------------|------|----------|-----------------|
| 1956 | VMI | VMI | 1970 | East Carolina | East Carolina |
| 1957 | Virginia Tech | The Citadel | 1971 | East Carolina | East Carolina |
| 1958 | VMI | Virginia Tech | 1972 | | *No meet held.* |
| 1959 | VMI | VMI | 1973 | East Carolina | VMI |
| 1960 | VMI | The Citadel | 1974 | East Carolina | East Carolina |
| 1961 | VMI | Fort Eustis, VA | 1975 | East Carolina | Appalachian State |
| 1962 | VMI | The Citadel | 1976 | East Carolina | Richmond |
| 1963 | The Citadel | The Citadel | 1977 | East Carolina | Furman |
| 1964 | Virginia Tech | The Citadel | 1978 | Marshall | VMI |
| 1965 | VMI | William & Mary | 1979 | Marshall | Furman |
| 1966 | East Carolina | The Citadel | 1980 | Marshall | VMI |
| 1967 | East Carolina | East Carolina | 1981 | Marshall | The Citadel |
| 1968 | East Carolina | East Carolina | 1982 | Marshall | Marshall |
| 1969 | East Carolina | East Carolina | | | |

*The 1961 VMI Keydets won the conference swimming and diving meet, the program's seventh championship in an eight-year span. (Virginia Military Institute archives)*

*A Proud Athletic History: 100 Years of the Southern Conference*

# MEN'S TENNIS

*Individual-flighted brackets only from 1928–1950. No team scoring until 1951.*
*Tournament Most Outstanding Player not selected until 1990.*
*Regular-season conference scheduling not official until 1992.*

| YEAR | REGULAR SEASON CHAMPION | TOURNAMENT CHAMPION | TOURNAMENT MOST OUTSTANDING PLAYER | TOURNAMENT HOST / SITE |
|---|---|---|---|---|
| 1928 | — | — | — | New Orleans |
| 1929 | — | — | — | New Orleans |
| 1930 | — | — | — | New Orleans |
| 1931 | — | — | — | New Orleans |
| 1932 | — | — | — | New Orleans |
| 1933 | — | — | — | North Carolina |
| 1934 | — | — | — | Virginia |
| 1935 | — | — | — | North Carolina |
| 1936 | — | — | — | North Carolina |
| 1937 | — | — | — | Richmond |
| 1938 | — | — | — | North Carolina |
| 1939 | — | — | — | William & Mary |
| 1940 | — | — | — | Duke |
| 1941 | — | — | — | Duke |
| 1942 | — | — | — | Duke |
| 1943–46 | *No tournament held due to war* | — | — | — |
| 1947 | — | — | — | North Carolina |
| 1948 | — | — | — | North Carolina |
| 1949 | — | — | — | North Carolina |
| 1950 | — | — | — | Davidson |
| 1951 | — | North Carolina | — | Davidson |
| 1952 | — | Duke | — | Davidson |
| 1953 | — | North Carolina | — | Davidson |
| 1954 | — | Davidson | — | Davidson |
| 1955 | — | Davidson | — | Davidson |
| 1956 | — | George Washington | — | William & Mary |
| 1957 | — | George Washington | — | Davidson |
| 1958 | — | George Washington | — | William & Mary |

| YEAR | REGULAR SEASON CHAMPION | TOURNAMENT CHAMPION | TOURNAMENT MOST OUTSTANDING PLAYER | TOURNAMENT HOST / SITE |
|---|---|---|---|---|
| 1959 | — | George Washington | — | Norfolk, VA |
| 1960 | — | George Washington | — | George Washington |
| 1961 | — | The Citadel | — | The Citadel |
| 1962 | — | George Washington | — | Virginia Beach, VA |
| 1963 | — | George Washington | — | George Washington |
| 1964 | — | George Washington | — | Davidson |
| 1965 | — | Davidson | — | Davidson |
| 1966 | — | Davidson | — | Richmond |
| 1967 | — | Davidson | — | Furman |
| 1968 | — | Davidson | — | VMI |
| 1969 | — | Furman | — | The Citadel |
| 1970 | — | Davidson | — | Davidson |
| 1971 | — | Davidson | — | William & Mary |
| 1972 | — | Furman | — | William & Mary |
| 1973 | — | Davidson | — | Furman |
| 1974 | — | Appalachian State | — | Appalachian State |
| 1975 | — | Appalachian State | — | The Citadel |
| 1976 | — | Furman | — | Richmond |
| 1977 | — | Furman | — | Davidson |
| 1978 | — | Chattanooga | — | Furman |
| 1979 | — | Chattanooga | — | Chattanooga |
| 1980 | — | Chattanooga | — | VMI |
| 1981 | — | Chattanooga | — | Appalachian State |
| 1982 | — | Chattanooga | — | The Citadel |
| 1983 | — | Chattanooga | — | Davidson |
| 1984 | — | Chattanooga | — | ETSU |
| 1985 | — | Chattanooga | — | Furman |
| 1986 | — | Furman | — | Chattanooga |
| 1987 | — | Furman | — | VMI |
| 1988 | — | Chattanooga | — | Western Carolina |
| 1989 | — | Chattanooga | — | Asheville, NC |
| 1990 | — | Furman | Yaser Zaatini, ETSU | Asheville, NC |
| 1991 | — | Furman | Ashley Gaines, Furman | Asheville, NC |
| 1992 | ETSU | ETSU | Luis Gonzalez, ETSU | Asheville, NC |

*A Proud Athletic History: 100 Years of the Southern Conference*

The doubles team of Juan Logu (left) and Taisei Miyamoto returns service for ETSU in 2018. The Buccaneers won the championship. (Frank Mattia, SoCon Photos)

Furman's Katarina Kozarov was the Most Outstanding Player at the 2019 SoCon Women's Tennis Tournament in Macon, GA. (SoCon Photos)

| YEAR | REGULAR SEASON CHAMPION | TOURNAMENT CHAMPION | TOURNAMENT MOST OUTSTANDING PLAYER | TOURNAMENT HOST / SITE |
|------|---|---|---|---|
| 1993 | Furman | Furman | Yaser Zaatini, ETSU | Davidson |
| 1994 | Georgia Southern | Georgia Southern | Gwinyai Tongoona, UTC | Davidson |
| 1995 | ETSU | ETSU | Sam Schroerlucke, Furman | Davidson |
| 1996 | Appalachian State & ETSU (tie) | ETSU | Jon Pastel, Davidson | Furman |
| 1997 | Davidson | Furman | Sam Schroerlucke, Furman | Davidson |
| 1998 | Furman | Chattanooga | Craig Hawkins, UTC | Furman |
| 1999 | ETSU | ETSU | Gustavo Gomez, ETSU | Wofford |
| 2000 | ETSU | Chattanooga | Jesse Koti, UTC | Chattanooga |
| 2001 | Furman & UNCG (tie) | Furman | James Cameron, Furman | The Citadel |
| 2002 | Furman | ETSU | Moises Serrano, ETSU | The Citadel |
| 2003 | Coll. of Charleston & ETSU (tie) | Coll. of Charleston | Timo Siebert, C of C | The Citadel |

| YEAR | REGULAR SEASON CHAMPION | TOURNAMENT CHAMPION | TOURNAMENT MOST OUTSTANDING PLAYER | TOURNAMENT HOST / SITE |
|---|---|---|---|---|
| 2004 | ETSU | ETSU | Oscar Posada, ETSU | The Citadel |
| 2005 | ETSU | ETSU | Felix Insaurraulde, ETSU | The Citadel |
| 2006 | Elon & Furman (tie) | Furman | Andy Juc, Furman | The Citadel |
| 2007 | Elon | Elon | Anuwat Dalodom, Elon | The Citadel |
| 2008 | Furman | Furman | Andy Juc, Furman | The Citadel |
| 2009 | Furman | Furman | Bo Ladyman, Furman | Elon |
| 2010 | Coll. of Charleston | UNCG* | Arsel Kumdereli, UNCG | The Citadel |
| 2011 | Coll. of Charleston & Elon (tie) | Samford | Carson Kadi, Samford | Chattanooga |
| 2012 | Coll. of Charleston & Samford* (tie) | Coll. of Charleston | Tom Delme, C of C | The Citadel |
| 2013 | Elon | Samford | Zac Dunkle, Samford | Elon |
| 2014 | Elon | Elon | Cameron Silverman, Elon | Chattanooga |
| 2015 | ETSU* | ETSU* | David Biosca, ETSU | Furman |
| 2016 | ETSU* | ETSU* | Rogerio Ribeiro, ETSU | Chattanooga |
| 2017 | ETSU* | ETSU* | David Biosca, ETSU | Furman |
| 2018 | ETSU* | ETSU | Sergi Fontcuberta, ETSU | Chattanooga |
| 2019 | ETSU | ETSU | Miguel Este, ETSU | Macon, GA |

*Championship subsequently vacated due to NCAA violations.*

## WOMEN'S TENNIS

| | | | | |
|---|---|---|---|---|
| 1984 | No regular-season play | Chattanooga | No selection | ETSU |
| 1985 | No regular-season play | Chattanooga | No selection | Furman |
| 1986 | Furman | Chattanooga | No selection | Chattanooga |
| 1987 | Furman | Furman | Janey Strause, Furman | Asheville, NC |
| 1988 | Chattanooga | Chattanooga | Joanie Elkins, Furman | Asheville, NC |
| 1989 | Furman | Furman | No selection | Asheville, NC |
| 1990 | Chattanooga | Chattanooga | Samantha Fletcher, UTC | Asheville, NC |
| 1991 | Furman | Furman | Meg Glass, UTC | Asheville, NC |
| 1992 | Furman | Furman | Gunda Pristauz-Telsnigg, Marshall | Davidson |
| 1993 | Furman | Furman | Elizabeth Nieto, GSU | Davidson |
| 1994 | Furman | Furman | Elizabeth Nieto, GSU | Davidson |

| YEAR | REGULAR SEASON CHAMPION | TOURNAMENT CHAMPION | TOURNAMENT MOST OUTSTANDING PLAYER | TOURNAMENT HOST / SITE |
|------|-------------------------|---------------------|-------------------------------------|------------------------|
| 1995 | Georgia Southern | Georgia Southern | Elizabeth Nieto, GSU | Davidson |
| 1996 | Georgia Southern | Georgia Southern | Elizabeth Nieto, GSU | Davidson |
| 1997 | Chattanooga & Marshall (tie) | Marshall | Anita Buggins, GSU | Furman |
| 1998 | Georgia Southern | Furman | Emelie Isaksson, Furman | Wofford |
| 1999 | Furman | Furman | Jarrell Starnes, Furman | Davidson |
| 2000 | Furman | Furman | Megan Dunigan, Furman | Chattanooga |
| 2001 | Furman | Furman | Megan Dunigan, Furman | The Citadel |
| 2002 | Furman | Furman | Gene Holman, Furman | The Citadel |
| 2003 | Furman | Coll. of Charleston | Rachel Magory, C of C | The Citadel |
| 2004 | Furman | Furman | Caroline Bentley, Furman | The Citadel |
| 2005 | Furman | Furman | Caroline Bentley, Furman | The Citadel |
| 2006 | Furman | Furman | Bonnie Baird, Furman | The Citadel |
| 2007 | Furman | Furman | Lauren Osborne, Furman | The Citadel |
| 2008 | Furman | Furman | Laura Gioia, Furman | The Citadel |
| 2009 | Furman | Coll. of Charleston | Anna Lee Evans, C of C | Elon |
| 2010 | Coll. of Charleston | Coll. of Charleston | Kinsey Casey, C of C | The Citadel |
| 2011 | Coll. of Charleston | Coll. of Charleston | Emma Hayman, C of C | Chattanooga |
| 2012 | UNCG | Coll. of Charleston | Kelly Kambourelis, C of C | The Citadel |
| 2013 | Coll. of Charleston | Coll. of Charleston | Cristin Newman, C of C | Elon |
| 2014 | Furman | Elon | Frida Jansaker, Elon | Chattanooga |
| 2015 | Samford | Samford | Jessica Northcutt, Samford | Furman |
| 2016 | Furman | ETSU | Lyn Yee Choo, ETSU | Chattanooga |
| 2017 | Furman | Furman | Danni Vines, Furman | Furman |
| 2018 | Furman | Furman | Danni Vines, Furman | Chattanooga |
| 2019 | Furman | Furman | Katarina Kozarov, Furman | Macon, GA |

VMI's Griffin Kowal clears the bar in pole vault competition held at the Corps Physical Training Facility, VMI's state-of-the-art indoor track and field venue. (Todd Drexler, SoCon Photos)

## MEN'S INDOOR TRACK AND FIELD

*No selection for Most Outstanding Athlete until 1970.*
*Most Outstanding Athlete selection not made between 2002–2007.*

| YEAR | MEET CHAMPION | MOST OUTSTANDING ATHLETE | TOURNAMENT HOST / SITE |
|------|---------------|--------------------------|------------------------|
| 1930 | Washington & Lee | — | North Carolina |
| 1931 | North Carolina | — | North Carolina |
| 1932 | North Carolina | — | North Carolina |
| 1933 | Duke | — | North Carolina |
| 1934 | North Carolina | — | North Carolina |
| 1935 | North Carolina | — | North Carolina |
| 1936 | Duke | — | North Carolina |
| 1937 | North Carolina | — | North Carolina |
| 1938 | Duke | — | North Carolina |
| 1939 | North Carolina | — | North Carolina |
| 1940 | North Carolina | — | North Carolina |

| YEAR | MEET CHAMPION | MOST OUTSTANDING ATHLETE | TOURNAMENT HOST / SITE |
|---|---|---|---|
| 1941 | North Carolina | — | North Carolina |
| 1942 | North Carolina | — | North Carolina |
| 1943–48 | *No championship held due to war.* | | |
| 1949 | North Carolina | — | North Carolina |
| 1950 | North Carolina | — | North Carolina |
| 1951 | North Carolina | — | North Carolina |
| 1952 | North Carolina | — | North Carolina |
| 1953 | Duke | — | North Carolina |
| 1954 | VMI | — | VMI |
| 1955 | VMI | — | VMI |
| 1956 | Virginia Tech | — | VMI |
| 1957 | William & Mary | — | VMI |
| 1958 | VMI | — | VMI |
| 1959 | VMI | — | VMI |
| 1960 | VMI | — | VMI |
| 1961 | Furman | — | VMI |
| 1962 | Furman | — | VMI |
| 1963 | Furman | — | VMI |
| 1964 | VMI & West Virginia (tie) | — | VMI |
| 1965 | VMI | — | VMI |
| 1966 | William & Mary | — | VMI |
| 1967 | William & Mary | — | VMI |
| 1968 | William & Mary | — | VMI |
| 1969 | William & Mary | — | VMI |
| 1970 | William & Mary | Charles Strode, W&M | VMI |
| 1971 | William & Mary | Howell Michael, W&M | VMI |
| 1972 | William & Mary | — | VMI |
| 1973 | William & Mary | — | VMI |
| 1974 | William & Mary | Mac Collins, W&M | VMI |
| 1975 | William & Mary | Carter Suggs, ECU | VMI |
| 1976 | Furman | Malcolm Grimes, VMI | VMI |
| 1977 | East Carolina | Malcolm Grimes, VMI | VMI |
| 1978 | VMI | Rex Wiggins, VMI | VMI |
| 1979 | VMI | Adrian Leek, ETSU | VMI |

| YEAR | MEET CHAMPION | MOST OUTSTANDING ATHLETE | TOURNAMENT HOST / SITE |
|---|---|---|---|
| 1980 | ETSU | Jody Weatherwax, VMI | VMI |
| 1981 | VMI | Adrian Leek, ETSU | VMI |
| 1982 | VMI | Robbie Mosley, App State | ETSU |
| 1983 | VMI | Dennis Stark, ETSU | VMI |
| 1984 | Appalachian State | Conrad Conneely, ETSU Sylvester Davis, VMI (tie) | ETSU |
| 1985 | Appalachian State | Dan Monahan, VMI | VMI |
| 1986 | Appalachian State | Marshall Pitts, App State | VMI |
| 1987 | Appalachian State | Michael Hanks, App State | ETSU |
| 1988 | Appalachian State | Greg Hatchett, VMI | ETSU |
| 1989 | Appalachian State | Lee Hawkins, App State | ETSU |
| 1990 | Appalachian State | James Hynes, ETSU | VMI |
| 1991 | VMI | Frank Allen, App State | ETSU |
| 1992 | Appalachian State | Seamus Power, ETSU | ETSU |
| 1993 | VMI | Shawn Miller, WCU | VMI |
| 1994 | Appalachian State | Seamus Power, ETSU | ETSU |
| 1995 | Appalachian State | Delevantie Brown, ETSU | ETSU |
| 1996 | VMI | Delevantie Brown, ETSU | VMI |
| 1997 | Marshall | Declan Fahy, ETSU | ETSU |
| 1998 | ETSU | Darrius Jackson, VMI | ETSU |
| 1999 | Western Carolina | Nic Crider, UTC | ETSU |
| 2000 | Appalachian State | Nic Crider, UTC | VMI |
| 2001 | VMI | Marcus Lunch, VMI | ETSU |
| 2002 | Appalachian State | — | ETSU |
| 2003 | Appalachian State | — | ETSU |
| 2004 | Western Carolina | — | ETSU |
| 2005 | Appalachian State | — | ETSU |
| 2006 | Western Carolina | — | Clemson, SC |
| 2007 | Appalachian State | — | Clemson, SC |
| 2008 | Western Carolina | Manteo Mitchell, WCU | Clemson, SC |
| 2009 | Appalachian State | Manteo Mitchell, WCU | Clemson, SC |
| 2010 | Appalachian State | Cordell Livingston, WCU | Clemson, SC |
| 2011 | Appalachian State | Cordell Livingston, WCU | Clemson, SC |
| 2012 | Western Carolina | Bo Ackerson-Gilroy, Samford | Birmingham, AL |

*A Proud Athletic History: 100 Years of the Southern Conference*

| YEAR | MEET CHAMPION | MOST OUTSTANDING ATHLETE | TOURNAMENT HOST / SITE |
|------|---------------|--------------------------|------------------------|
| 2013 | Appalachian State | Brandon Hairston, WCU | Winston-Salem, NC |
| 2014 | Western Carolina | Brandon Bassett, Samford | Winston-Salem, NC |
| 2015 | Western Carolina | Tripp Hurt, Furman | Birmingham, AL |
| 2016 | Western Carolina | Jamie Brown, WCU | Birmingham, AL |
| 2017 | Western Carolina | Patrick Taylor, ETSU | ETSU |
| 2018 | Western Carolina | Marquis Barnes, Samford | VMI |
| 2019 | Western Carolina | Trini Feggett, WCU | VMI |

## WOMEN'S INDOOR TRACK AND FIELD

*No Most Outstanding Athlete selection made, 2003–07.*

| | | | |
|------|---------------|--------------------------|------|
| 1988 | Appalachian State | Lamonda Miller, App State | ETSU |
| 1989 | Appalachian State | Sabrina Keeton, ETSU | ETSU |
| 1990 | Appalachian State | Monica Teeter, App State | VMI |
| 1991 | Appalachian State | Cate Pichon, Furman | ETSU |
| 1992 | Appalachian State | Melissa Morrison, App State | ETSU |
| 1993 | Appalachian State | Melissa Morrison, App State | VMI |
| 1994 | Appalachian State | Shiree Cutts, Furman | ETSU |
| 1995 | ETSU | Shelli Clendenon, ETSU | ETSU |
| 1996 | Western Carolina | Heather VandeBrake, Furman | VMI |
| 1997 | Western Carolina | Daree Thompson, WCU | ETSU |
| 1998 | Chattanooga | Taneisha Robinson, ETSU | ETSU |
| 1999 | Western Carolina | Taneisha Robinson, ETSU | ETSU |
| 2000 | Western Carolina | Rosalyn Hood, WCU | VMI |
| 2001 | Appalachian State | Tyleana Hanner, UTC | ETSU |
| 2002 | Appalachian State | LaShana Poole, App State | ETSU |
| 2003 | Appalachian State | — | ETSU |
| 2004 | Appalachian State | — | ETSU |
| 2005 | Appalachian State | — | ETSU |
| 2006 | Appalachian State | — | Clemson, SC |

| | | | |
|---|---|---|---|
| 2007 | Appalachian State | — | Clemson, SC |
| 2008 | Western Carolina | Kerrie Savery, WCU | Clemson, SC |
| 2009 | Appalachian State | Lynndsey Hyter, GSU | Clemson, SC |
| 2010 | Western Carolina | Janet Carothers, WCU | Clemson, SC |
| 2011 | Appalachian State | Lynndsey Hyter, GSU | Clemson, SC |
| 2012 | Appalachian State | Dena O'Brien, C of C | Birmingham, AL |
| 2013 | Western Carolina | Breanna Alston, App State & Lauren D'Alessio, Samford (tie) | Winston-Salem, NC |
| 2014 | Western Carolina | Breanna Alston, App State | Winston-Salem, NC |
| 2015 | Western Carolina | Xaviera Bass, WCU & Allie Buchalski, Furman (tie) | Birmingham, AL |
| 2016 | Samford | Allie Buchalski, Furman | Birmingham, AL |
| 2017 | Samford | Katrina Seymour, ETSU | ETSU |
| 2018 | Samford | Selena Popp, Samford | VMI |
| 2019 | Samford | Selena Popp, Samford | VMI |

*Western Carolina's Sally Woerner warms up for the hurdles at the 2019 championship meet. (Todd Drexler, SoCon Photos)*

*A Proud Athletic History: 100 Years of the Southern Conference*

# MEN'S OUTDOOR TRACK AND FIELD

*No selection for Most Outstanding Athlete until 1978.*
*Most Outstanding Athlete selection not made between 2002–2007.*

| YEAR | MEET CHAMPION | MOST OUTSTANDING ATHLETE | TOURNAMENT HOST / SITE |
|------|---------------|--------------------------|------------------------|
| 1923 | Mississippi State | — | Montgomery, AL |
| 1924 | Virginia (Northern meet) | — | Virginia |
|      | *Mississippi State (Southern meet)* | — | Montgomery, AL |
| 1925 | Mississippi State | — | Sewanee |
| 1926 | North Carolina | — | North Carolina |
| 1927 | LSU | — | LSU |
| 1928 | LSU | — | Birmingham, AL |
| 1929 | LSU | — | Birmingham, AL |
| 1930 | North Carolina | — | Birmingham, AL |
| 1931 | Tulane | — | Birmingham, AL |
| 1932 | LSU | — | Georgia Tech |
| 1933 | North Carolina | — | Duke |
| 1934 | North Carolina | — | Duke |
| 1935 | North Carolina | — | Duke |
| 1936 | Duke | — | Duke |
| 1937 | Duke | — | Duke |
| 1938 | North Carolina | — | Duke |
| 1939 | North Carolina | — | North Carolina |
| 1940 | North Carolina | — | William & Mary |
| 1941 | Duke | — | William & Mary |
| 1942 | North Carolina | — | North Carolina |
| 1943 | North Carolina | — | North Carolina |
| 1944–45 | *No championship held due to war.* | | |
| 1946 | Duke | — | North Carolina |
| 1947 | North Carolina | — | North Carolina |
| 1948 | North Carolina | — | North Carolina |
| 1949 | North Carolina | — | North Carolina |
| 1950 | North Carolina | — | North Carolina |
| 1951 | Maryland | — | North Carolina |
| 1952 | Maryland | — | North Carolina |

| YEAR | MEET CHAMPION | MOST OUTSTANDING ATHLETE | TOURNAMENT HOST / SITE |
|------|---------------|--------------------------|------------------------|
| 1953 | Maryland | — | Duke |
| 1954 | VMI | — | Ft. Eustis, VA |
| 1955 | VMI | — | Ft. Eustis, VA |
| 1956 | Virginia Tech | — | William & Mary |
| 1957 | William & Mary | — | William & Mary |
| 1958 | William & Mary | — | William & Mary |
| 1959 | The Citadel | — | William & Mary |
| 1960 | The Citadel | — | William & Mary |
| 1961 | The Citadel | — | William & Mary |
| 1962 | Furman | — | Norfolk, VA |
| 1963 | Furman | — | Charleston, WV |
| 1964 | West Virginia | — | William & Mary |
| 1965 | Furman | — | Furman |
| 1966 | William & Mary | — | Ft. Eustis, VA |
| 1967 | William & Mary | — | Ft. Eustis, VA |
| 1968 | William & Mary | — | Ft. Eustis, VA |
| 1969 | William & Mary | — | Ft. Eustis, VA |
| 1970 | William & Mary | — | Ft. Eustis, VA |
| 1971 | William & Mary | — | Ft. Eustis, VA |
| 1972 | William & Mary | — | Furman |
| 1973 | William & Mary | — | Furman |
| 1974 | William & Mary | — | Richmond |
| 1975 | William & Mary | — | William & Mary |
| 1976 | East Carolina | — | Davidson |
| 1977 | East Carolina | — | Furman |
| 1978 | VMI | David Washington, VMI | Marshall |
| 1979 | VMI | Adrian Leek, ETSU | Appalachian State |
| 1980 | Appalachian State | Lafette Jordan, App State | Charleston, SC |
| 1981 | VMI | Robbie Mosley, App State, Adrian Leek, ETSU & David Washington, VMI (tie) | Appalachian State |
| 1982 | VMI | Kevin Johnson, ETSU | Furman |
| 1983 | VMI | Dale Davis, VMI & James Barham, ETSU (tie) | VMI |
| 1984 | Appalachian State | Sylvester Davis, VMI | Marshall |

| YEAR | MEET CHAMPION | MOST OUTSTANDING ATHLETE | TOURNAMENT HOST / SITE |
|------|---------------|--------------------------|------------------------|
| 1985 | Appalachian State | Curtis Handy, The Citadel | Appalachian State |
| 1986 | Appalachian State | Michael Hanks, App State | Marshall |
| 1987 | Appalachian State | Michael Hanks, App State | Appalachian State |
| 1988 | VMI | Leigh Hawkins, App State | VMI |
| 1989 | Appalachian State | Leigh Hawkins, App State | Marshall |
| 1990 | VMI | James Hynes, ETSU | Appalachian State |
| 1991 | VMI | Mario Small, VMI | VMI |
| 1992 | Appalachian State | Shawn Miller, WCU | Marshall |
| 1993 | Appalachian State | Jason Dalton, App State | Appalachian State |
| 1994 | VMI | Shawn Miller, WCU | VMI |
| 1995 | Appalachian State | Jeff Capps, WCU | Marshall |
| 1996 | Appalachian State | Robert Johnson, App State | ETSU |
| 1997 | VMI | Will Dickerson, App State | Appalachian State |
| 1998 | VMI | Declan Fehy, ETSU | VMI |
| 1999 | Western Carolina | Phillip Johnson, WCU | ETSU |
| 2000 | VMI | Marcus Lynch, VMI | Appalachian State |
| 2001 | Appalachian State | Ben Bissette, App State | VMI |
| 2002 | Appalachian State | — | ETSU |

*Dakota Lamont holds the baton aloft after running the anchor leg for the victorious Western Carolina distance medley relay team in 2018. (SoCon Photos)*

*Wofford's Hannah Steelman won the SoCon steeplechase in 2019 and placed third in the NCAA championships, earning All-America honors. (SoCon Photos)*

| YEAR | MEET CHAMPION | MOST OUTSTANDING ATHLETE | TOURNAMENT HOST / SITE |
|------|---------------|--------------------------|------------------------|
| 2003 | Appalachian State | — | Appalachian State |
| 2004 | Appalachian State | — | Appalachian State |
| 2005 | Appalachian State | — | Western Carolina |
| 2006 | Western Carolina | — | Georgia Southern |
| 2007 | Western Carolina | — | Appalachian State |
| 2008 | Appalachian State | Manteo Mitchell, WCU | Western Carolina |
| 2009 | Western Carolina | Manteo Mitchell, WCU | Georgia Southern |
| 2010 | Appalachian State | Malcolm Styers, App State | Appalachian State |
| 2011 | Appalachian State | Cordell Livingston, WCU | Samford |
| 2012 | Appalachian State | Jared Stalling, App State | Western Carolina |
| 2013 | Western Carolina | Ben Davies, Samford | Georgia Southern |
| 2014 | Samford | Steven Bastien, Samford | Spartanburg, SC |
| 2015 | Samford | Sidney Jordan, Samford | Samford |
| 2016 | Western Carolina | Jordan White, VMI | Western Carolina |
| 2017 | Western Carolina | Ben Johnson, ETSU | Samford |
| 2018 | Western Carolina | Scott Peretin, WCU | Western Carolina |
| 2019 | Western Carolina | Ben Johnson, ETSU | Samford |

## WOMEN'S OUTDOOR TRACK AND FIELD

*Most Outstanding Athlete selection not made between 2002–07.*

| | | | |
|------|---------------|--------------------------|------------------------|
| 1987 | Appalachian State | Meg Warren, App State | Appalachian State |
| 1988 | Appalachian State | Lamonda Miller, App State | VMI |
| 1989 | Appalachian State | Whitney Ball, App State | Marshall |
| 1990 | Appalachian State | Vanessa Kosmala, App State | Appalachian State |
| 1991 | Appalachian State | Von Ross, WCU | VMI |
| 1992 | Appalachian State | Leigh Wallace, App State | Marshall |
| 1993 | Appalachian State | Melissa Morrison, App State | Appalachian State |
| 1994 | Appalachian State | Rita Roberts, WCU | VMI |
| 1995 | Appalachian State | Angela Rowe, WCU | Marshall |
| 1996 | ETSU | Rahma Mateen, WCU | ETSU |

| YEAR | MEET CHAMPION | MOST OUTSTANDING ATHLETE | TOURNAMENT HOST / SITE |
|------|---------------|--------------------------|------------------------|
| 1997 | Western Carolina | Daree Thompson, WCU | Appalachian State |
| 1998 | Appalachian State | Taneisha Robinson, ETSU | VMI |
| 1999 | Western Carolina | Mary Jayne Harrelson, App State | ETSU |
| 2000 | Western Carolina | Tyleana Hanner, UTC | Appalachian State |
| 2001 | Western Carolina | Tyleana Hanner, UTC & Virginia LaCombe, WCU (tie) | VMI |
| 2002 | Appalachian State | — | ETSU |
| 2003 | Appalachian State | — | Appalachian State |
| 2004 | Appalachian State | — | Appalachian State |
| 2005 | Appalachian State | — | Western Carolina |
| 2006 | Appalachian State | — | Georgia Southern |
| 2007 | Georgia Southern | — | Appalachian State |
| 2008 | Western Carolina | Brittani Williams, App State | Western Carolina |
| 2009 | Appalachian State | Lily Tallent, App State | Georgia Southern |
| 2010 | Western Carolina | Felicia Paulding, WCU | Appalachian State |
| 2011 | Appalachian State | Zakiyyah Stewart, WCU | Samford |
| 2012 | Appalachian State | Breanna Alston, App State | Western Carolina |
| 2013 | Western Carolina | Ashley Cope, Samford | Georgia Southern |
| 2014 | Samford | Jasmin Walker, GSU | Spartanburg, SC |
| 2015 | Western Carolina | Tayla Carter, WCU & Demeteria Edgecombe, ETSU (tie) | Samford |
| 2016 | Western Carolina | Hailey Cook, WCU & Sarah Sanford, Samford (tie) | Western Carolina |
| 2017 | Samford | Kyra Atkins, ETSU | Samford |
| 2018 | Western Carolina | Selena Popp, Samford | Western Carolina |
| 2019 | Samford | Maggie Johnston, Samford | Samford |

*A pair of Samford blockers rise up as Chattanooga's Kristy Wieser lines up a shot in the 2016 championship match, won by Samford. (SoCon Photos)*

# WOMEN'S VOLLEYBALL

| YEAR | REGULAR SEASON CHAMPION | TOURNAMENT CHAMPION | TOURNAMENT MOST OUTSTANDING PLAYER | TOURNAMENT HOST / SITE |
|------|------|------|------|------|
| 1983 | Western Carolina | Western Carolina | — | ETSU |
| 1984 | Appalachian State | Appalachian State | — | Western Carolina |
| 1985 | Western Carolina | Western Carolina | Emily Holliday, WCU | Appalachian State |
| 1986 | Appalachian State & Western Carolina (tie) | Western Carolina | Michelle Barrett, WCU | Furman |
| 1987 | ETSU | Chattanooga | Dina Parris, UTC | Marshall |
| 1988 | ETSU | Marshall | Cindy Bryant, Marshall | Chattanooga |
| 1989 | ETSU & Western Carolina (tie) | ETSU | Pam Flinchum, ETSU | ETSU |
| 1990 | Appalachian State | Furman | Jennifer Wilson, Furman | Western Carolina |
| 1991 | ETSU | Appalachian State | Rachael Wade, App State | Appalachian State |
| 1992 | Appalachian State | ETSU | Jennifer Garriga, ETSU | Furman |

*A Proud Athletic History: 100 Years of the Southern Conference*

| YEAR | REGULAR SEASON CHAMPION | TOURNAMENT CHAMPION | TOURNAMENT MOST OUTSTANDING PLAYER | TOURNAMENT HOST / SITE |
|---|---|---|---|---|
| 1993 | Furman | Appalachian State | Heidi McElhaney, App State | Marshall |
| 1994 | Appalachian State | Appalachian State | Sheri Leverette, App State | Chattanooga |
| 1995 | Appalachian State | Marshall | Jessica Braga, Marshall | Davidson |
| 1996 | Marshall | Chattanooga | Jennifer Breasse, UTC | Georgia Southern |
| 1997 | Chattanooga | Chattanooga | Rachel Evans, UTC | Georgia Southern |
| 1998 | Chattanooga | Chattanooga | Rachel Evans, UTC | Appalachian State |
| 1999 | Davidson | Davidson | Mara Mordini, Davidson | Western Carolina |
| 2000 | Davidson | Davidson | Mara Mordini, Davidson | Coll. of Charleston |
| 2001 | Coll. of Charleston | Georgia Southern | Camila Schmitz-Rower, GSU | UNCG |
| 2002 | Coll. of Charleston & Georgia Southern (tie) | Coll. of Charleston | Mary Sabatino, C of C | Davidson |
| 2003 | Appalachian State (North) *Coll. of Charleston & Georgia Southern (tie South)* | Georgia Southern | Martina Veiglova, GSU | Chattanooga |
| 2004 | Appalachian State (North) *Coll. of Charleston (South)* | Coll. of Charleston | Amanda Timmers, C of C | Western Carolina |
| 2005 | Coll. of Charleston | Coll. of Charleston | Tiffany Blum, C of C | Georgia Southern |
| 2006 | Coll. of Charleston | Coll. of Charleston | Tiffany Blum, C of C | Appalachian State |
| 2007 | Coll. of Charleston | Coll. of Charleston | Tiffany Blum, C of C | Chattanooga |
| 2008 | Samford (North) *Coll. of Charleston (South)* | Furman | Alison West, Furman | UNCG |
| 2009 | Samford (North) *Furman (South)* | Coll. of Charleston | Ginny Phillips, C of C | Furman |
| 2010 | Elon (North) *Coll. of Charleston (South)* | Georgia Southern | Kate Van Dyke, GSU | Appalachian State |
| 2011 | Samford (North) *Coll. of Charleston (South)* | Samford | Lexi Bauer, Samford | Samford |
| 2012 | Samford (North) *Georgia Southern (South)* | Coll. of Charleston | Sloane White, C of C | Davidson |
| 2013 | Georgia Southern | Georgia Southern | Jamie DeRatt, GSU | Furman |
| 2014 | Furman | Samford | Chelsi Carter, Samford | UNCG |
| 2015 | Chattanooga | Furman | Jo Wilks, Furman | Western Carolina |
| 2016 | ETSU | Samford | Erin Bognar, Samford | Samford |
| 2017 | Furman | ETSU | Rylee Milhorn, ETSU | Western Carolina |
| 2018 | ETSU | Samford | Taylor Anderton, Samford | UNCG |

*Chon Porter of the Citadel (in blue) battles with Chase McKinney of Gardner-Webb at the 2019 wrestling championships in Boone, NC. (Todd Drexler, SoCon Photos)*

## WRESTLING

*Regular-season scheduling officially implemented in 1994.*
*Conference tournament held intermittently between 1927–1940.*
*Tournament's Most Outstanding Wrestler chosen 1948–53;discontinued in 1954; restored in 1961.*

| YEAR | REGULAR SEASON CHAMPION | TOURNAMENT CHAMPION | TOURNAMENT MOST OUTSTANDING PLAYER | TOURNAMENT HOST / SITE |
|---|---|---|---|---|
| 1927 | Virginia Tech | — | — | — |
| 1928 | Duke | — | — | — |
| 1929 | Duke | — | — | — |
| 1930 | — | VMI | — | Lexington, VA |
| 1931 | North Carolina, VMI, Washington & Lee (tie) | — | — | — |
| 1932 | Washington & Lee | — | — | — |
| 1933 | — | Washington & Lee | — | Lexington, VA |

| YEAR | REGULAR SEASON CHAMPION | TOURNAMENT CHAMPION | TOURNAMENT MOST OUTSTANDING PLAYER | TOURNAMENT HOST / SITE |
|---|---|---|---|---|
| 1934 | — | Washington & Lee | — | Virginia Tech |
| 1935 | — | VMI | — | Lexington, VA |
| 1936 | — | Washington & Lee | — | Lexington, VA |
| 1937 | VMI, Washington & Lee (tie) | — | — | — |
| 1938 | — | VMI | — | Virginia Tech |
| 1939 | VMI, Washington & Lee (tie) | — | — | — |
| 1940 | VMI, Washington & Lee (tie) | — | — | — |
| 1941 | — | Washington & Lee | — | Maryland |
| 1942 | — | North Carolina | — | Greensboro, NC |
| 1943 | — | VMI | — | Waynesboro, VA |
| 1944–46 | *Limited participation due to war.* | | | |
| 1947 | — | North Carolina | — | Lexington, VA |
| 1948 | — | Washington & Lee | Fred Moyer, VMI | Lexington, VA |
| 1949 | — | Washington & Lee | Phil Kemp, UNC | Lexington, VA |
| 1950 | — | Washington & Lee | Jerry Gallagher, Duke | Maryland |
| 1951 | — | VMI | Ted Lonergan, W & L | Lexington, VA |
| 1952 | — | Maryland | Ernie Fischer, Maryland | Lexington, VA |
| 1953 | — | Maryland | Rodney Norris, Maryland | Lexington, VA |
| 1954 | — | West Virginia | — | Lexington, VA |
| 1955 | — | Virginia Tech | — | Lexington, VA |
| 1956 | — | Virginia Tech | — | Lexington, VA |
| 1957 | — | VMI | — | Lexington, VA |
| 1958 | — | Virginia Tech | — | VMI |
| 1959 | — | West Virginia | — | The Citadel |
| 1960 | — | Virginia Tech | — | Davidson |
| 1961 | — | Virginia Tech | Jeff Hartsell, The Citadel | West Virginia |
| 1962 | — | Virginia Tech | Jeff Hartsell, The Citadel | Virginia Tech |
| 1963 | — | Virginia Tech | Jose Barcelo, The Citadel | West Virginia |
| 1964 | — | West Virginia | Bruce Schwanda, The Citadel | Davidson |
| 1965 | — | West Virginia | Henry Seymour, Va. Tech | VMI |
| 1966 | — | West Virginia | John Luckini, WVU | William & Mary |
| 1967 | — | The Citadel | Ed Steers, The Citadel | West Virginia |
| 1968 | — | William & Mary | Bob Hobson, W&M | VMI |
| 1969 | — | William & Mary | John Wood, The Citadel | The Citadel |

| YEAR | REGULAR SEASON CHAMPION | TOURNAMENT CHAMPION | TOURNAMENT MOST OUTSTANDING PLAYER | TOURNAMENT HOST / SITE |
|---|---|---|---|---|
| 1970 | — | William & Mary | Bob Hobson, W&M | William & Mary |
| 1971 | — | William & Mary | Lonnie Parker, W&M | William & Mary |
| 1972 | — | East Carolina | John Kaila, W&M | East Carolina |
| 1973 | — | East Carolina | Mark Belknap, W&M | William & Mary |
| 1974 | — | East Carolina | Chris Jacobsen, App State | Appalachian State |
| 1975 | — | East Carolina | Mark Belknap, W&M | Richmond |
| 1976 | — | East Carolina | Mike Regner, The Citadel | The Citadel |
| 1977 | — | William & Mary | Phil Mueller, ECU | East Carolina |
| 1978 | — | Chattanooga | Randy Batten, UTC | Appalachian State |
| 1979 | — | Chattanooga | Tom Flanagan, UTC | Chattanooga |
| 1980 | — | Chattanooga | Larry Meierotto, UTC | The Citadel |
| 1981 | — | Chattanooga | Larry Meierotto, UTC & Todd Sumter, App State (tie) | Appalachian State |
| 1982 | — | Chattanooga | Charlie Heard, UTC | VMI |
| 1983 | — | Chattanooga | Bill Moss, UTC | Chattanooga |
| 1984 | — | Appalachian State | Charlie Heard, UTC & John Munno, VMI (tie) | The Citadel |
| 1985 | — | VMI | Amaro Lamar, App State | Appalachian State |
| 1986 | — | Chattanooga | Ben Walker, VMI | VMI |
| 1987 | — | Chattanooga | Amaro Lamar, App State | Chattanooga |
| 1988 | — | Chattanooga | Clay Ogden, The Citadel & Tom Sell, UTC (tie) | Davidson |
| 1989 | — | Chattanooga | Charlie Buckshaw, UTC | Furman |
| 1990 | — | Chattanooga | Michael Murray, VMI | The Citadel |
| 1991 | — | Chattanooga | Bret Gustafson, UTC | Appalachian State |
| 1992 | — | Chattanooga | Bret Gustafson, UTC | Asheville, NC |
| 1993 | — | Chattanooga | Victor Balmeceda, App State | Asheville, NC |
| 1994 | Appalachian State, Chattanooga & VMI (tie) | Chattanooga | Charlie Branch, VMI | Asheville, NC |
| 1995 | VMI | Appalachian State & VMI (tie) | David Barden, UTC | Asheville, NC |
| 1996 | VMI | Appalachian State | Aaron Mickiewicz, VMI | UNCG |
| 1997 | Appalachian State | Appalachian State, UNCG & VMI (tie) | Leslie Apedoe, VMI | UNCG |
| 1998 | Appalachian State, Chattanooga & UNCG (tie) | Chattanooga | Bob Hanson, UTC | UNCG |

| YEAR | REGULAR SEASON CHAMPION | TOURNAMENT CHAMPION | TOURNAMENT MOST OUTSTANDING PLAYER | TOURNAMENT HOST / SITE |
|---|---|---|---|---|
| 1999 | Appalachian State, Chattanooga & VMI (tie) | Chattanooga | Jeremy Hart, App State | UNCG |
| 2000 | Chattanooga | Chattanooga | Heath Eslinger, UTC | Chattanooga |
| 2001 | Appalachian State | Appalachian State | Jeremy Hart, App State | Chapel Hill, NC |
| 2002 | Chattanooga | Chattanooga | Mark Fee, App State | Raleigh, NC |
| 2003 | Appalachian State | Appalachian State | Adam Britt, VMI | Appalachian State |
| 2004 | The Citadel | The Citadel | Josh Keefe, UTC | Charlottesville, VA |
| 2005 | Chattanooga | Chattanooga | Jon Sioredas, UTC | UNCG |
| 2006 | Chattanooga | Chattanooga | Matt Keller, UTC | VMI |
| 2007 | Chattanooga | Chattanooga | Scott Ervin, App State | Raleigh, NC |
| 2008 | Chattanooga | Chattanooga | Cody Cleveland, UTC | Chattanooga |
| 2009 | Chattanooga | Chattanooga | Cody Cleveland, UTC | The Citadel |
| 2010 | Chattanooga | UNCG* | Victor Hojilla, UNCG | Davidson |
| 2011 | Chattanooga | Chattanooga | Kyle Blevins, App State | Appalachian State |
| 2012 | Appalachian State | Chattanooga | Austin Trotman, App State | Chattanooga |
| 2013 | Chattanooga | Chattanooga | Anthony Elias, Davidson | VMI |
| 2014 | Chattanooga | Chattanooga | Corey Mock, UTC | Campbell |
| 2015 | Chattanooga | Chattanooga | Connor McMahon, SIUE | Asheville, NC |
| 2016 | Appalachian State, Chattanooga & Gardner-Webb (tie) | Appalachian State | Kamaal Shakur, UTC | Asheville, NC |
| 2017 | Appalachian State | Campbell | Ryan Mosley, Gardner-Webb | The Citadel |
| 2018 | Appalachian State | Appalachian State | Irvin Enriquez, App State | The Citadel |
| 2019 | Appalachian State, Campbell & Chattanooga (tie) | Campbell | Neal Richards, VMI | Appalachian State |

*Championship subsequently vacated due to NCAA violations.*

# RESOURCES

## WEBSITES

Allstatesugarbowl.org

Baseballreference.com

Bigbluehistory.net

Bigblueview.com

Boydsworld.com

Chroniclingamerica.loc.gov

Collegian.psu.edu

Cstv.com

Encyclopediaofarkansas.net

Findagrave.com

Flotrack.org

Greatbutforgotten.blogspot.com

History.com

Library.la84.org

Livingplaces.com

Marinechat.com

Missamerica.org

Nationalfootballfoundation.org

Ncpedia.com

Nctennisfoundation.com

News.ncsu.edu

Nola.com

Pgatour.com

Profootballreference.com

Sportsday.dallasnews.com

Stpetecountryclub.com

Theappalachianonline.com

Thisdayinaviation.com

Upi.com

Ussporthistory.com

Vasportshof.com

Vintagecarsofamerica.com

Wikipedia.com

## NEWSPAPERS

*Bluefield* (WV) *Daily Telegraph*, Apr. 7, 1976

*Bluefield* (WV) *Daily Telegraph*, Nov. 25, 1964

*The Buffalo News*, July 7, 2018

*Bristol* (TN) *Herald Courier*, Oct. 1, 2009

*Charlotte* (NC) *Observer*, June 14, 2014

*The Collegian*, University of Richmond student newspaper, Oct. 21, 1993

*Columbia University Spectator*, Sept. 12, 1940

*The* (NJ) *Courier-Post*, Jan. 18, 2018

*The Daily Tar Heel*

*Daily Telegraph*, Bluefield, WV, Aug. 29, 1959

*Dominion Post*, Morgantown, WV

*The Gettysburg Times*

*Greensboro News & Record*, Jan. 7, 1991

*Greenville* (SC) *News*, June 15, 2018

*Los Angeles Times*, Nov. 27, 1990

*New York Times*, June 3, 1990

*New York Times*, Sept. 14, 1986

*Northwest Georgia News*, April 13, 2017

*The Oklahoman*, March 20, 2015

*The Oklahoman*, Sept. 6, 1992

*Pittsburgh Tribune*, March 21, 2010

*Raleigh News & Observer*, Oct. 8, 1991

*The Salt Lake Tribune*, January 15, 2018

*Spartanburg Herald-Journal*, June 9, 1983

*Spartanburg Herald-Journal*, March 6, 2015

*Staunton* (VA) *News Leader*, Apr. 2, 1933

*The Times of West Virginia*, May 16, 2008

*Tuscaloosa News*, Dec. 16, 2013

*The Washington Post*, March 2, 1994

*West Virginia Gazette Mail*, December 13, 2015

## BOOKS

Bailey, John Wendell. *Handbook of Southern Intercollegiate Track and Field Athletics, 1894–1924*. Starkville, MS: Mississippi Agricultural and Mechanical College Press, 1924.

Bezilla, Michael. *Penn State: An Illustrated History*. University Park, PA: Pennsylvania State University Press, 1985.

Chibbaro, Mike. *The Cadillac: The Life Story of University of South Carolina Football Legend Steve Wadiak*. Greenville, SC: Thirty-Seven Publishing, 2014.

Lazenby, Roland and Mike Ashley. *Best Regrets*. Lexington, VA: Full Court Press Inc. and the VMI Keydet Club, 2014.

Wallenfeldt, E. C. *The Six-Minute Fraternity: The Rise and Fall of NCAA Tournament Boxing, 1932–60*. Westport, CT: Praeger Publishers, 1994.

Winstead, Roger and Tim Peeler *N.C. State Basketball: 100 Years of Innovation*. Chapel Hill, NC: University of North Carolina Press, 2010.

## PERIODICAL ARTICLES

Bracken, Chris. "How Yale lost football." *Yale Daily News* (November 4, 2016).

Edds, Kevin. "Death of a conference." *Virginia. Sportswar.com* (December 2, 2014).

Fimrite, Ron. "Battle of His Life." *Sports Illustrated* (August 24, 1987).

"How College Sports Lost Its Way." The Brookings Institution (2017).

Hylton, J. Gordon. "Recent college football realignments are nothing new." *Marquette University Law School Faculty Blog* (November 7, 2011).

Jackson, Roger. "In the SC 22 Will Get You Three" *Sports Illustrated* (January 19, 1981).

Jacobs, Barry. "ACC anniversary marks a milestone for power conferences." *Charlotte Observer* (May 10, 2017).

Jares, Joe. "The Agony of Lefty Driesell." *Sports Illustrated* (March 8, 1965).

Megargee, Steve. "Three-point shot got its start from Ronnie Carr." *Rivals.com* (May 24, 2007).

Neely, Jack. "A Southern mutiny: The birthplace of the Southeastern Conference." *Metropulse* (September 5, 2012).

Reid, Whitelaw. "Lights Out." *Virginia Magazine* (Summer 2017).

"Retail prices, 1890 to 1927." US Department of Labor study (1929).

Traughber, Bill. "Vandy wins 1927 championship." Vanderbilt University Athletics (March 17, 2010).

## COLLEGE YEARBOOKS

*Agromeck*, North Carolina State University

*Blue Print*, Georgia Tech University

*The Bomb*, Virginia Military Institute

*Bonhomie*, Furman University

*The Bugle*, Virginia Tech University

*Calyx*, Washington & Lee University

*The Chanticleer*, Duke University

*Garnet and Black*, The University of South Carolina

*Howler*, Wake Forest University

*Jambalaya*, Tulane University

*Quips and Cranks*, Davidson College

*Reveille*, University of Maryland

*Taps,* Clemson University

*The Web*, University of Richmond

*Yackety Yack*, University of North Carolina

## OTHER RESOURCES

Southern Conference official minutes, 1921 to present

Southern Conference media guides and record books

Media guides of members, former members, and other conferences

Member and former member athletic websites

Southern Conference 75th Anniversary Record Book

# INDEX